A F R I C A N

AMERICAN

CHURCH

LEADERSHIP

OTHER PARKER BOOKS

Elijah's Mantle, edited by Diane Proctor Reeder
Making Your Vision a Reality by Paul Cannings

PARKER BOOKS

AFRICAN AMERICAN CHURCH LEADERSHIP

Principles for Effective Ministry and Community Leadership

Lee N. June, PhD
Christopher C. Mathis Jr., PhD
Editors

*African American Church Leadership: Principles for Effective Ministry
and Community Leadership*

© 2013 by Lee N. June and Christopher C. Mathis Jr.

Published by Kregel Publications, a division of Kregel, Inc., P.O. Box 2607, Grand Rapids,
MI 49501.

Parker Books was conceived by Matthew Parker, the president of the Institute for Black
Family Development, Detroit, MI, and is an imprint that provides books for Christian ministry leaders.

ISBN 978–0–8254–4273–5

Printed in the United States of America
13 14 15 16 17 / 5 4 3 2 1

CONTENTS

PREFACE

Leadership Principles
in the African American Church

Matthew Parker Sr.

As I have often said, "the best leaders accomplish goals without making people feel that they have been led." Since 1986, as president of the Institute for Black Family Development, I have been successfully meeting educational and leadership needs among African American churches and Christian organizations.

Despite my focus on the big picture, I haven't forgotten the influences in my life that came from one-on-one relationships. Losing my parents (Matt and Ruth Parker) who provided the foundation for my spiritual and leadership development, I turned to two individuals, asking them to become my spiritual parents (the late Barbara Walton and Lloyd Blue). Moreover, the late Tom Skinner became my mentor on leadership development and networking. These three have been very instrumental in shaping the decisions that I have made in my life. They allowed me to watch them interact with their spouses, children, friends, and ministries. The precious insights and principles received from them made strong walls for the foundation provided by my parents. Their investments are some of the reasons for my accomplishments, and I want to pass on what they gave me.

This book is written by individuals and leaders who also want to pass on wisdom. Some of the qualities and character they possess are expressed in their own way. These individuals lift up the value of coaching and supporting people, praising them for good performance more often than criticizing them for problem performance.

Above all, the contributors demonstrate high levels of integrity in the church, home and community. As you read this volume, it is my desire that this collage of knowledge, wisdom, and skills will enhance your effectiveness as leaders, or as persons interested in effective leadership.

Matthew Parker Sr.

INTRODUCTION

Lee N. June and
Christopher C. Mathis Jr.

The purpose of this book is to share practical information regarding a broad range of issues faced by leaders, followers, and organizations concerned about the implementation of effective leadership principles and strategies within the Christian community. A particular focus is placed on African American churches and the potential they have for impacting African American communities. As has been one of the traditions of the Institute for Black Family Development, we have again assembled the expertise and wisdom of individuals from a broad range of backgrounds who are thinkers, doers, and on the front line of providing services to the African American community.

In 1995, under the auspices of the Institute for Black Family Development, Eugene Seals and Matthew Parker edited a book entitled *Call to Lead: Wisdom for the Next Generation of African American Leaders.* In some ways, this volume is an extension of that book. We have utilized some of the excerpts from that book in chapter two. We also are republishing four chapters (7–10) originally published in 2003 in the book *Help! for Your Leadership* (PriorityOne Publications: Detroit, MI). However, what is unique about this book is that it contains a mixture or blend of leadership principles and discussions on how to implement practices that can enhance effective leadership as well as how to remove practices that impede effective leadership. Leaders carry an enormous burden and there are factors, barriers, and issues that can impede their progress and success. Leaders can possess great leadership skills, but unless the leaders also pay attention to the factors that can impede their leadership, they will not be successful. This book addresses both of those areas.

Some of the books readily available in the leadership area have focused more on management and administration. Such books are most valuable for the day-to-day elements of African American church administration and management, but they do not focus on leadership as a holistic concept as this volume does. Among such books are Massey and McKinney (2003, originally published in 1976) and Flake, Flake and Reed (2005).

Another source of leadership materials and information is the Skinner Leadership Institute (*www.skinnerleadership.org/resources.htm*). This Institute, now under the leadership of Dr. Barbara Williams-Skinner, continues the work of the late Tom Skinner, a pioneering evangelist to the African American community. His leadership impacted thousands over the years. The book *Becoming an Effective 21st Century Leader* by Barbara Williams-Skinner (Skinner Leadership Institute, 2000) is also a valuable resource, and is described on the Skinner Leadership Institute's website as follows:

> This workbook by Barbara Williams-Skinner will challenge you to change the world around you. It is about helping people who feel a call to leadership but lack the leadership skills to know where to begin. It also shows experienced leaders how to be more effective in their leadership skills. This is a book for those who dream of a better world and are willing to assume responsibility for creating that world.

The book you now hold, *African American Church Leadership: Principles for Effective Ministry and Community Leadership*, is divided into four parts. Part one, entitled "Leadership in Perspective," consists of two chapters. Hank (Henry) Allen, a sociologist and professor, lays out in chapter one in scholarly, but readable fashion, the overall state of leadership in the early part of the twenty-first century. What makes the chapter valuable is that he outlines what can and what needs to be done to make leadership effective from a macro perspective. In chapter two, we present the voices of a variety of persons from all walks of life (including youths— our future leaders), who briefly give their views of what leadership is and its essential characteristics. Some of the individuals highlighted are now deceased, but were powerful in their lifetimes, either on the national scene or behind the scenes, influencing their times and serving as mentors to today's leaders. While their words differ, there is much commonality in their views. We encourage you, as you read this chapter, to not only heed their advice, but also construct your own definition of leadership and to make a list of what you think are the essential characteristics of effective leaders.

Part two of the book is entitled "Some How-tos of Leadership" and consists of four chapters (3–6). In chapters three through five, Paul Cannings, an experienced pastor, covers some of the essential principles and how-tos of leadership. A leader understands the people with whom one is working, and can maximize the gifts of the followers. People in an organization must also understand what the elements of effective leadership are so that they and the leader can form a team. Additionally, there are various roles to play as part of a leadership team. These roles are also discussed by Cannings. In chapter six, Lloyd Blue, a veteran in the field and a mentor of many current leaders (particularly pastors), writes passionately and persuasively regarding what needs to be done to motivate and mobilize a congregation for effectiveness. Recent figures suggest that there are some 320,000 Protestant congregations in America, of which approximately 75,000 can be described as primarily African American. Just imagine how powerful the Christian community would be if all of these congregations were to implement the principles that Blue shares.

Part three of the book is entitled "Handling the Pressures of Leadership" and consists of four chapters (7–10). Too often leaders neglect the personal side of their lives. Some become so involved in helping others that their family, their health, and their effectiveness deteriorate. Others who are around such persons typically see these negative signs and effects before the leaders themselves. Thus in chapter seven, Christina Dixon covers an area that is most essential, yet often neglected. We routinely talk about balancing our budgets and our checkbooks, but less frequently do we focus on balancing our mind and ministry. All leaders need to reflect on whether there is such a balance in their lives.

Chapter eight by Sabrina Black, a counselor and a prolific writer, explores the area of stress and its impact on leaders. She offers practical stress management tips. If heeded, leaders will not only be more effective in their leadership roles, but also there will be improvement in their health and personal lives.

Pamela Hudson, in chapter nine, deals with the broad question of leadership in crisis. It is crucial that a leader not only detect the crisis in the movement or organization that he or she is leading, but must also be able to detect the crisis that might be brewing in their personal lives. Being unaware of either is detrimental to effective leadership.

Brenda A. Jenkins, in chapter ten, challenges us to not be Lone Rangers. Leadership involves people and effective leaders cannot be isolated from the people they serve. Proverbs 24:6 tells us that "in multitude of counsellors there is safety."

The final section of the book is entitled "Some Special Aspects of Leadership" and consists of four chapters (11–14). In chapter eleven, Michael and Maria Westbrook, a husband-and-wife team with extensive experience working with youth, lay out some of the challenges and opportunities that face our precious resources—our youth. For a people to continue to advance, one must invest in and develop the next generation. One of the greatest indictments on a generation is for the next generation to rise up and "know not the Lord." Thus this chapter deals with what we need to be doing with our youth and how the church has assisted in helping our youth to develop leadership skills.

The next two chapters (12–13) focus on the issues typically faced by females and young Black males. In chapter twelve, Patricia Robinson Williams and Shirley Spencer June, who have extensive experience working with women, discuss and share some of the unique opportunities and challenges that are present when females exercise leadership in the church and Christian community. This chapter is presented in a scholarly yet practical manner, and includes references to the personal challenges and experiences of the authors. In chapter thirteen, Christopher C. Mathis who has extensive experience working with males, discusses some of the unique factors, opportunities, and challenges that confront young Black males. Specifically, he discusses what needs to be done to prepare young Black males for effective future leadership. Finally, Lee N. June, in chapter fourteen, surveys some of the recent literature on leadership and discusses the area of servant leadership, the leadership style of Jesus, biblical principles of leadership, and the concept of leader as steward. The words "servant leadership" have been in leadership literature since the 1970s and have gained increased attention. Servant leadership reflects what Jesus Christ himself practiced. In addition, this chapter reviews some of the writings that have look specifically at Jesus's style of leadership, biblical principles of leadership, and steward leadership.

Lee N. June and Christopher C. Mathis Jr.

The contributors to this book represent individuals from a variety of church and leadership backgrounds. Their viewpoints are both indications of the diversity of gifts and the diversity of ideas within the body of Christ. The views expressed do not necessarily represent those of the Institute for Black Family Development, but are worthy of public presentation and examination.

It has been a pleasure to work with the various contributors and to assemble this volume. As we present it to the public, it is our sincerest hope that the content will be useful to those who are personally grappling with the issues of leadership, or who simply want to be more effective as leaders. Through this work, may the area of leadership be better understood and God's kingdom advanced "on earth as it is in heaven".

Lee N. June and Christopher C. Mathis Jr.

REFERENCES

Black, Sabrina D., Christina Dixon, Pamela J. Hudson, and Brenda A. Jenkins, 2009. *Help! for Your Leadership: Healing, Encouragement, and Loving Perspective for Overwhelmed Leaders*. Detroit: PriorityOne Publications.

Flake, Floyd H., Elaine. M. Flake, and Edwin C. Reed, 2005. *African American Church Management Handbook*. Valley Forge, PA.: Judson Press.

Massey, Floyd and Samuel B. McKinney, 2003 (rev. ed.). *Church Administration in the Black Perspective*. Valley Forge, PA.: Judson Press.

Seals, Eugene and Matthew Parker, ed., 1995. *Call to Lead: Wisdom for the Next Generation of African American Leaders*. Chicago: Moody Press.

Williams-Skinner, Barbara, 2000. *Becoming an Effective 21st Century Leader*. Tracy Landing, MD: Skinner Leadership Institute.

CONTRIBUTORS

Lee N. June (Editor)

A native of Manning, South Carolina, Dr. Lee N. June is currently a professor in Honors College, Department of Psychology, and African American and African Studies at Michigan State University (MSU).

On December 31, 2010, he stepped down from the roles of associate provost for Academic Student Services and Multicultural Issues, and vice president for Student Affairs and Services, after serving concurrently in both roles for sixteen years. He previously served for three years as senior advisor to the Provost for Racial, Ethnic and Multicultural Issues, and for eight and a half years as director of the Counseling Center, both at MSU.

Lee earned a bachelor's degree from Tuskegee University in Biology, and a Masters of Education in Rehabilitation Counseling and MA and PhD in Clinical Psychology from the University of Illinois, Champaign-Urbana. He also has a certificate in Theology from the Interdenominational Theological Center, Atlanta, Georgia and did post-baccalaureate study in psychology at Haverford College and sabbatical study at Duke University Divinity School.

A licensed psychologist, he has particular research and scholarly interests in the art and science of effective service delivery to students, brief-focused counseling and psychotherapy, factors affecting the persistence and graduation rates of students of color, multicultural psychology, religion and psychology, and the psychology of the African American church.

He is the author or coauthor of some thirty journal articles and book chapters and the author, editor, or coeditor of five books: *The Black Family: Past, Present, and Future* (1991); *Men to Men* (1996); *Evangelism and Discipleship in African American Churches* (1999); *Counseling for Seemingly Impossible Problems* (2002); and *Yet with a Steady Beat: The Black Church through a Psychological and Biblical Lens* (2008).

He is active with his local church (New Mount Calvary Baptist), where he serves on the ministerial staff and teaches Sunday school. He is also chair of the board of directors of the Institute for Black Family Development.

Lee is married to Shirley Spencer June, and they are the parents of two sons, Brian L. and Stephen A. June.

Christopher C. Mathis Jr. (Coeditor)

Dr. Christopher C. Mathis Jr. is a senior research director of 1890 Research and Extension Services, the director for the Center of Agricultural Systems, Food Production, Safety and Security, and adjunct professor for the graduate program, where he teaches the two core courses entitled "Introduction to Statistic Analysis," and "Understanding Educational Research" in the School of Education, Humanities, Arts, and Social Sciences at South Carolina State University, where he had been since August 2000.

Christopher was reared in Newberry, South Carolina, earned a BS degree in biology and chemistry from Johnson C. Smith University, a MA degree in student affairs and higher administration, and a PhD in agricultural extension education from Michigan State University. Currently, he is enrolled at Payne Theological Seminary (Wilberforce, Ohio) as a candidate for the MDiv degree.

He serves as a Licentiate for the men's ministry at the historical Williams Chapel, African Methodist Episcopal Church (AMEC), under the leader of senior pastor Dr. Caesar R. Richburg, located in Orangeburg, South Carolina.

Mathis spent a year abroad as an international intern with Africare in Niger, West Africa, under the International Foundation of Education Self-Help (IFESH) program founded by the late Rev. Dr. Leon Sullivan.

He has been at South Carolina State University for eleven years, and he serves as the principle advisor to a student group entitled Minorities in Agriculture Natural Resources and Related Sciences (MANRRS), as well as the coordinator for the national program called AgDiscovery, which has been in existence since 2010, sponsored by the U. S. Department of Agriculture, Animal and Plant Health Inspection Service (APHIS), and Marketing and Regulatory Programs Business Services (MRPBS).

He is married to Gossie C. Mathis, M.D., and they are parents to Courtney, Tamilia, Sterling, and Christopher.

Matthew Parker Sr. (Consulting Editor)

Matthew Parker Sr. is president of The Institute for Black Family Development, a multifaceted ministry that designs and coordinates programs to strengthen Black families and churches. He is also founder of the Summit Group and Parker Books.

Matthew earned a BA in sociology from Wheaton College, a diploma from the Grand Rapids School of Bible and Music, and a MA in educational administration from the University of Detroit.

He has served as staff for Campus Crusade for Christ, associate vice president for urban academic affairs at William Tyndale College (Farmington Hills, Michigan), and on the editorial boards of Zondervan Press and Moody Press. He is highly sought-out consultant for many organizations

Matthew is the author of *Teaching Our Men—Reaching Our Fathers* (2010), coeditor of *Called to Lead* (1995), *Planting Seeds of Hope* (2000); and consulting editor to numerous books, including *The Black Family: Past, Present, and Future* (1991); *Evangelism, Discipleship in African American Churches* (1999), *Men to Men* (1996), and *Women to Women* (1996).

With his gift of administration, teaching and networking with churches, Christian organizations, Christian colleges, foundation, banks, healthcare agencies, publishers, associations, denominations, trainers, and volunteers, he has equipped, mentored and coached over one million people. His efforts have generated approximately 50 million dollars in revenue from book sales, grants, products, training, sponsorships and in-kind contributions. In addition, he has been involved in the starting of thirty-five churches, organizations, and programs.

Matthew is married to Karon Parker and they are the parents of five children—Matthew Jr., Tiffany, Michael, Kelley, and Justin.

Henry (Hank) Lee Allen

Dr. Henry Lee Allen is professor of Sociology and chair of the Department of Sociology and Anthropology at Wheaton College (Illinois). He has a biblical studies degree from Wheaton College and a PhD from the University of Chicago. Born in Joiner, Arkansas, and raised in Phoenix Illinois, he is married to Juliet Cooper Allen.

He has previously held faculty positions at the University of Rochester (New York), Bethel College (Minnesota), and Calvin College (Michigan). The author of numerous articles, his current research is focused on developing mathematical models to analyze global scientific developments in societies and their systems of postsecondary education. Under the auspices of the National Education Association, he has completed research on such matters in the United Kingdom, Canada, Israel, and the United States.

Along with teaching the adult Sunday School class at Jubilee Baptist Church in Bolingbrook, Illinois for nearly a decade, he has worked on projects with international leaders in law enforcement.

Paul Cannings

Dr. Paul Cannings is the founder and senior pastor of Living Word Fellowship Church in Houston, Texas. He is also the president of Power Walk Ministries, a national and global training ministry for clergy and lay leaders.

Cannings studied at Oxford University (England) and holds a doctorate in Philosophy/Theological Studies in Religion and Society from Oxford Graduate School in Dayton, Tennessee. He earned a MA in Christian Education from Dallas Theological Seminary and received a BA from Austin College (Sherman, Texas).

He is the author of numerous books, including the newest release, *Making Your Vision a Reality* (2013). He has also written *Give Fear a Knock Out Punch* (2010) and the most requested *Leadership Training Manual* (2012). He can be heard daily in Houston on KHCB 105.7 FM, where he also hosts a live question-and-answer program, Oneplace.com, and is seen on local My20 Houston.

Paul and his wife Everette are the parents of two adult sons, Paul Jr. and Pierre, who are married to Tanisha and Monica respectively. They have four grandchildren.

Lloyd C. Blue

Dr. Lloyd C. Blue is a product of California Baptist College, Riverside, California, where his studies included religion, sociology, and business administration. In August 1985, he received a Doctor of Ministry Degree from the University of Central America. Dr. Blue worked for approximately fifteen years with Campus Crusade for Christ International, assisting pastors in training the laity to personally share their faith using "The Four Spiritual Laws," and assisting pastors in implementing the principles of "Pastoral Management." He served as Senior Pastor for thirty years and has trained and assisted pastors for twenty-six of those years. He is professor emeritus of Aspen Christian College & Seminary, Aurora, Colorado.

Blue is both nationally and internationally acclaimed for his lectures in the areas of personal evangelism, the ministry of the Holy Spirit, abundant Christian living, building disciples, church growth, family enrichment, pastoral management, the mechanics of expository preaching, and instruction on how to conduct city/countywide revivals.

He has been guest speaker for numerous national and international Christian organizations of all cultures, including The Keswick Convention (Barbados), The National Black Pastors Conference, The Greenbelt Festival (South Shore England), Here's Life Black America Conference, Southern Baptist Evangelism Conference, In Contact Ministries (London, England), and the E. K. Bailey Expository Preaching Conference.

Known to many as a leading authority on church growth, he was led of the Holy Spirit to enter into full-time ministry as a consultant on church growth and he is responsible for the organization of Church Growth Unlimited, Inc.

He is one of the most gifted and sought-after preachers in the contemporary Black church. His compelling understanding of the gospel and its relationship to the complexities of our culture has made him one of the most requested lecturers of our day.

In addition to his duties with Church Growth Unlimited, Inc., he ministers to husbands and fathers, serves as senior associate pastor of the Cornerstone Baptist Church of Arlington, Texas, and is executive director of Pastoral Development Ministries, Baptist Ministers Conference, Dallas, Texas.

He is a native of North Carolina. He and his wife Tressie are the parents of one son, Lloyd II.

The author of several book chapters and self-help manuals, he is also author of the book *Developing Oneness in Marriage: A How-to for Husbands* (Dallas: Searchlight Press, 2011).

Christina Dixon

Christina Dixon brings contagious enthusiasm to whatever she does. As a publisher and writing coach, she has spent over a decade equipping writers as they go from manuscript to marketplace.

In January 2001 she released her first book entitled *How to Respect an Irresponsible Man.* She is a contributing writer to the *Wisdom and Grace Devotional Bible for Young Women of Color* (2002), by Nia Publishing, and co-author of the award winning book *HELP! for Your Leadership* (2003) by

PriorityOne Publications where she is founder and president, as well as five years an inspirational columnist for the e-magazine *WOW! Women of the Word*. She also serves as vice president of the American Christian Writers— Metro Detroit Scribes for Christ. As a family-life educator and counselor, she helps single and couples build, maintain, and restore healthy relationships through seminars, workshops, and keynotes at conferences, churches, rehabilitation centers, prisons, and community events. Christina serves as vice chair of the board of directors of the Marriage Resource Center. A graduate of Great Lakes Christian College, Christina is also a certified biblical counselor through Christian Research and Development.

An active member of the United Christian Women's Ministries (UCWM), she has served as local church president (New Hope Progressive Church of Christ (Holiness, USA), district president for churches in Michigan and Ohio, as well Northern Diocese secretary. A licensed missionary, in June 2012, she was selected as the UCWM Northern Diocese Woman of the Year.

Skilled at speaking to both secular and faith-based organizations, Christina has inspired people from all walks of life for more than twenty years. No matter what "hat" she wears, Christina can be found encouraging others to be all that God has designed them to be, while challenging them to overcome the obstacles they face and inspiring them to take the next step.

A wife, mother, and grandmother, Christina and her husband, Elder Michael Dixon, lives in Detroit, Michigan.

Sabrina D. Black

Dr. Sabrina Black is an author, professor, counselor, mentor, life coach, missionary, and Bible scholar. She is the founder of *Global Projects for Hope, Help, and Healing* (GPH3), a non profit 501c3 Missions Agency that has served five continents. She is a modern-day abolitionist in the fight against human trafficking. She is also vice chair of *MIRRC—the Michigan Rescue and Restore Coalition*. She is the recipient of the Great Commission Humanitarian of the Year Award, Who's Who in Black Detroit, 2010 Spirit of Detroit Award, the 2011 Community Icon Award, and the 2011 Kingdom Dreamer Award for Global Impact.

With more than twenty years on the mission field, Dr. Black was one of four hundred delegates from the US chosen to be a part of four thousand leaders from more than two hundred nations in Cape Town for the 2010 Lausanne World Congress, where she was communication liaison for the African American delegates. She was also coordinator for the 2010 Lausanne Gathering in Detroit, Michigan. In 2010, she was appointed by the Movement for African National Initiative (MANI) as deputy continental coordinator for Africans in the Diaspora, in charge of North America. She is a cofacilitator for the Global Impact Strategy Meeting in Maryland, and served as affinity speaker for Mission America. Sabrina served as a volunteer and counseling mentor at the European Leadership Forum in Budapest, Hungary in 2010.

Dr. Black is in private practice and the clinical director of Abundant Life Counseling Center, which emphasizes spiritual values. She is a limited licensed professional counselor, certified addictions counselor and certified biblical counselor with twenty years of experience in individual, marriage, family, and group counseling. She has degrees in psychology and counseling and expertise in gambling addiction, sexual addiction and sexual abuse, relational problems due to substance addiction, issues relating to clergy and ministry leaders, marital conflict and communications, boundaries and spiritual growth, stress, anxiety, burnout, anger management, and depression.

Dr. Black is an expert talent on such video training projects as Domestic Violence, DivorceCare, GriefShare, and Single Parenting. and a national and international speaker for conferences, retreats, and workshops.

Sabrina is contributing author to the *Soul Care Bible*; coauthor of *Prone to Wander: A Woman's Struggle with Sexual Sin and Addiction*; coeditor of *Counseling in African American Communities* (title changed to *Counseling for Seemingly Impossible Problems*); author of *Can Two Walk Together: Encouragement for Spiritual Unbalanced Marriages* and *Effective Strategies for Counseling African American Men*; coauthor of *HELP! for Your Leadership* and several workbooks.

She has served as adjunct faculty to several colleges, universities, and seminaries, as well as with Christian Research and Development. She is a member of Evangel Ministries (Christopher Brooks, pastor). She is president of the National Biblical Counselor Conference, past chairperson of the Black African American Association of Christian Counselors and a member of the American Counselors Association, and International Association of Marriage and Family Counseling.

Sabrina lives in Detroit, Michigan with her husband Warren José Black. She has one son and four grandchildren. She has traveled to Romania,

London, Budapest, the West Indies, Italy, Bulgaria, Spain, Nigeria, South Africa, Liberia, and Uganda, teaching, preaching, and reaching the masses with the gospel of Jesus Christ. She is an ordained elder and chaplain who has written more than one hundred songs of praise and worship.

Pamela J. Hudson

A certified biblical counselor and life coach, Pamela counsels singles, married, and youth. She is president of ACMS Coaching Service, LLC, director of the WRAP writing group, and executive director of Global Projects, an international non-profit organization.

She is coauthor of *HELP! for Your Leadership* (2003), a contributing writer in the *Wisdom and Grace Bible for Young Women of Color* (2002), and the e-book *Coaching Keys to Living Victorious* (2012).

Authors of multiple articles in national publications, she has published through Nia Publishing, PriorityOne Publications and *Grapevine Magazine*, as well as several counseling associations.

Pamela resides in Detroit, Michigan. She has one adult daughter and two granddaughters.

Brenda A. Jenkins

Brenda is an associate minister and director of parenting ministry at New Hope Missionary Baptist Church in Southfield, Michigan. She is a certified biblical counselor and adjunct instructor for Christian Research and Development (CRD). Brenda started the counseling ministry at New Hope and assisted other churches in the Detroit area to get counseling ministries started under CRD.

Brenda is a member of the National Speakers Association and has served in multiple capacities at the Michigan chapter board of directors. She is working on a doctorate in education (which she expects to complete in Organizational Leadership in 2013).

Brenda has her own business, ARIEL Connections, and serves as a consultant, speaker, and author. She is coauthor of the books *HELP! for Your Leadership* and *He Is Not Left Behind ... He Is with Me!*

Brenda is the mother of four adult children, grandmother of fourteen, and great grandmother of three.

Michael T. Westbrook

Michael Thomas Westbrook was born in Summit, New Jersey, and grew up in Summit and Newark. Raised by a single mother, who encouraged community outreach programs and the church to assist in his growth, he recognized at an early age the lack and need of family restoration. He attended William Penn University (Iowa) and was recognized by the president and professors as an effective speaker and advocate for student rights. This served as the foundation for his later works. He is a Rutgers University Common Ground Leadership and Executive Leadership Programs graduate and has studied in the masters' program in Urban Work at Alliance Theological Seminary.

Michael has served several institutions in leadership development and management, including the YMWCA and Fountain Baptist Church of Summit. He recalled a Bill Moyers special report on the worst city in the U.S. in 1986—Newark! Thus, he gave up dreams of a football career to begin a journey of rebuilding and restoration of youth, families, communities of Newark, and elsewhere by joining the staff of Young Life, Inc., as an area director in Newark. He served seventeen years on staff as urban training director, regional director, vice president of Multicultural & Urban Ministry Eastern Division, and on the President's cabinet. He also served as assistant of St. John UF Baptist Church, Newark, and is currently treasurer for Metropolitan Annual Conference.

Identifying the need to expand outreach to also include youth, families, and the entire community, in 2003, Michael became president/CEO & cofounder of Greater Life, Inc. He is also pastor of Greater Life Christian Fellowship Church, alongside his wife, Maria who serves as assistant pastor.

During his twenty-five years of service to more than 50,000 people, Michael has served many organizations and groups in various capacities throughout the country, focusing on the concerns relating to youth, gang, and street culture, family restoration, and community development, including as vice president of the 5th District Newark Police Department Clergy Alliance; dean of several institutions, including Eastern University Institute for Urban Ministry Training; advisory boardmember at the Essex County (New Jersey) Youth Detention Facility; founder and chairman of the board of Gateway Pregnancy Centers (headquartered in Irvington, New Jersey); member of board of directors of Fourth Generation Ministries, Montclair, New Jersey, and Restore Ministries, Elizabeth, New Jersey; Boy Scouts Northern NJ Lenape district vice-chair of development and Newark Scout Master; Newark Anti-Human-Trafficking Coalition; cochairman of the Weequahic Homeowners Coalition; and vice president of Newark North Jersey Committee of Black Churchmen.

Michael is a contributing author of the books *Planting Seeds of Hope* (2002) and *Men of Color Study Bible* (2002), and is a recipient of many honors and awards, including Who's Who Amongst American Christian Leaders and the International Peace Prize.

A resident of Newark, New Jersey, he is married to Maria A. Westbrook. They have six godchildren, have "parented" orphaned children of murdered and deceased parents, and have assisted parents in crisis situations for twenty-five years.

Maria A. Westbrook

Rev. Maria Antoinette (Rimmel-Ellis-)Westbrook was born and raised in the "projects" of Pittsburgh, and shortly thereafter, moved to Compton (Los Angeles). As a teenager, she was thrust into a world of hatred, misery, homelessness, and utter loneliness. When she was sixteen, God spared her life by introducing her to a teen-focused community outreach program and church that enhanced her spiritual and academic growth.

Maria attended William Penn University (Iowa) and earned a degree in Business Administration and Economics, with later education through Fuller Seminary (California), Eastern Bible College (Pennsylvania), and is a graduate of Metropolitan Bible Institute (New Jersey).

She worked for more than a decade in a business career at Kemper Insurance in Collection Accounting & Underwriting (which included working at the World Trade Center). While volunteering after work, she realized that God was calling her to serve full-time to give back what she had gained, to young people, parents, families, and the community of Newark.

Over the years, Maria has directly impacted more than fifty thousand people. She has served in the areas of accounting, underwriting, administration, nonprofit organizational, fundraising, and leadership development. She has served as a women's counselor and women's seminar leader, establishing teen programs, gang intervention and prevention programs, and young married couples' counseling and gatherings along with her husband, Michael. She and her husband also helped to pioneer Young Life in Newark (a street outreach to teenagers) in 1986 through 2003, where she also served as administrator, trainer, and fund developer for Young Life's vice-president's office of Multicultural & Urban Ministries in the Eastern Division of the U.S.

Maria currently serves more than fifteen hundred residents per year in the city of Newark, as cofounder and vice president of Greater Life, Inc. (an expanded holistic outreach to youth, families, and communities) and as cofounder and assistant pastor of Greater Life Christian Fellowship Church, alongside her husband Michael.

Maria has graduated from various programs and been certified in several areas, including the Executive Leadership Program of The Institute for Black Family Development, urban youth work, crisis pregnancy counseling to women and families, grant writing, consultation, and fund development, and the Newark Community Orientation Course. She has also been professionally trained in music and has participated in concerts and recordings with statewide choirs, musicals, and solo productions. Maria also presents workshops on Black sacred music.

Maria is listed in the "National Who's Who" Directory, and has received numerous other awards for her service to others, including the State of New Jersey First Lady Award. She has volunteered her time over the years for several organizations, including Local Boys' and Girls' Club, Youth Advocate Program, Youth Employment & Referral Network (YERN), YMWCA, Cochair of the Newark Historic Robert Treat Boy Scouts, Newark Police Clergy Alliance, Gateway (Crisis) Pregnancy Centers in NJ, Newark Anti-Human-Trafficking Coalition, Essex County Youth Detention Facility, Newark Police Clergy ride-a-longs, Newark-North Jersey Black Churchmen, and several organizations' board of directors.

A resident of Newark, Maria is married to Pastor Michael T. Westbrook. They have six godchildren, and have been "parenting" orphaned children and assisting parents in crisis situations for twenty-five years.

Patricia R. Williams

Patricia Robinson Williams is minister of congregational care and development of the Wheeler Avenue Baptist Church located in Houston, Texas. She holds the PhD in literature and linguistics from the University of Illinois in Champaign-Urbana. She has also earned a Certificate in Bible and Theology from the College of Biblical Studies—Houston, is certified in Telios Therapy from the Houston Center for Christian Counseling; is recipient of the MA in pastoral counseling and psychology from Houston Baptist University; as well as holder of a specialization in marriage and family therapy from Houston Graduate School of Theology. Additionally, she is a licensed marriage and family therapist and an American Association of Pastoral Counselors specialist in Pastoral Care.

She has nineteen years of experience as a ministry professional, commencing in 1993 as adjunct professor at the College of Biblical Studies—Houston, later becoming department chair and professor of general studies at this institution. She was a trustee of the Board of the College of Biblical Studies from 1996–2001, during which time she served as accreditation consultant to the college—a role that resulted in full accreditation. She has also served as adjunct professor at the Houston Graduate School of Theology, 2005–2008, in the counseling program. Since 2004, Williams has held the position of minister of congregational care and development of the Wheeler Avenue Baptist Church of Houston, Texas, where she cares for congregants experiencing short-term and long-term illnesses and provides support for those experiencing grief, as well as offers counseling and growth group opportunities for congregants. Dr. Williams is also responsible for congregational development through initial discipleship of new members and subsequent involvement of these individuals in the work and witness of the church. In these roles, she leads and assists in the development of three ministry teams, one of which is a Stephen Ministry group.

During her career, she has received numerous awards, among these the Zeta Phi Beta Sorority Ordinary People Doing Extraordinary Things in 2011. A published author, she recently completed the unpublished manuscript, *Healing for Souls Under Siege.*

She is the wife of Rev. Dr. Warren Williams and the mother of Mr. Jerrel, Rev. Jaclyn P. and Mr. Julian (Mrs. Jaclyn K.) Williams.

Shirley Ann Spencer June

A native of Thomasville, Georgia, Shirley earned a BS degree in biology from Knoxville College, a MS degree in zoology from the University of Illinois (Champaign-Urbana), a MA in counseling ministries from Cornerstone University/Grand Rapids Theological Seminary (Grand Rapids, MI), and is a limited licensed professional counselor. She also did a year of postbaccalaureate study in biology at Knox College (Galesburg, Illinois), has a certificate in Theology from the Interdenominational Theology Center (Atlanta, Georgia), and is also a graduate of the Mount Hope Bible Training Institute (Lansing, Michigan).

Prior to retiring from Michigan State University, she worked first in the medical school in electron microscopy and later in the undergraduate university division as an academic advisor.

The author of two book chapters, she is a member of the ministerial staff at the New Mount Calvary Baptist Church (Lansing, MI) and serves as the superintendant of Sunday school.

She is married to Lee N. June, and they are the parents of two sons, Brian L. and Stephen A. June.

PART 1
LEADERSHIP IN PERSPECTIVE

Chapter 1

LEADERSHIP IN AFRICAN AMERICAN CHURCHES: NEW HORIZONS FOR THE TWENTY-FIRST CENTURY[1]

Henry L. Allen

No other ethnic group in history has accomplished more good by overcoming greater odds and opposition than have African Americans. Yet the societal and global populace is rarely aware of this salient fact. African Americans have always lived in perilous times throughout their collective sojourn in the United States of America. As the only ethnic group that has survived the multiple onslaughts of involuntary migration, genocidal oppression, racist dehumanization, slavery, segregation, prejudice, discrimination, poverty, civilized inhumanity, and chronic social injustice *simultaneously*, few experts understand the internal and external consequences of these intergenerational malignancies (Rothenberg 2008).

Few religious or civil authorities (and organizations) have the social capital that provides tangible wisdom for dealing with the ongoing plight of African Americans. While it is extremely popular to engage in historical amnesia or a denial of responsibility, the nation itself has been implicated for

---

1. This paper was initially prepared for and presented to the President's Institute, Institute for Black Family Development on January 12, 2009. Some editorial changes have been made.

multiple generations in the degradation of African Americans. Inconsistent, intermittent social progress since the 1960s cannot obviate the lethal radioactive damage accumulated from 1619–1959! Often new immigrants have been treated with more sympathy and provided more systemic, tangible assistance than have African Americans whose labors have subsidized the nation's economy, and whose soldiers have died for it across generations. While it is indeed proper to rejoice at the incredible election of President Obama, one must never lose sight of the very complicated problems that transcend his immediate era. African Americans face internalized and external threats well beyond other ethnic groups.

Leadership always matters for African American families and communities. Authentic biblical leaders require a truthful assessment of our times. Standing in the gap for those created in God's image, these exemplars of spirituality are tangible, living incarnations of God's truth. Given these timeless premises, the gist of this chapter is about developing fresh social, scientific, and organizational innovations for biblical leadership in African American churches during the twenty-first century. What can a new generation of leaders do to address these complications in the African American churches? How might they move God's precious people and new converts beyond the "ball of confusion"? Statistical disparities can illuminate the breadth, depth, and range of African American social experiences, but they fail to probe the deeper human meanings behind the tabulations. Our task in this chapter is to offer up salient perspectives that target the needs of the most disadvantaged.

EMBRACING ETERNAL TEMPLATES

Authentic biblical wisdom always offers redemption and hope for every age and generation. For example, the cosmological prophet Daniel instructs us to discern the acute [though inconspicuous] ideological and global social trends among the nations in order to visualize how the Lord of Hosts is working in any epoch (Daniel 12:3). Generations earlier, in the book of Genesis, the visionary strategic planner Joseph exemplified the sufferings of minority status as he rose in social mobility from a slave to become the prime minister of an ancient Egyptian dynasty. With his strategic vision and planning across more than fourteen years of prosperity and famine, Joseph displayed for succeeding generations how to anticipate God's purposes across multiple conditions and time sequences.

Henry L. Allen

King David was actively and tenaciously engaged in building God's kingdom, in order to celebrate God's holiness and fulfill his everlasting purposes. One can peruse Psalms 145 to observe the nuggets of wisdom that permeated his soul. Moreover, Mordecai, Nehemiah, Joshua, Caleb, Barnabas, Paul, Timothy, Deborah, and Mary provided eternal templates of leadership for God's people. Through his atonement, Messiah Yeshua (Christ Jesus) left us all an enduring legacy of truth, sacrificial love, and redemption. From snippets of these brief portraits of godliness, we can deduce that authentic, biblical, church-related leadership must have a foundation of incarnational worship (Messiah), sacrificial love (Messiah), redemption (Messiah), multinational vision (Daniel), dedicated struggle (David), and strategic planning (Joseph).

God holds all leaders to a higher standard of responsibility to care for the disadvantaged. In the Pentateuch, Moses included the Year of Jubilee to counteract entrenched levels of social stratification, allowing the disadvantaged the hope of a new start every seven years. In Isaiah 58, the prophet warned leaders not to exploit workers or reject those in need. In Ezekiel 34, God angrily confronts self-indulgent leaders who fail to care for his flock. In Jeremiah 22, God indicts false leaders and false ideas that lead his people astray. In chapters three and five of the New Testament epistle of James, God holds leaders accountable for the impact of their leadership over those under their jurisdiction. Meanwhile, the most blistering remarks ever given by our Messiah were directed at leaders who neglected the weightier matters of the law: justice, equity, and mercy (Matthew 23). No ethnic group can escape these biblical principles and ultimately thrive.

Leadership in our times must carefully match innate spiritual dispositions with strategic opportunities, wise decisions, the best scientific expertise, precise timing, and collaborative social networks. Leaders must see ahead, see clearly with integrity, act responsibly, and visualize their role in the biblical agendas of God's unfolding kingdom. Our journey in this chapter will begin by identifying key contextual traits that characterize the emergent twenty-first century. Secondly, we shall identify the territorial gulfs that African American church leaders must face. Thirdly, we will probe core elements needed to produce a collaborative strategic plan. Finally, we suggest ways to move beyond the current intellectual malaise in religion, politics, and society.

DELVING INTO THE TWENTY-FIRST CENTURY

Like every other person, African Americans who live in the twenty-first century must engage global, regional, and local spheres of social reality. International events like distant wars, terrorism, foreign policies, interlocking technologies, and multinational markets or organizations frame global domains. Regional domains include proximate governments, confederations, and other forms of consortia. Local spheres revolve around families, schools, communities, churches, and businesses. We must negotiate informal, private interactions and public, formal ceremonies. It is delusional for us to act in a parasitic fashion as others use us to subsidize their interests, markets, and wealth. Far too many of us naively assist those sinister barons who want to rob, kill, and destroy our God-given treasures.

African Americans must operate on the basis of implicit theories about their plight, along with practical policies of survival, at both telescopic and microscopic levels. We must pursue life inexorably within existing social institutions and societal norms. We must take a panoramic view, incorporating short-term and long-term time frames in the national narrative. Astute biblical leadership has to inculcate the above frames of reference in an era of diversity, globalization, inequalities, and contingencies. Leadership matches innate dispositions (or character traits), behavioral experiences, and inspired vision with relevant trends, networks, conditions, and appropriate timing.

I have seen these abstract ideas operate tangibly in multiple roles, up close and personal. For some twenty-seven years, I have taught sociology at predominately White institutions of higher education in Illinois, Minnesota, Michigan, and New York. I have been a consultant on postsecondary educational matters with the National Education Association [an organization with more than three million members] for sixteen years. I have advised major organizations such as the American Bible Society, public school districts, the University of Oxford Round Table, and the FBI National Academy. I have belonged to scientific associations like the New York Academy of Sciences, the Game Theory Society, the American Mathematical Society, the American Academy of Social and Political Science, etc. I have joined the NAACP, the Urban League, and founded the African American Leadership Roundtable (Illinois). For forty-two years, I have been an active member of evangelical-oriented churches, mainly in African American congregations. My research has covered issues related to church denominations, colleges and universities, ethnicity, gender, productivity and work, labor markets, science, and future generations in society.

As a mathematical sociologist, I am especially attuned to the mathematics that typify the hidden network of social relationships that structure and process observable outcomes (Miller and Page, 2007). I am deeply interested in how and why negative outcomes are generated for African Americans and others—along with feedback loops, patterns of social organization and disorganization. Specifically, I watch the construction of norms, roles, and institutions that affect human societies according to their implications for theoretical explanations, methods of evidence, policy matters, and practical concerns across levels involving individuals, groups, social networks, communities or neighborhoods, complex organizations, institutions, markets, industries, and social systems.

These social factors imply that leadership in any African American domain—especially churches—is not at all easy. Even with the best expertise and motives, anyone who aspires to lead must face the insidious temptations of pride and the unpopular pathos of rejection. Leaders must see farther ahead than their followers. They must probe deeper aspects of reality than those they supervise and serve. Table 1.1 below displays the conceptual rubric that should guide twenty-first century leaders in each dimension (formal and informal) of the strategic planning process. The formal dimension pertains to overt or visible phenomena, while the informal dimension captures the invisible features of what goes on behind the scenes. The best leaders must address all these domains, directly or indirectly.

TABLE 1.1. A MATRIX OF SOCIOLOGICAL ANALYSES FOR STRATEGIC PLANNING

Levels	Theory	Methods	Policy	Practice
Social system				
Markets				
Industry				
Organization				
Community				
Social network				
Group				
Individual				

Each column must guide thoughtful deliberations for each level of analysis. Church leaders ought to engage these intersections in their thoughts and plans. Theories account for *why* things occur, including the intersections between the observations we make and the codifications of our assumptions about reality. Methods refer to the techniques we adopt to measure or scrutinize the scope, rigor, and quality of empirical evidence used in making decisions. Policy domains involve the prescriptions or proscriptions we solicit in addressing human problems. Finally, the realm of *practice* depicts how our leadership or plans tangibly affect how people eat, sleep, acquire shelter or healthcare, and remedy other practical needs. Mental and spiritual needs are incorporated, too. Leaders can adapt this intellectual tool or social technology to their own capacities and interests. Beyond this tool, leaders can subsequently popularize their acquired insights for the convenient consumption of their constituencies.

What fresh challenges must a new generation of African American church leaders meet? I remind the reader that Figure 1 pertains to each of these in at least two basic dimensions, notably formal (visible, public) and informal (invisible, private). We must be alert to the impact and role of tipping points, thresholds of complexity, and chaos in our best laid plans (Gladwell 2000). Mere discursive morality and traditional spiritual polemics alone are not sufficient for addressing these challenges. African American leaders in the twenty-first century must be conversant about mathematics and statistics, science and technology, climate change, and population trends. Note the list of items below:

- The glut of information overload in media or World Wide Web (Mastering these electronic technologies helped President Obama win a momentous election.)

- The implications of social intelligence (toxic social relations)

- Allostatic load/catastrophic stress levels (poverty, illiteracy, etc.)

- An organizational underdevelopment crisis

- Disintegration of African American marriages, families, and communities

Henry L. Allen

- Complexities, contingencies, and persistent inequalities in housing, healthcare, education, technology, entrepreneurship, safety and security, immigration, mental health

In these pressured times, all citizens face an information glut exacerbated by a technology gap for many needy African Americans (Wright 2007). Too much information can impede critical judgments or cloud our discernment, thereby inhibiting our discretion. Moreover, many of our neighborhoods are plagued with negative social factors that inhibit healthy identities or relationships (Diamond 2005). Unfortunately, far too many of us have reached salient tipping points in moral turpitude, vulgar sexuality, profane speech, vanity, the incarceration of African American males, and in ignoring the ongoing marital eligibility crisis for African American women. These maladies far too often breed senseless violence against women, children, and youth! Gender wars are frequently concealed among the disadvantaged even as many of our assimilated elites abandon our collective interests. Potential talents and expertise have been siphoned off into tar pits of destruction, often for cheap commercial profit or greedy material indulgence. Many of our church or moral leaders are afraid to expose the vulgarity of many cultural fads and fashions. Some even bring such vanities and delusions into church! They fear being called outdated or facing the backlash of irrelevance.

Our communities lack coherence, as they disintegrate into enclaves of hyper-segregation, economic turmoil, and pathological violence. Economic distress is endemic, a cancer destroying any hopes for sustained, intact African American communities. Much more important than mere faddish concerns with social capital is the organizational and institutional expertise that is needed to survive in the global marketplace (Goleman 2006). For the size of our population, we lack sufficient social institutions that we control (Tobert 2009). Our neighborhoods are chronically underdeveloped outside the typical confines of churches, funeral homes, small businesses, and civil rights associations. This is the burden we inherit from our history in this nation. All these conditions increase allostatic load and render catastrophic stresses for most African Americans, vitiating the patriotic myth of equality of opportunity in education and society (Goleman 2006). We also have the burdens of exposing and ameliorating White privilege (Rothenberg 2008). Statistical data simply bear out the variations and ranges that structure the distributions of these and other variables.

REMEDYING THE GULFS AND CHASMS

How might African Americans remedy the challenges identified above in an age of oversaturated mass media? As a simple scholar, I know that no long-term progress can be made apart from engaging the academic systems that umpire and legitimate the division of labor in society (Newfield 2008). Sociologist Emile Durkheim realized that ideology and solidarity are the outcomes of the division of labor, the structure of occupations and jobs in society. Great scientific and technological advances are rooted in the global competition surrounding mathematics and science (Trefil 2008). There can be no genuine freedom as long as any ethnic group has a pariah status within these intellectual domains. Universities sculpt the leaders of tomorrow. During the twenty-first century, the most innovative African American churches and their leaders must grapple with statistical trends, computer simulations, and the mathematical thinking that fuels the third scientific revolution (Gowers 2008).

TABLE 1.2. A TYPOLOGY OF AFRICAN AMERICAN LEADERSHIP STYLES

Transformative Style	
Adversarial Leadership Promotes leader's moral vision Power over and through others	**Democratic, Empowering Leadership** Promotes democracy and social empowerment Power with others
Authoritarian Leadership Promotes maintenance of status quo Power over others	**Facilitative Leadership** Promotes more humane organizational climate and individual empowerment Power through and power over others
Transactional Style	

Source: Adapted from Blase, Joseph and Gary L. Anderson. 1995. *The Micropolitics of Educational Leadership*. New York: Teachers College Press; cited at a workshop on educational issues at the Margaret S. Warner Graduate School of Education, the University of Rochester, Rochester, NY, 1991–1996.

What are the leadership proclivities of African American leaders? Insights from organizational studies of educational leadership might offer some possibilities as shown in Table 1.2. This profiles four hypothesized styles of leadership on a vertical axis that ranges from *transformative* aims at the top to *transactional* objectives at the bottom. On the horizontal axis, the range—left to right—is from closed patterns to open patterns of collaboration. Four cells are created from the intersection of these two axes. The upper left cell depicts *adversarial leadership*, a style that promotes the leader's moral vision via power over and power through other human beings. The lower left cell reveals an *authoritarian* style of leadership that promotes the status quo through power over others. Adversarial leaders focus on transforming organizational conditions, while authoritarian leaders maintain existing social transactions. African American church leaders and pastors can conform to each of these patterns, which were indicative of twentieth-century mind-sets.

For the twenty-first century, more open styles of leadership are needed for success. The upper right cell displays *empowering leadership* that promotes democracy and encourages power in collaboration with others. The lower right cell targets leaders that are point guards, those who promote an organizational climate that maximizes the individual potential of all organizational actors: power through and over others in ways that *facilitate* active ownership or engagement. New generations embrace these modalities of leadership, as the election strategies of President Barack Obama in 2008 demonstrated.

Experts realize that twentieth-century patterns of organizational leadership differ appreciably from twentieth-first century leadership patterns (Hickman 1998). Table 1.3 illustrates this:

TABLE 1.3. CHANGES IN LEADERSHIP PATTERNS

From: Twentieth-Century Leadership Patterns	To: Twenty-First-Century Leadership Patterns
Few leaders, mainly at the top	Leaders at every level; fewer managers
Leading by goal-setting (return on investment)	Leading by vision—new directions for long-term business growth
Downsizing, benchmarking for low cost, high quality	Also creating domains of uniqueness, distinctive competencies
Reactive/adaptive to change	Anticipative/futures creative
Designer of hierarchical organizations	Designer of flatter, distributed, more collegial organizations; leader as social architect
Directing and supervising individuals	Empowering and inspiring individuals, but also facilitating teamwork
Information held by a few decision-makers	Information shared with many, both internally and with outside partners
Leaders as boss, controlling processes and behaviors	Leader as coach, creating learning organizations
Leaders as stabilizer, balancing conflicting demands and maintaining the culture	Leader as change agent, creating agenda for change, balancing risks, and evolving the culture and technology base
Leader responsible for developing good managers	Leader also responsible for developing future leaders; serving as leader of leaders
Source: Hickman 1998, 7.	

Anticipating these emerging changes in leadership patterns as the twenty-first century unfolds, one expert (Hickman 1998, 7) writes:

> Since no organization can possibly be all things to all people, the leader will be constantly challenged to forge major alliances and partnerships with others to achieve mutual goals. Thus the role of leader as social architect will be expanded, and skills such as negotiation, technology assessment, and design of organizational cultures could grow in importance for aspiring leaders.

All these changes will create a need for millions of new leaders in the future. In the end, leaders who succeed best will be those who are best able to (1) set direction during turbulent times, (2) manage change while still providing exceptional customer service and quality; (3) attract resources and forge new alliances to accommodate new constituencies; (4) harness diversity on a global scale; (5) inspire a sense of optimism, enthusiasm, and commitment among their followers; and be a leader of leaders, especially regarding knowledge workers. Leadership in the twenty-first century is not a job for wimps, but then, it never was. President Obama, for example, embodies many of these leadership traits.

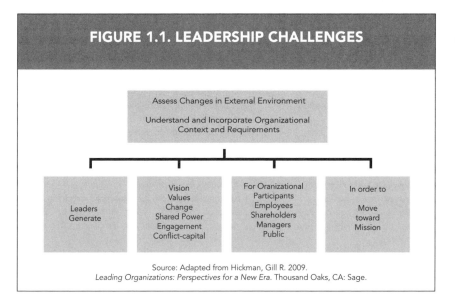

FIGURE 1.1. LEADERSHIP CHALLENGES

Source: Adapted from Hickman, Gill R. 2009. *Leading Organizations: Perspectives for a New Era.* Thousand Oaks, CA: Sage.

Henry L. Allen

Leaders must confront the changing social conditions of the twenty-first century. As the diagram above indicates, leaders must examine external environments, understand organizational matters, posit vision and values for all participants, and move toward the organization's mission. They must create viable structures, align goals, frame culture, and build capacity in order to generate organizational contributions to society.

LOOKING AHEAD: TWENTY-FIRST-CENTURY CHALLENGES AND STRATEGIC VISTAS

African American leaders must be prepared for ecological catastrophes or natural disasters like Hurricane Katrina, which are unexpected, ominous threats to natural and social climates (see Jared Diamond, *Collapse: How Societies Choose to Fail or Succeed,* 2005). Government intrusions, the improper surveillance of civilians, police brutality and misconduct, nefarious youth gangs, unemployment crises, criminal justice problems, prison reforms, academic achievement gaps, gaps in wealth, technological gaps, intergenerational turnover, aging populations, the decline of U.S. world dominance, traditional theological controversies, *plus* scientific revolutions in biotechnology, quantum computers, complex systems science, and information technologies likewise deserve the attention of new leaders. The exact details relevant to each of these complications exceed the scope of this general inquiry. One can add these topics to those that noted talk-show host Tavis Smiley and his cadre of leaders have investigated as they have evaluated the status of African Americans in the last decade.

Every extraordinary challenge offers strategic opportunities for faith, innovation, resiliency, and achievement. What an opportunity for transformational leaders in the "Obama era"! We need African American mathematicians, physicists, chemists, biologists, and other scientists, thus moving beyond those disciplines we habitually enter. Imagine a thousand Ben Carsons or Percy Julians! Imagine African Americans as forty or more percent of scholars in the National Academy of Sciences, at California Institute of Technology, at MIT, and other premier universities. Table 1.4 illustrates the extent of our current plight in academia:

As a scholar of the sociology of American higher education, I can attest that there can be no real freedom for any ethnic group on this planet without collectively mastering the intricacies of mathematics. We need a new cadre of leaders in law enforcement: an FBI director, terrorism and crime experts, criminologists, and prison psychiatrists. We need to explore new vistas in parenting education, solar technologies, community development, and corporate leadership. Branching out beyond roles in movies, sports, and entertainment industries, we need new leaders to refurbish our social networks to include the worst of the poor—motivating them to reach their God-given potential.

TABLE 1.4. PROGRESS OF FULL-TIME BLACK FACULTY AT THE NATION'S HIGHEST UNIVERSITIES

Institution	1999	2002	2005	Change 1999–2005
Vanderbilt U.	2.2%	3.1%	4.3%	+2.1%
Northwestern U.	2.7%	2.0%	4.4%	+1.7%
UNC-Chapel Hill	4.1%	4.4%	5.7%	+1.6%
Carnegie Mellon	1.7%	1.6%	3.0%	+1.3%
Washington U.	2.6%	3.4%	3.9%	+1.3%
Johns Hopkins U.	2.9%	3.5%	3.9%	+1.0%
Princeton U.	2.0%	2.3%	3.0%	+1.0%
Harvard U.	2.2%	2.7%	3.1%	+0.9%
CalTech	0.6%	0.6%	1.4%	+0.8%
Brown U.	3.3%	3.7%	4.0%	+0.7%
Cornell U.	2.7%	3.3%	3.4%	+0.7%
Stanford U.	2.6%	2.6%	3.2%	+0.6%
U. Penn.	2.6%	3.2%	3.2%	+0.6%
Yale U.	2.7%	2.8%	3.2%	+0.5%
U. Chicago	2.4%	2.7%	2.8%	+0.4%
Duke U.	3.6%	3.7%	3.9%	+0.3%
U. Michigan	4.8%	4.7%	5.1%	+0.3%
Georgetown U.	4.5%	3.7%	4.6%	+0.1%
U. Notre Dame	2.2%	2.8%	2.3%	+0.1%
Dartmouth C.	4.1%	3.2%	4.1%	0.0%
MIT	2.9%	3.0%	2.9%	0.0%
U. Virginia	3.0%	3.2%	3.0%	0.0%
Rice U.	2.0%	2.1%	1.5%	–0.5%
Columbia U.	7.2%	7.2%	6.4%	–0.8%
U. Cal. Berkeley	3.1%	2.9%	2.1%	–1.0%
Emory U.	7.1%	6.9%	5.2%	–1.9%
Source: *Journal of Blacks in Higher Education*, Summer 2005, No. 48, 79.				

Henry L. Allen

We must accentuate our roots and embrace our legacy, for the Lord has always used our collective suffering to bring civil redemption to this nation. We must innovate beyond the conservative inertia of an insensitive or impotent evangelicalism. We must dream big, much bigger than the obvious dimensions of political institutions. We need to celebrate tradition without being imprisoned by it. Proactive, innovative leaders must move us beyond "churchanity" to spiritual optimality. Invisible ideas—rooted in goodness and truth—always have produced visible benefits. A new generation must postulate fresh vision and robust meanings to move us forward in the twenty-first century. If we pursue these vistas with integrity and excellence, this will be the African American century!

CONCLUSION

We live in an unprecedented age of innovation and opportunity, of poverty amidst great prosperity, of confusion despite an information explosion, of progress and pathos for African Americans. Typically, the United States' general populace suffers from ongoing historical amnesia and moral shortsightedness about the most disadvantaged African Americans amidst the usual pomposity of patriotic fervor. Yet, all is never entirely gloomy. Joy surrounded the inauguration of President Obama in 2009, while the deepest sorrows pervade the lives of poor and struggling families when innocent youth are murdered by senseless violence. Horrific, abominable crimes occur when human beings are treated like animals in the worst segments in our cities.

Technological gadgets and scandals abound. Leaders fall from corruption and the lack of integrity. The goddess of sexual immorality is worshipped via commercials, the Internet, cell phones, and the altars of pornography. AIDS, gangs, teenage pregnancies, violence, and stupidity are sometimes glamorized by materialistic fetishes plus unrealistic vanities as profits fuel mass media, music, and entertainment industries. Generations atrophy. The thief robs, kills, and destroys, while various religious, cultural, civic, and political elites wallow in petty self-indulgence. Delusions of apostasy engulf popular culture and elite society alike. We need a domestic and foreign policy to address the loss of virtue in many of our remaining intact communities. Let us learn assiduously from the successes of Barack Obama, Tony Dungy, Venus and Serena Williams, Ben Carson, Cathy Hughes, Mike Tomlin, Deval Patrick, Corey Booker, David Patterson, Michelle Obama, Linda Johnson-Rice, and other achievers.

Religious officials must revive as well as renew the organizational effectiveness of churches away from antiquated instruction, cultural traditionalism, musical addictions, and petty moralizations. We need a new generation of authentic church leaders whose lives are rooted in integrity and excellence, love, compassion, dignity, diligence, and an incarnational gospel rooted in the African American experience. Responsible church leaders must be organizational, spiritual, and educational innovators who eagerly grasp new horizons in the twenty-first century. They must jettison conservative mind-sets that are rooted in traditions of theological irrelevance and rediscover proactive biblical solutions to the most complicated woes facing humanity. Many unbelievers and agnostics reject "conservative mind-sets" rather than Messiah, mistaking the latter for the former. A new, more courageous generation must arise and shine to show the difference, as Isaiah 60 invites. If we can accomplish the feat of harnessing and controlling the intellectual property that the Lord of hosts has bequeathed to us as African Americans, young and old, get ready for the greatest accumulation of wealth that any oppressed ethnic group has ever experienced in history, even greater than the ascendancy of Barack Obama to the U.S. presidency. On to the African American century!

REFERENCES

Diamond, Jared. 2005. *Collapse: How Societies Choose to Fail or Succeed.* New York: Penguin.

Gladwell, M. 2000. *The Tipping Point.* Boston: Little, Brown, and Company. "Tipping points" refer to the numerical thresholds underlying the transitions to popular fads or fashions.

Goleman, D. 2006. *Social Intelligence.* New York: Bantam Books.

Gowers, Timothy, ed. 2008. *Princeton Companion to Mathematics.* Princeton, NJ: Princeton University Press.

Hickman, G. R. 1998. *Leading Organizations.* Thousand Oaks, CA: Sage.

Miller, John H. and Scott E. Page. 2007. *Complex Adaptive Systems.* Princeton, NJ: Princeton University Press.

Henry L. Allen

Newfield, C. 2008. *Unmaking the Public University*. Cambridge, MA: Harvard University Press.

Rothenberg, P. 2008. *White Privilege*. 3rd ed. New York: Worth Publishers.

Tolbert, P. S. and R. H. Hall. 2009. *Organizations: Structures, Processes, and Outcomes,* 10th ed. Upper Saddle River, NJ: Pearson/Prentice Hall.

Trefil, J. 2008. *Why Science?* New York: Columbia University Teachers College.

Wright, Alex. 2007. *Glut*. Washington, DC: Joseph Henry Press.

ABRIDGED BIBLIOGRAPHY OF RESEARCH IN SOCIAL COMPLEXITY, EDUCATION, AND SOCIETY

Allen, H. L. 1991. "The Mobility of Black Collegiate Faculty Revisited: Whatever Happened to the Brain Drain?" *Journal of Negro Education* 60: 97–109.

_____. 1994. "Faculty Workload and Productivity in an Accountability Era." *The NEA 1994 Almanac of Higher Education*: 25–38.

_____. 1995. "Workload and Productivity: Case Studies." *The NEA 1995 Almanac of Higher Education*: 21–32.

_____. 1996. "Faculty Workload and Productivity in the 1990s: Preliminary Findings." *The NEA 1996 Almanac of Higher Education*: 21–34.

_____. 1997. "Faculty Workload and Productivity: Ethnic and Gender Disparities." *The NEA 1997 Almanac of Higher Education*: 25–42.

_____. 1997. "Tenure: Why Faculty, and the Nation, Need It." *Thought and Action*, XIII, 2:75–88.

_____. 1998. "Faculty Workload and Productivity: Gender Comparisons." *The NEA 1998 Almanac of Higher Education*: 29–44.

_____. 1999. "Workload and Productivity in an Era of Performance Measures." *The NEA 1999 Almanac of Higher Education*: 27–44.

_____. 2000. "Tenure: Why Faculty, and the Nation, Need It." *Thought and Action* (republished with new postscript): 95–110.

_____. 2001. "Faculty Workload and Productivity in an Era of Organizational Change." *The NEA 2001 Almanac of Higher Education*: 59–74.

_____. 2002. "The Organizational Demography of Faculty Tenure: 1980–2000." *The NEA 2002 Almanac of Higher Education*: 59–72.

_____. 2002. "The Best of Times, the Worst of Times: Scenarios for Higher Education in the 21st Century." *Thought and Action*: 91–102.

_____. 2003. "Diversity, Nonstandard Work, and Academic Employment in the 21st Century." *The NEA 2003 Almanac of Higher Education*: 27–38.

_____. 2004. "Employment at the Margins: Nonstandard Work in Higher Education." *The NEA 2004 Almanac of Higher Education*: 27–38.

_____. 2006. "The Ghost of Veblen Revisited: Faculty Workload and Productivity in an Era of Privatization and Assessment." *The NEA 2006 Almanac of Higher Education*: 81–94.

_____. 2007. "The Evolving Nexus of Diversity: Ethnic Minority Faculty Views on Workload and Productivity." *The NEA 2007 Almanac of Higher Education*: 41–48.

Annals of the New York Academy of Sciences. 2000. Vol. 901. *Closure: Emergent Organizations and Their Dynamics*. New York: The New York Academy of Sciences.

Annals of the New York Academy of Sciences. 2001. Vol. 935. *Unity of Knowledge.* New York: The New York Academy of Sciences.

Annals of the New York Academy of Sciences. 2002. Vol. 959. *Increasing Healthy Lifespan.* New York: The New York Academy of Sciences.

Annals of the New York Academy of Sciences. 2003. Vol. 1001. *The Self: From Soul to Brain.* New York: The New York Academy of Sciences.

Annals of the New York Academy of Sciences. 2004. Vol. 1036. *Youth Violence.* New York: The New York Academy of Sciences.

Arnold, V., et al. 2000. *Mathematics: Frontiers and Perspectives.* Providence, RI: American Mathematical Society.

Arons, A. B. and A. M. Bork, ed. 1964. *Science and Ideas.* Englewood Cliffs, NJ: Prentice Hall.

Bailey, K. D. 1994. *Sociology and the New Systems Theory.* Albany, NY: State University of New York.

Barrow, J. 1998. *Impossibility.* New York: Oxford University Press.

Bar-Yam, Y. 1997. *Dynamics of Complex Systems.* Reading, MA: Addison-Wesley.

_____. 2000. "Significant Points in the Study of Complex Systems." *Unifying Themes in Complex Systems: Proceedings of the First International Conference on Complex Systems,* Vol. 1. Cambridge, MA: Westview.

_____. 2004. *Making Things Work.* Cambridge, MA: NECSI Knowledge Press.

Ben-David, J. 1972. *American Higher Education.* New York: McGraw-Hill.

_____. 1984. *The Scientist's Role in Society*. Chicago: University of Chicago Press.

Blalock, H. M. 1969. *Theory Construction: From Verbal to Mathematical Formulations*. Englewood Cliffs, NJ: Prentice Hall.

Blau, P. M. 1964. *Exchange and Power in Social Life*. New York: Wiley.

_____. 1973. *The Organization Of Academic Work*. New York: Wiley.

_____. 1994. *Structural Contexts of Opportunities*. Chicago: University of Chicago Press.

Bok, D. 1993. *The Cost of Talent*. New York: Free Press.

_____. 2003. *Universities in the Marketplace*. Princeton, NJ: Princeton University Press.

Boorstin, D. 1983. *The Discoverers*. New York: Random House.

Bourdieu, P. 1988. *Homo Academicus*. Stanford: Stanford University Press.

Bourgine, P. and J. Johnson, eds. 2006. "Living Roadmap for Complex Systems Science." ftp://ftp.cordis.europa.eu/pub/fp7/ict/docs/fet-proactive/press–13_en.pdf.

Bowles, S. 2004. *Microeconomics*. Princeton, NJ: Princeton University Press.

Brewer, D. J., S. M. Gates, and C. A. Goldman. 2005. *In Pursuit of Prestige*. New Brunswick, NJ: Transaction Publishers.

Buchanan, M. 2002. *Nexus*. New York: WW Norton and Company.

Camerer, Colin. 2003. *Behavioral Game Theory*. Princeton, NJ: Princeton University Press.

Henry L. Allen

Caplow, T. and R. McGee. 1958. *The Academic Marketplace*. New York: Basic Books.

Carroll, G. and M. Hannan. 2000. *The Demography of Corporations and Industries*. Princeton, Princeton University Press.

Casti, J. 1994. *Complexification*. New York: HarperCollins.

Chaitin, G. 1998. *The Limits of Mathematics*. Singapore: Springer-Verlag.

Clark, B. 1983. *The Higher Education System*. Berkeley, CA: University of California Press.

Cole, J. R. and S. Cole. 1973. *Social Stratification in Science*. Chicago: University of Chicago Press.

Coleman, J. S. 1990. *Foundations of Social Theory*. Cambridge, MA: Belknap/Harvard University Press.

Crane, D. 1972. *Invisible Colleges*. Chicago: University of Chicago Press.

Derber, C. 1998. *Corporation Nation*. New York: St. Martin's Griffen.

Diamond, J. 2005. *Collapse: How Societies Fail or Succeed*. New York: Viking.

Dickinson, Boonsri. 2007. "Map: Science's Family Tree." *Discover Magazine*: 14.

DiMaggio, P. 2001. *The Twenty-First-Century Firm*. Princeton, NJ: Princeton University Press.

Durkheim, E. 1996. *The Division of Labor in Society*. New York: Free Press.

Feemster, Samuel L. 2007. "Spirituality: The DNA of Law Enforcement Practice." *FBI Law Enforcement Bulletin*.

Ferris, T., ed. 1991. *The World Treasury of Physics, Astronomy, and Mathematics*. Boston: Little, Brown and Company.

Finer, S. E. and D. Mirfin. 1966. *Vilfredo Pareto: Sociological Writings*. New York: Praeger.

Forrester, J. 1973. *World Dynamics*. Cambridge, MA: Wright-Allen Press.

_____. 1976. *Principles of Systems*. Cambridge, MA: Wright-Allen Press.

Gladwell, M. 2000. *The Tipping Point*. Boston: Little, Brown, and Company.

Goleman, Daniel. 2006. *Social Intelligence*. New York: Bantam Books.

Gowers, Timothy, ed. 2008. *Princeton Companion to Mathematics*. Princeton, NJ: Princeton University Press.

Hickman, G. R. 1998. *Leading Organizations*. Thousand Oaks, CA: Sage.

Hubler, A. 2005. "Predicting Complex Systems With a Holistic Approach." *Complexity* 10:3:11–16.

Hunt, Earl. 2007. *The Mathematics of Behavior*. New York: Cambridge University Press.

Iberall, A. S. 1985. "Outlining Social Physics for Modern Societies— Locating Culture, Economics, and Politics: The Enlightenment Reconsidered." *Proceedings of the National Academy of Sciences* 82:5582–5584.

Karp, D. A., W. C. Yoels, and B. Vann, ed. 2004. *Sociology in Everyday Life* Long Grove, IL: Waveland Press.

Kaku, M. 1997. *Visions*. New York: Anchor Books, Doubleday.

Henry L. Allen

Lax, Peter D. 2008. "Mathematics and Physics." *Bulletin of the American Mathematical Society* 45:1:135–152.

Lightman, A. 2005. *The Discoveries*. New York: Pantheon.

Lindley, Dennis V. 2006. *Understanding Uncertainty*. Hoboken, NJ: Wiley.

Mackenzie, D., and B. Cipra. 2006. *What's Happening in the Mathematical Sciences*. Providence, RI: American Mathematical Society.

Mandelbrot, B. 2004. *The (Mis)behavior of Markets*. New York: Basic Books.

Miller, J. H. and S. E. Page. 2007. *Complex Adaptive Systems*. Princeton, NJ: Princeton University Press.

Newfield, C. 2008. *Unmaking the Public University*. Cambridge, MA: Harvard University Press.

Odin, J. and P. T. Manicas, ed. 2004. *Globalization and Higher Education*. Honolulu, HI: University of Hawaii Press.

Page, S. E. 2007. *The Difference*. Princeton, NJ: Princeton University Press.

Parsons, T. and G. R. Platt. 1968. *The American Academic Professions*. Cambridge, MA: Harvard University Press.

_____. *The American University*. Cambridge, MA: Harvard University Press.

Penrose, R. 2005. *The Road to Reality*. New York: Alfred A. Knopf.

Piel, G. 2001. *The Age of Science*. New York: Basic Books.

Rhodes, F. T. 2001. *The Creation of the Future*. Ithaca, NY: Cornell University Press.

Rothenberg, P. S. 2008. *White Privilege,* 3rd ed. New York: Worth
Publishers.

Siegfried, Tom. 2005. *A Beautiful Math.* Washington, DC: Joseph Henry
Press.

Simon, H. A. 1957. *Models of Man.* New York: Wiley.

_____. 1997. "Can There Be a Science of Complex Systems?" *Unifying
Themes in Complex Systems.* Cambridge, MA: Perseus Press 1:3–14.

Stewart, S. 2002. "The Complexity Complex." *University of Chicago
Magazine* 38–45.

Tolbert, P. S. and R. H. Hall. 2009. *Organizations: Structures, Processes, and
Outcomes,* 10th ed. Upper Saddle River, NJ: Pearson/Prentice Hall.

Trefil, J. 2008. *Why Science?* New York: Columbia University Teachers
College.

Urry, J. 2004. "Small Worlds and the New Social Physics." *Global Networks*
4:2:109–130.

Von Neumann, J. and O. Morgenstern. 2004. *Theory of Games and
Economic Behavior* (Sixtieth Anniversary Edition). Princeton, NJ:
Princeton University Press.

Von Neumann, John. 1986. "John von Neumann on Technological
Prospects and Global Limit." *Population and Development Review*
12:1:117–126.

Wagner, T. 2008. *The Global Academic Achievement Gap.* New York: Perseus
Books.

Wallace, W. L. 1983. *Principles of Scientific Sociology.* New York:
Aldine.

Weidlich, W. and G. Haag. 1983. *Concepts And Models of a Quantitative Sociology*. New York: Springer-Verlag.

Wolfram, S. 2002. *A New Kind of Science*. Champaign, IL: Wolfram Research.

Wright, A. 2007. *Glut*. Washington, DC: Joseph Henry Press.

Yellin, J. "A Model of Research Problem Allocation Among Members of a Scientific Community." *Journal of Mathematical Sociology* 2:1–36.

Young, H. Peyton. 2001. *Individual Strategy and Social Structure*. Princeton, NJ: Princeton University Press.

Chapter 2

LEADERSHIP VOICES—PAST, PRESENT, AND FUTURE

Lee N. June, Matthew Parker Sr., and Christopher C. Mathis Jr.

This chapter contains a collection of statements written by past leaders (now deceased), current leaders, and youth (our future leaders) from throughout the country. Each of these individuals were asked to briefly define leadership and to indicate what they believe are the characteristics of an effective leader. These statements represent various views on what leadership is and what makes for effective leadership. A special thanks to all of the contributors to this chapter.

All of those who lead have their definitions. While they are different, they share much in common. The reader is encouraged to construct his or her own definition of leadership as this chapter is read. The first seven statements on leadership were abstracted from an earlier publication. They are repeated here because of their timelessness and continued applicability to those who lead.

While the reader will be challenged by all the statements, particularly insightful are the voices of our youth (eighth–twelfth graders and college students, at the time this chapter was written). These youths are mentored through a program called The Generals under the auspices of the Institute for Black Family Development, Matthew Parker, president.

Dr. John M. Perkins, Founder and Chairman, Christian Community Development Association; President of John Perkins Foundation

One model of an effective leader can be seen in the book of Esther. After the death of her parents, Mordecai raised the orphaned Esther as his own daughter. Being a wise man full of integrity, at an early age, Mordecai instilled these five notable qualities in Esther:

- Know yourself.

- Be who you are. Avoid trying to appear being what you are not. Develop your strengths. Find others to compensate for your weakness.

- Communicate clearly and precisely.

- Take advantage of every opportunity. Most people do not want to be told what to do. A real leader gets people together and goes over a game plan, making sure everyone knows what part he or she plays.

- Make decisions. The faster you make a decision the more effectiveness you will have as a leader. Do not make decisions in a vacuum. You need a keen sense of when to act.

- Have well-defined goals.

- Do what is necessary to see that the goals are reached.

- Strive to develop an individual's self-confidence to supersede their current level of performance expectations.

Leaders enrich others and are known by the personalities they enrich as they allow others to achieve aims and goals that they have for themselves Perkins 1995, 34–35).

Joseph C. Jeter Sr., Founder and President, Have Christ Will Travel Ministries

Without prayer, the Christian leader is helpless, whether missionary, pastor, preacher, teacher, or auxiliary leader. The leader must understand that the program, the project and the people are the Lord's. The leader has no power to do what needs to be done. Jesus said that all power was given unto Him. A leader must stay in constant touch with the Lord, who alone knows the way and has the power to cause it to occur (Jeter 1995, 51).

Dolphus Weary, Founder and Chairman, Real Christian Foundation

Every ministry that wants to survive must pass on the vision to what I call the second generation of leaders. These are the apprentices who will succeed the current leadership and carry the ministry to new heights. Owning the vision is very important because a ministry often dies in the second or third generation if there is no commitment to the original vision (Weary 1995, 59).

The Late Dr. Mary Ross, Former President of Women's Department, National Baptist Convention, U.S.A., Inc.

Women are beginning to see today that Jesus did not display a demeaning view of women in word or deed. Moreover, Jesus adamantly stood up to his contemporaries to defend women.

In order to be a good leader, the Black woman must have a faith fit to live by, a self fit to live with, and work fit to live for. She knows as Joyce Ladner says, "The Black women's life has been characterized by two major focuses: high achievement and excellence by a limited few, and a cycle of poverty that engulfs the lives of many."

In spite of the many problems that have been thrust upon her historically, the Black woman continues to fight for self-determination, equal opportunity, and a life that is void of discrimination based on sex, race, or social class (Ross 1995, 139, 142).

Beverly Yates, Past President, Chicago and Christian Women's Conference

In Exodus 18: 17–23, we see how Jethro advised that great leader Moses regarding his leadership of the children of Israel in the wilderness. Moses was burdened with the people and their problems, trying to do all the leading himself, until Jethro showed him a better way…

In summary, Jethro advised Moses to:

- Choose capable people.

- Train them

- Organize them.

- Delegate work to them.

- Hold them accountable.

Jethro's advice is appropriate for us, and it works. Confident leaders learn to share authority and are not afraid to allow others to make mistakes. Good leaders rejoice when their associates do a good job and are generous with applause.

Wouldn't it be a wonderful sight to see the local church alive with everyone's gifts being discovered, developed, and displayed (Yates 1995, 108–9)?

The Late Barbara Walton, Mentor to Matt Parker and Others

My advice to all leaders and would-be mentors is not to stifle your commendable desire to help develop young people and to help them them grow spiritually. Give them lots of room to try their wings. Remember, we learn from failures as well as from successes—but stay around to help them pick up the pieces. Hopefully, there will be more celebrations than failures (Walton 1995, 174–75).

Lorraine Elizabeth Williams, Producer and On-Air Personality of "Let's Talk"

Leadership is generic, neither male nor female. Leaders are accountable. They are servants. Leaders have integrity in all things. Leadership is constructive. Leaders stress quality in addition to or instead of quantity. They trust the spoken word, intuition, and their "gut." Effective leaders value teamwork and cooperation.

A leader is people-oriented and capable of listening. A leader is honest, emphasizing motivating people. A good leader promotes affirming group relations while motivating the team to get the job done (Williams 1995, 167–68).

The Late Tom Skinner, Founder and President, Tom Skinner Associates and Mentor to Many

"Leadership is the ability to motivate people to move from one point to another and get them to like it. It is creating an atmosphere to help others succeed" (Williams-Skinner 2000, 5).

Leah Gaskin Fitchue, President, Payne Theological Seminary

Ronald A. Heifetz and Marty Linsky, authors of *Leadership on the Line*, are correct when they state that "leadership requires disturbing people—but at a rate they can absorb" (Heifetz 2002, 20). I also believe that John Kotter is right in *Leading Change*, when he describes "establishing a sense of urgency" as the first step in creating major change in an organization (Kotter 1996, 35). The art of leadership involves knowing how to be bold and risky in sounding the alarm for change, disturbing the status quo in the process, while also helping those whom the change will benefit understand the value of the change and the consequences of not doing so in an urgent manner. The decision to change must reside in the will of the people if the end product is going to last, and this will only happen if personal transformation is the glue.

A leader must be in two places at the same time. A leader must be out in front of the people to show the way. Being out front requires a leader to be a trustworthy authority if he or she is going to be successful in taking people where they otherwise would not go. But a leader must also walk beside the people to acknowledge the moans and groans that are inherent in loss, so that stability is maintained, chaos is avoided, and the integrity of the change process can be honored.

Realizing that grief accompanies pain and loss when a new paradigm edges out the old, a leader must be willing to respect the dialectic struggle in search of the higher truth.

Finally, a leader must also be fully aware that authentic growth and change is best obtained by both/and rather than either/or.

Dr. Ken Staley, Pastor of Shepherd Care, Philadelphia, PA, and Ms. Sheila Staley, Therapist, Diane Langberg and Associates, Philadelphia, PA

Leadership is the ability of a person [with authority] to direct [lead, focus, encourage] a group of people, by influence [teaching, maturity, unity] to work together to complete a defined [understandable] task that benefits the group and/or community.

Bernard Fuller, Senior Pastor, New Song Bible Fellowship, Glendale, MD—*Moving from Existing to Effectiveness in Ministry: Twelve Behaviors of Effective Christian Leaders*

Are you an effective Christian leader? I define Christian leadership as "A person(s) involved in taking initiative in *a process of influencing* others with the love of God to accomplish clear-cut biblical purposes by means of godly character, conduct, communication, and competency to achieve specific results for the good of mankind and the glory of God."

- Effective Christian leaders are *committed* to the lordship of Jesus Christ and lead through taking initiative and using the influence of godly character, conduct, communication, and competency.

- Effective Christian leaders *count the cost* of doing ministry before taking on ministry assignments.

- Effective Christian leaders *cast* the vision, mission, and values of the ministry organization in which they serve.

- Effective Christian leaders *create* strategic plans with specific goals to align their ministries with the vision, mission, and values of their ministry organization.

- Effective Christian leaders *connect* the dots of their ministry goals with specific action steps.

- Effective Christian leaders *choose* team members who are uniquely gifted and passionate for their ministry area.

- Effective Christian leaders *communicate* clearly and frequently with those on their ministry team the vision, mission, values, and goals.

- Effective Christian leaders *cultivate* a healthy loving ministry atmosphere in order to mobilize and motivate their ministry team members to carry out their mission mandate.

- Effective Christian leaders *challenge* their team members to live godly and to walk by faith, trusting God to do impossible tasks through them.

- Effective Christian leaders *configure* well organized systems, in order to network resources and to manage information that *saves* you shame, time, energy, money, and stress (S.Y.S.T.E.M.S.) in ministry.

- Effective Christian leaders *coach* by modeling, motivating, assessing, and assisting, their team members in developing their God-given potential.

- Effective Christian leaders *celebrate* with their team members in their ministry accomplishments and victories, as well as *comfort* them in their ministry defeats.

Michael Lyles, Senior Partner, Lyles and Crawford Clinical Consulting, P. C., Roswell, GA

On the wall of my psychiatric office is a framed collection of photos of my mentors—the people who have served as leaders in my life spiritually and professionally. It is there to show my patients that we all are impacted by the people in our lives—positively or negatively. Thus we need to actively seek out people who will invest positively in our lives. Considering the topic of leadership gave me pause to consider what characteristics that these mentors shared as leaders—at least in my life. What caused their impact to be so significant that thousands of patients have been influenced by their leadership investment in my life? The following "traits" characterize these leaders in my experience of them.

1. Availability—These men spent a lot of time with me with little in return. Dr. Bill Wilson opened his home to students for prayer breakfasts and Bible studies for years. He listened to our travails and translated difficult concepts into very understandable and applicable terms. He put his life on display as a tangible example of how God works to disciple someone. Love is truly spelled T I M E —time spent with someone.

2. Authenticity—Because of the time spent with these men, I was afforded the privilege of seeing them as real people. Dr. David Larson would unnerve me by discussing his failures and insecurities—but balanced that by modeling how he was trusting God with them. He was years later awarded a national award for excellence for one of the activities that he was most insecure about. I had the ringside seat in seeing God transform this humble servant into a national leader—because Dave was transparent and real (authentic) with me.

3. Vision—Dr. James Carter was a highlight-reel leader in my life, but I did not realize it at the time. He was pushy and demanding with me and never satisfied that I had performed to the best of my abilities. I later (much later) found out that it was because he saw something in me that I did not see. He was trying to "stir up" the gift in me, but I did not see the gift. He saw outside the box, when I was happy to have a box. He was a leader with vision trying to lead a follower who was "blind."

4. Perseverance—All of these men toiled without much recognition or results for years but were true to their calling. Leaders care too much to quit. Darrel Heide was a spiritual leader in my life. I witnessed him having his heart broken by the spiritual callousness and apathy of people that he tried to disciple. To this day I remember his commitment when I am tempted to quit on a patient or mentee.

5. Humility—All of these leaders had servant attitudes. They were not arrogant or full of themselves. Their passion to minister to others flowed from the experience of their relationship with God and the work of the Holy Spirit in their lives. They considered their leadership positions to be a divinely appointed privilege and an opportunity to serve.

J. T. Roberson, Professor, Payne Seminary Transformational Leadership in Black Family/Community Development

Transformational leadership can be defined as helping people to discover the calling on their lives and then to move them to a position whereby they are able to live out that calling. This is a key component in Black family progress. The challenge is to first be transformed oneself and then to function in a transformational role to empower the family and community. The environment we find ourselves in does not necessarily avail itself to emancipated leadership. With such social ills as racism, classism, nepotism, and economics, it is easy for persons in the Black community to be stifled in developing their leadership abilities. It therefore becomes necessary for one from this community to first get past, what Jack Mezirow calls their "formative learning" and to engage in "transformative learning." Transformative learning will usher in an emancipatory learning that frees the individual to develop their full potential, especially in the area of leadership. Once this potential is activated, persons are then freed to empower their family and their community.

Lee N. June, Matthew Parker Sr., and Christopher C. Mathis Jr.

As a transformational leader in the Black family and community, persons are able to empower others in the community. From a personal perspective, it was necessary for me to be transformed before I could utilize all of my leadership potential. Having grown up in the south and experiencing the various social ills mentioned above, I had to experience what Mezirow calls a "disorienting dilemma" before I could make myself open to new learnings. Once this was done, I was then able to appropriate new learnings and to take full advantage of what leadership abilities I have. Once transformed, I was able to provide a transformative leadership function for my family, my church, my school, and my community.

John M. Wallace Jr., Professor, University of Pittsburgh, School of Social Work

There are many kinds of leaders, but at the most basic level, leadership is simply the ability to work with and through others to get things done. Key leadership qualities include honesty, integrity, emotional maturity, vision, and the willingness to give away credit for success and to accept responsibility for setbacks and failure.

Bishop Samuel Duncan Jr., Bishop of the Third Ecclesiastical Jurisdiction of Southwest Michigan (Church of God in Christ) and Pastor of Lansing Church of God in Christ, Lansing, MI

I believe that the definition of leadership has changed over the past few years. It was in a broad's sense described as "influence" and using that influence to direct, inspire and motivate others to achieve a desired end or result. But now because of the complexity of the workplace, unusual demands, and a paradigm shift in human material resources and education, leadership takes on a new look.

In today's times an effective leader must possess confidence and a positive attitude. They must remain confident regardless of circumstances and recognize and appreciate confidence in others. Confidence empowers and a good leader has the ability to instill within people confidence in the leader and in others. Confidence is so important, because insecure leaders are dangerous to themselves, others, and the organization they lead. A leadership position becomes an amplifier of the things done and seen.

There must be a continual winning of the servants'/followers' hearts. The leader must always be mindful that a leader/servant denies self, develop others, accept mistreatment, pursues harmony, and remains teachable.

Finally, leaders do not have to pretend to know everything, but in giving vision and direction, there has to be clarity and not certainty.

Reverend Will Stokes, Pastor of Little Rock Missionary Baptist Church, Lansing, MI

Leadership involves directing, teaching, and living. Key characteristics of an effective leader are the ability to identify with the people, being humble, and showing love, kindness, and long suffering. Great leaders are often reluctant to lead, and sometimes operate from behind the scene. They also exhibit the characteristics listed for bishops in 1 Timothy 3:1–7.

Reverend Marc Williamson, Pastor of True Light Missionary Baptist Church, Lansing, MI

Leadership consists of developing and strengthening others. Key characteristics of effective leadership are patience and long suffering. Leadership is often handed to you because of what others see in you.

Reverend Charles Howard, Chair of the Deacon Board, Associate Minister, and Church Administrator, Southern Heights Baptist Church, Fort Wayne, IN

Leadership Defined. In the Christian context, leadership is exhibited as it relates to service in the local church. It is the recognition, by the elders of the congregation as seen in Acts 6: 1–7, of the maturity and ability to, by their godly example, positively influence the church's Christians; and it is the willingness to be used by the Lord in areas of responsibility and service (ministry) to the congregation.

Characteristics of Leadership. The prerequisites for a leader are (1) Christian/spiritual maturity as defined in Galatians 5:22–23, which results in the ability to lovingly relate to your fellow believers, and (2) a knowledge of the Bible with its doctrines and principles for Christian living. The practical functioning of these characteristics, as it applies to leadership, will be the ability to manage (lead) varied personalities and to provide service to the church community, as spelled out in 1 Timothy 3; 6; 2 Timothy 2; and Titus 1:5–9; 2:1–15.

Norvella Carter, Professor of Urban Education and Endowed Chair in Urban Education, Texas A & M University

As a Christian and professor of graduate students at a tier-one research institution, I have adopted many different components that define and form my leadership style. I believe in the "servant leadership" model that was first set forth by Jesus Christ during his time on earth before his resurrection.

Modern day theorists claim this theory of leadership, but in actuality, it was Jesus who first modeled it. I define servant leadership as: 1) being able to stand alone when needed; 2) encouraging and supporting the personal and professional growth of individuals; and 3) helping others to achieve goals that are focused on the enhancement and betterment of our society.

I also believe in "transformational leadership," which I define as leadership that causes or enhances positive change in others and assists them in becoming leaders themselves. Again, I attribute this definition to the model that Jesus provided for us as Christians. The characteristics that are imbedded in both of these styles are courage; the ability to listen to others; kindness; competence in a specific field of expertise that has been developed through hard work; enthusiasm; patience; perseverance; the ability to encourage others; and a vision that has been given by the Lord. I believe these characteristics are essential elements for an effective leader within the academy and within life itself.

Reverend Dr. Warren E. Williams, Professor, Texas Southern University, and Minister of Christian Marriage and Counseling, Wheeler Avenue Baptist Church, Houston, TX.

Leadership is the gift (Rom. 12:8) of being able to move a collection of followers from Point A to Point B in the most expedient manner. It is identifying or being called to a need. Sometimes it is being a committee of one.

Effective leaders:

1. have been mentored by effective leaders (Moses, for example mentored Joshua; David mentored Solomon)

2. work diligently on being whole regarding body, soul, and spirit (1 Thessalonians 5:23)

3. are able to choose persons who fit the task rather than by favoritism or fearing possible successors

4. provide those whom they supervise with the tools, materials and environment necessary to have the maximum chance to succeed

5. believe in integrity and ethics regarding personnel and practices

6. are not afraid to take ownership of mistakes before being forced

7. require accurate information from those they supervise, thus being aware of sparks before they become flames

8. realize that the small, seemingly less important items contribute significantly to the big picture

9. are able to listen to varying viewpoints, and truly utilize and value wisdom in all forms

Melvin J. Holley, Executive Director, United Conference for Men

The United Conference for Men began in 1977, to provide a weekend retreat for males, focused on the discipleship of males that were followers of Jesus Christ. Principally, we purposed to address their role in their local church and community. We also sought to challenge other men who were unchurched, but needed reassurance that God could accept them and mold them as he saw fit.

My role as executive director was to be committed to biblical truth and be a dedicated Christian believer and man of character. The use of learned administrative skills, personal integrity, generosity, principled standards, and servant-devotion in my commitment to Christ the King has been my reason for continuing with the organization and its present team of men who assist in the carrying out the mission. Learning to work with other men in the planning has required my listening to their ideas, and helping them to build their relationship to Jesus Christ as well. Looking back over those years, I have many memories of numerous men who were renewed in their faith and life because of the retreats.

I am convinced that a leader is really a chosen follower who decides to be committed to the vision given and understood, for him or her, because of the examples displayed by others who preceded them in their devotion to our Sovereign Lord. The letter to Hebrews addresses the walk of the follower: "Wherefore seeing we also are compassed about with so great a cloud of witnesses, let us lay aside every weight... and the sin which easily... beset us..., run with patience the race that is set before us, looking unto Jesus the author and finisher of our faith" (Hebrews 12:1–2 KJV).

Verna D. Holley, President, The United Conference for Women

The United Conference for Women began in November 1976 as a nondenominational, Christ-centered outreach. Its organizing group was made up of several women from Detroit, Michigan who had been a dedicated group of friends from the Christian Brethren Assemblies of Detroit. Encouraged by Ethel Holley of Detroit's Berean Tabernacle, the women bonded and selected officers for the fledgling organization and began inviting women from other churches to join them at the first retreat held at Adrian College, Adrian, Michigan. The board and officers chose the theme: "Daily Strength for Daily Needs."

My role has been to lead in preparing documents required for incorporation, securing nonprofit status, leading in planning meetings, make site visits, contracting to secure adequate facilities, ensuring the means to fund the meetings, securing speakers, topical leaders, and musicians, arrange for printing, bookstore resources, and other administrative responsibilities as I lead the organization. All of this performance required working smoothly with several competent men and women to accomplish the goal each year with effective teamwork, while balancing my role as a wife and teacher, with family responsibilities, church duties, etc. However, as a child of the King, I found that my personal integrity, moral beliefs, and principles of living directed me in my leadership responsibilities. As I view it after so many years now, God had prepared me for work with accomplishing the organization's goals. God allowed me to be a partner for discouraged, hurting women seeking a place of truth and peace.

Reverend Dr. Lonnie J. Chipp, Pastor, New Mount Calvary Baptist Church, Lansing, MI

As one seeks to gain knowledge and understanding regarding the importance of being a "godly leader," one must keep in mind that there is a vast difference between worldly leadership and godly leadership. Worldly leadership is self-driven and self-directed, while godly leadership is Word-driven and Spirit-directed.

First and foremost, a godly leader understands that leadership is a calling. John 15:16 says, "Ye have not chosen me, but I have chosen you, and ordained you, that you should go and bring forth fruit, and that your fruit should remain" (KJV). Godly leaders understand that they are called to fulfill God's purpose and not their own.

Godly leaders have a humbleness of spirit. They understand the benefit of Peter's instruction in 1 Peter 5:5b–6: "Yea, all of you be subject one to another, and be clothed with humility; for God resisteth the proud, and giveth race to the humble, Humble yourself under the mighty hand of God, that he may exalt you in due time" (KJV). A godly leader knows the importance of being led. He or she respects the elders and they listen and learn from everyone. They don't concern themselves with worrying about position, status, or recognition, because godly leaders know that God's recognition counts more than any human praise.

Godly leaders desire to be taught. In Matthew 4:23a; 5:1–2 it is stated that "Jesus went about all Galilee, teaching in their synagogues…. And seeing the multitudes, he went up into a mountain, and when he was set, his disciples came unto him: And he opened his mouth, and taught them" (KJV). Thus, a godly leader understands just how vital it is to consistently and diligently study the Word of God.

Godly leaders know the value of *follow*ship. They have committed themselves to the instruction given in Luke 9:23: "If any man will come after me, let him deny himself, and take up his cross daily, and follow me" (KJV). Godly leaders know that following Christ may be costly, but they are willing to deny themselves of selfish desires, because they know that serving God is well worth it.

Godly leaders know the importance of being a student of the Word of God. Second Thessalonians 2:15 tells us that we must "stand fast, and hold the traditions which ye have been taught, whether by word, or our epistle" (KJV). Godly leaders realize that they will face many challenges: persecution, false teaching, idleness, and apathy; but they are committed to stand fast and hold on to the truths that they have been taught through the Word of God.

Finally, godly leaders know that God has divine ownership. Psalm 24:1 says that "the earth is the LORD's and the fullness thereof; the world, and they that dwell therein" (KJV). Godly leaders know that all things belong to God and that they are only stewards or caretakers. They know that they have been assigned to properly manage that which God has entrusted to them.

Marvin Lynch, Director, Compensation and Performance Management, Office of Human Resources, Howard University.

I believe that a leader should be a superior listener. My leadership experience bears this out. My effectiveness as a leader has been directly tied to the degree to which I have listened to subordinate staff and others over which I have had responsibility. It is a studied fact that effective communication involves not only talking but listening. It is important for a leader to be the kind of listener who really hears what those over whom he/she has responsibility are saying. The best way to demotivate those over whom one leads is not to listen to their ideas, suggestions, and comments. Being a leader doesn't mean that one makes all the decisions; instead. he or she takes in all relevant information, especially from those who are closer to the "front line." The leader can then make the best possible decisions for his or her group.

I believe that a leader should not try to do it all, and that in advancing toward a goal to take it in steps—one step at a time. I have learned over the years that it is important to break up projects into stages, not try to do too much at once as a team in moving toward their goal. A leader can and should have a clear vision of what he or she wants to accomplish, but it should be manageable by the group and make use of the group's best skills. I'm reminded of the woman who climbed the Himalayan mountains sometime in the 1980s. She was asked by a news reporter what went through her mind while she was climbing up one of the world's most challenging mountain peaks. In response to the reporter she replied, "The only way to eat an elephant is one bite at a time." Small progress is what the leader has to keep in mind as he or she is moving toward that ultimate goal that is worthy of pursuing, and toward which he or she is leading others.

Reverend James C. Offutt, Pastor, Mt. Carmel Baptist Church, Canton, IL and Past President of Peoria Black Chamber of Commerce

Leadership is often the perception of what others see in the perspective leader that the person may or may not see in him or herself. For example, when Saul was identified by Samuel, he initially hid (see 1 Samuel 10:17–25). David, at first, was not initially on the scene when the process of selecting a king began (see 1 Samuel 16). Gideon had to be persuaded to get involved (see Judges 6). Thus leaders are often reluctant to lead and the identification process often happens outside of oneself.

Key characteristics of effective leaders are discipline, dedication, discernment, and development.

Hilton Thomas, Executive Director of Meridian Professional Psychological Consultants and Professional Psychological and Rehabilitation Services, and Pastor of Paradise Baptist Church, Lansing MI; and Bari Thomas, Director of the Division of Administrative Office Services, Michigan State Housing Development Authority.

Leaders who aspire to positions of power often become frustrated with the results. Power inspires fear, control, and obedience, but it stifles creativity and diminishes trust in any relationship; especially between leaders and those who would follow. Influence, though requiring the use of skill, insight, and patience, provides a better yield.

Successful leaders are those who use their influence to inspire trust and loyalty. They do what they say they're going to do and trust others to do the same. They create a vision for achievement and coach others to live in the vision through mentoring, shadowing and training.

Influential leaders know that they have to listen to their followers and understand their needs. These leaders understand what motivates them may not be motivating to their followers. They know that their success is largely contingent upon the success of those around them, and they take the time to learn what each person needs to achieve. Influential leaders know that what motivates them to achieve at high levels does not necessarily work for others. It is understood that the leader is responsible to listen and learn so that each person that follows can find their individual path to success, but also share their talents for group achievement.

There are differences between secular leaders and those serving in the spiritual realm. In the secular world, the mission is defined by the organization and is often profit-driven. In the spiritual realm, the mission is defined by God. Spiritual leaders lead people to God and the mission is saving souls. Spiritual leaders need to be servant leaders, not autocratic dictators. A true servant leader realizes this difference in secular and spiritual leadership. This does not mean that a successful secular leader would not choose to be a servant leader.

In short, those who aspire to leadership do well not to be drunk with power, but rather to be servant leaders. This is imperative in a spiritual leader and certainly useful with secular leaders.

Karon Parker, Parent and Teacher

Leadership is learning from one's journey how to read and obey the traffic lights of life, comprehending when God says yes, no, or wait.

Leadership is through godly character and integrity glorifying God and pointing others to the Jesus of the Bible.

Leadership is more about who you follow rather than who you lead because everyone follows something. Thus leadership is godly character and integrity infused with a lifestyle that embraces oneness with God.

Leadership is living a life without regret because the journey and the memories are solidified with oneness with God.

Henry Well III, Pastor, Great Commission Fellowship Church and PhD Student at Wayne State University (Detroit, MI).

A leader is a person who lives selflessly in order to seek the highest good of others. This is lived out with a level of integrity that is seen equally in their private life, as well as their public life.

VOICES FROM YOUTH
(K8–12 AND COLLEGE STUDENTS—THE GENERALS)

These were their grade levels at the time of the writing of this chapter.

Breanna Brown (8th grade—Great Oaks Academy)

I believe that leadership is the ability to guide someone to the right path. Leadership is being a role model and setting a positive example for others.

Devaughn Munson-Dowell (8th grade—Forsythe Middle School)

To me a leader is a person who does good things for other people. A leader doesn't care for himself and is always looking for things that will make a person's day. A leader sets examples for other people to follow like finish high school, college, and other things that a person may want to achieve. A leader shows good character, treats everybody the same just as he would want to be treated, and sets goals for other people who don't believe they could accomplish them. A leader is always on task for what he has to do and is a person everyone would either like to be, or become one day. A leader inspires people in many different ways and never stops working hard. A leader should also have a good reputation from the people around him. A leader should always stay on the right path and out of as much trouble as he or she can.

Lakay Via Golden (8th grade—Advanced Tech Academy)

Leadership is taking action or standing up for what is right. To be a leader means to lead so that the people who look up to you follow by example in a positive way.

Justin Parker (9th grade—Southfield Christian School)

Leading others in a common cause. Mentoring others so they can become future leaders and erudite learners. This is what I think leadership is.

Robert Wells (10th grade—Winans Academy of Performing Arts)

To me leadership is when you do something so well everyone wants to follow it. You know you are a leader if you do a certain thing and the next day you see someone else doing it. There are good leaders and bad leaders and even the bad leaders try to follow good leaders, though they may twist everything the good leader is doing.

Daniel Valentine (12th grade—Henry Ford Academy)

Leadership is when a person knows when and how to guide and provide good authority and direction to others.

Angelo Thompson (12th grade—Consortium College Preparatory High School)

Leadership is to have knowledge and good social skills in taking charge of a team or activity.

Kelly Parker (12th grade—Southfield Christian High School)

Leadership is having the patience to listen and the wisdom to utilize those ideas appropriately and realistically. In addition, the goal of the leader is to supply what people need and not necessarily what they want. Without both of these terms, you will either be an unsuccessful leader or a selfish dictator.

Rodney Jones Jr. (12th grade—Harrison High School)

Leadership is an important factor that consists of a major level of accountability and integrity of an individual. Being a leader compels someone to be mindful and strive for excellence.

Brittany Folmar (12th grade—Michigan Collegiate)

In my opinion, leadership is not being a follower but having others follow you. You are your own person and a person someone can look up to.

Alwalkie Barber Jr. (12th grade—King High School)

Leadership is something one takes in his or her own hands and doesn't abuse. To have leadership is to have confidence in making wise decisions. Leadership is earned through being a positive role model—rising above the negative and never falling out of the square.

Tiffany Parker (12th grade—Westside Christian Academy)

Leaders exhibit dependability, first to God and then to others.

VOICES OF COLLEGE STUDENTS

These were their class levels at the time of the writing of this chapter

Cortland P. Medy (freshman—Wayne County Community College)

Leadership is the act of guiding someone through hard and confusing times; it is a relationship that provides advice and counsel.

Michael Parker (sophomore—University of Michigan-Dearborn)

Leaders are individuals that have the skills to develop others through their words and actions. With this ability, they are able to encourage others to not only reach their goals but become leaders themselves.

Tiffany Parker (senior—Wayne State University)

Leadership is not being afraid to go against the grain and the courage to face fears by taking a leap of faith.

VOICES OF YOUNG ADULTS

Brian L. June, Technology Specialist, Lansing, MI

I believe that leadership means being a servant. Some of the greatest leaders are servants. In thinking of leadership, I am reminded of the passage that says that the greatest among you must be a servant.

Some of the major characteristics of an effective leader include patience, humility, and courage. These characteristics were evidenced in leaders like the biblical Moses, Dr. Martin Luther King Jr., and Harriett Tubman. These individuals, and many others, inspire and encourage us all.

Matthew L. Parker Jr., Ernst and Young

Leadership is the ability to lead with the foresight to know when to follow. Every leader attempts to execute a strategy, however, great leaders develop others so they will have the ability to lead themselves.

Stephen A. June, Recreation and Fitness (Building Operator, Student Supervisor)

A leader is someone who paves the way, or goes before others, showing them where to go, and tell them how to get there. They direct others. Leaders should be charismatic, articulate, engaging, and diplomatic. Leadership is the action of, or service of one who demonstrates the above.

CONCLUSION

The above represents the voices of a variety of individuals who have made, are making, and will make major contributions to our world and the Christian community. They show that while leadership may be variously defined, it shares much in common. Particularly insightful are the voices of our youth and college students. Their voices show that they are watching what leaders do and are keenly aware of what it takes to be an effective leader.

REFERENCES

Heifetz, Ronald A. and Marty Linsky. 2002. *Leadership on the Line*. Boston: Harvard Business School Press.

Jeter, J. C. 1995. "Prayer in Leadership." *Call to Lead: Wisdom for the Next Generation of African American Leaders.* Matthew Parker and Eugene Seals. eds. Chicago: Moody Press.

Kotter, John P. 1996. *Leading Change*. Boston: Harvard Business School Press.

Perkins, J. M. 1995. "Filling the Leadership Vacuum." *Call to Lead: Wisdom for the Next Generation of African American Leaders.* Matthew Parker and Eugene Seals, eds. Chicago: Moody Press.

Ross, M. 1995. "The African American Woman: Her Undeniable, Undebatable Leadership in Church and Society." *Call to Lead: Wisdom for the Next Generation of African American Leaders*. Matthew Parker and Eugene Seals, eds. Chicago: Moody Press.

Walton. B. 1995. "Mentoring Tomorrow's Leaders." *Call to Lead: Wisdom for the Next Generation of African American Leaders*. Matthew Parker and Eugene Seals, eds. Chicago: Moody Press.

Weary, D. 1995. "Second Generation Leadership Development." *Call to Lead: Wisdom for the Next Generation of African American Leaders.* Matthew Parker and Eugene Seals, eds. Chicago: Moody Press.

Williams, L. E. 1995. "Some Leaders Are Born Women." *Call to Lead: Wisdom for the Next Generation of African American Leaders.* Matthew Parker and Eugene Seals, eds. Chicago: Moody Press.

Williams-Skinner, Barbara. 2000. *Becoming an Effective 21st Century Leader.* Tracy Landing, MD: Skinner Leadership Institute.

Yates, B. 1995. "Always Work Yourself out of a Job." *Call to Lead: Wisdom for the Next Generation of African American Leaders.* Matthew Parker and Eugene Seals, eds. Chicago: Moody Press.

PART 2
SOME HOW-TOS OF LEADERSHIP

Chapter 3

GENERAL LEADERSHIP PLANNING AND DEVELOPMENT

Paul Cannings

Planning and developing a team of leaders is significant to the health and strength of the church (Acts 20:24–35). The strength and effectiveness of the church, in caring and developing the Lord's people, are as strong or weak as its leadership team. Leaders shape the character and nature of the church (1 Timothy 3:15; 4:16). This is why the process for planning and developing a leadership structure must never be implemented for political gains. The process must honor God. This must be done in compliance with God's Word and with much prayer (Acts 14:23). Leaders must pray and seek God with an open heart. The Spirit of God must guide the process through his Word and for his glory. Paul gives us a great example of this when Timothy was provided to him by the leaders in Derbe and Lystra, as explained in Acts 16.

During Paul's visit to Derbe and Lystra, the brethren spoke highly of Timothy. They recognized that Timothy was a true disciple of Jesus Christ. Not only did the leaders speak in this manner (1 Timothy 4:14), so did many members of the church also. It was the consistency of Timothy's work in the church, the fruit of that work (Acts 16:4–5), and his commitment to serve Christ that caused the leaders to ordain and send him with Paul. Timothy's life and maturity are what caused him to be promoted from a disciple to a pastor. It was not his friendship with Paul, the amount of money he gave Paul to do effective ministry, or his loyalty to Paul that allowed him to gain this promotion. It was Timothy's love for Christ, commitment to God's Word, and willingness to serve. Note what Paul said about Timothy.

> Do not neglect the spiritual gift within you, which was bestowed on you through prophetic utterance with the laying on of hands by the presbytery. Take pains with these things; be absorbed in them, so that your progress will be evident to all. Pay close attention to yourself and to your teaching; persevere in these things, for as you do this you will ensure salvation both for yourself and for those who hear you (1 Tim. 4:14–16).

It is stated that "Some leaders are outgoing; some introverted. Some can talk their way out of any situation, while others perform their way out" (Myra 1987). A leader's commitment must be to first focus on applying themselves to the principles of God, and then lead others. This will ultimately empower the church to accomplish the purposes of God (Ephesians 1:9–11) and to impact the world (Matthew 5:13–16).

> For I did not shrink from declaring to you the whole purpose of God. Be on guard for yourselves and for all the flock, *among which the Holy Spirit has made you overseers*, to shepherd the church of God which He purchased with His own blood. I know that after my departure savage wolves will come in among you, not sparing the flock; and from among your own selves men will arise, speaking perverse things, to draw away the disciples after them. Therefore be on the alert, remembering that night and day for a period of three years I did not cease to admonish each one with tears. And now I commend you to God and to the word of His grace, which is able to build you up and to give you the inheritance among all those who are sanctified (Acts 20:27–32, emphasis mine).

Planning and developing a leadership process must be in line with the principles of God's Word to prevent the establishment of a new foundation that is not biblically based.

> According to the grace of God which was given to me, as a wise master builder I laid a foundation, and another is building upon it. But let each man be careful how he builds upon it. *For no man can lay a foundation*

other than the one which is laid, which is Jesus Christ (1 Corinthians 3:10–11, emphasis mine).

ORGANIZING THE LEADERSHIP PLAN: BIBLICAL PRINCIPLES FOR THE SUPPORT OF A PASTOR, ELDERS, AND DEACONS LEADERSHIP STRUCTURE

Due to the vast nature of a pastoral position (a biblical outline of this is provided below), the ministry of elders and deacons play a significant role in the overall development of the church (Exodus 18:19–23; Numbers 11:10–18; Acts 6:1–6; 1 Timothy 3:1–15). This comes as a result of the diverse needs of God's sheep and the work that Christ has ordained the church to do.

An example of this can be seen by the manner in which the Godhead functions. This process demonstrates how God the Father, God the Son, and God the Holy Spirit powerfully care for the diverse needs of all creation. Understanding this process may serve as a model in directing the leadership of the local church while effectively nurturing the diverse needs of God's sheep. This helps the believers to progressively mature into the fullness of Christ.

The role of God the Father, God the Son, and God the Holy Spirit toward the church, is an illustration of how God cares for the spiritual and physical needs of each believer. God provides the direction for the development of humankind (Genesis 12:1–3; John 3:16; Ephesians 1:11). Christ provides the means by which human's spiritual life is established based in God's plan (Genesis 3:15; John 1:1; Ephesians 1:7–10; Colossians 1:15–18). The Holy Spirit is Christ's helper just like Christ was and is, God's helper (John 14:16–17). The Holy Spirit provides direction (John 16:13), comfort (John 14:25–27), gives victory over the attacks of Satan (1 John 4:4), and power in our daily prayer life (Romans 8:26) so that we can do *"all things through Christ* (since the Holy Spirit is his helper) *who strengthens us"* (Philippians 4:13). We are able to do all things because of the fruit of the Spirit (Galatians 5:22–24). This process allows us to do exactly what Christ did, and that is walk in step with the Spirit (Galatians 5:25) and allow Christ to accomplish the goal of his death on Calvary (2 Corinthians 3:18). This Trinitarian process is transferred to the church in two ways; (1) the leadership structure (1 Timothy 3:1–15), (2) and in the use of spiritual gifts (1 Corinthians 12:4–8).

The pastor is God's representative to the people (Exodus 18:19; Jeremiah 3:15)) and must be called by God for this position (Ephesians 4:11). Elders can desire to be elders because no call is necessary (1 Timothy 3:1). The pastor must be gifted to teach the Word of God to his people (Exodus 18:20; 1 Timothy 4:11; 2 Timothy 4:2–3) whereas elders can be skilled to teach ("apt") but no gift is required (1 Timothy 3:2):

> I solemnly charge you in the presence of God and of Christ Jesus, who is to judge the living and the dead, and by His appearing and His kingdom: preach the word; be ready in season and out of season; reprove, rebuke, exhort, with great patience and instruction (2 Timothy 4:1–2).

It is the Scriptures that equips the man of God for every good work (2 Timothy 3:17). This is why the pastor must study to show himself approved, "as a workman who does not need to be ashamed" (2 Timothy 2:15). The pastor has assistants to help oversee the spiritual development of the people in the same way that Christ fulfilled the will of God (Acts 20:27–31; 2 Corinthians 3:18). Christ being God's helper even though he is equal to God in nature but has a different function. The same takes place for the pastor and elders. Therefore, teaching of the Word is the primary responsibility of the pastor, and this is shared by the elders who are skilled to teach (1 Timothy 3:2). Elders are gifted by God with knowledge and understanding because they assist the pastor in overseeing the spiritual needs of God's people, unlike deacons who care for physical needs (Jeremiah 3:15; Acts 20:27–29; 6:4). Likewise, elders must be "apt to teach," and Paul does not prescribe this for deacons (1 Timothy 3:2; 3:8–11). It does not mean that deacons cannot teach as we would see the case of Philip (Acts 8:25–40). It is not a function that is one of their responsibilities with the leadership structure of the church). Deacons function under the elders (1 Timothy 3:1–13) to assist in shepherding the flock so that they do not become prey to every beast in the field, as is stated in Ezekiel 34:4–8. Deacons must have wisdom (Acts 6:3) which is something someone prays for (James 1:5–8), and it comes after knowledge and understanding are applied (Colossians 1:9–10). However, deacons oversee the physical needs of the body as each believer lives out the biblical principles that are taught primarily by the pastor and sometimes by elders (Acts 6:2–4; 1 Timothy 3:8–13).

By developing this system of leadership the kingdom work of God is reestablished within the local church (Ephesians 1:22–23). Through this process each believer is functionally challenged to grow and to mature (Ephesians 4:12–13; Colossians 1:28–29; Hebrews 13:7). It also provides believers a living example of spiritual maturity that they observe (Matthew 28:19), because their spiritual, as well as their physical life, is being nurtured. The development of a biblical leadership structure becomes crucial to the effectiveness and strength of the church (1 Timothy 3:15). The importance of this structure is highlighted when Moses became frustrated and upset with God when the Israelites became tired of eating the same food day after day.

In Numbers 11, the people wanted meat rather than the same diet God had provided. God came to Moses and told him to gather the elders and officers that he knew to be faithful and to bring them before Him at the tent of meeting. Once Moses completed the task he was instructed to do; God said, "*I will come down and speak with you there*" (Numbers 11:17, emphasis mine). Notice that God did not say I will come down and speak with everyone. He said he would come down and speak with Moses. This is because Moses needed to share the load (Exodus 18:18). Even though leaders are in place to provide leadership, they must share the pastor's load as they endeavor to faithfully serve God.

Leadership begins with one person—the leader. A thousand people may be led or a dozen management skills exercised, but ultimately the leadership equation may be reduced to a lone person, one individual whom people follow (Myra 1987).

Someone must explain the mind of God to the people (Exodus 18:19). There are those who must ensure that the principles taught are implemented into the lives of the people as well as into the life of the body (Exodus 18:21–22). Someone must ensure that the physical needs of the people are effectively served (Numbers 11:16; officers). This process serves as a blessing for the kingdom of God and strengthens the lives of his people.

> If you do this thing and God so commands you, then you will be able to endure, and all these people also will go to their place in peace (Exodus 18:23).

These individuals make up the church's leadership. Explaining the mind of God is the pastor's responsibility, with assistance from the elders. Serving the physical needs of the community is the deacons' responsibility (Acts 6:3–6).

When planning a leadership team, it is essential that the structure implemented is not determined by denominational expectations. The structure must be controlled, even dominated, by principles outlined in the Word of God. God has provided for us an administration that is suitable for the fullness of times. As a result there is no need to change it. The Bible puts it this way:

> He made known to us the mystery of His will, according to His kind intention which He purposed in *Him with a view to an administration suitable to the fullness of the times, that is, the summing up of all things in Christ, things in the heavens and things on the earth.* In Him also we have obtained an inheritance, having been predestined according to *His purpose who works all things after the counsel of His will,* to the end that we who were the first to hope in Christ would be to the praise of His glory (Ephesians 1:9–12, emphasis mine).

This structure was established by a foundation that was laid by the apostles with Christ Jesus as its cornerstone (1 Corinthians 3:10; Ephesians 2:20).

> So then you are no longer strangers and aliens, but you are fellow citizens with the saints, and are of God's household, *having been built* on the foundation of the apostles and prophets, Christ Jesus Himself being the corner stone, in whom the whole building, being fitted together, is growing into a holy temple in the Lord, in whom you also are being built together into a dwelling of God in the Spirit" (Ephesians 2:19–22, emphasis mine).

This structure is implemented into a system that is empowered by each believer who has been given spiritual gifts through the ministry of the Holy Spirit for the proper operation of the body of Christ for the glory of God (1 Corinthians 12:4-8).

> As each one has received a special gift, employ it in serving one another as good stewards of the manifold grace of God (1 Peter 4:10).

> Now there are varieties of gifts, but the same Spirit. And there are varieties of ministries, and the same Lord. There are varieties of effects, *but the same God who works all things in all persons. But to each one is given*

the manifestation of the Spirit for the common good (1 Corinthians 12:4–7, emphasis mine).

This process is powerful because it provides Christ the opportunity to functionally operate as the head of the church (provided everyone is willing to allow the Word of God to control how the church operates), and the body to be shaped by ministries outlined in his Word (1 Corinthians 12:4–8; 12–31). When the world experiences the church as a viable organism, lives are powerfully impacted for the glory of God. This does not occur as a result of a variety of church programs, but by ministries, structured and developed based on the Word of God. When individuals (saved or unsaved) experience Christ as they function in the church, or as a result of the impact made when the church gets involved in the community, lives are not just impacted they are transformed into the fullness of Christ (Ephesians 4:12–13; 2 Corinthians 3:18).

When forming a leadership structure, the importance of biblical support is crucial. We must keep in mind that there is a difference between what the Bible gives as a structure and what the government may require. The difference is noted in the development of trustees. This office is required by government and viewed as the contact for the resolution of an organization in the event that it is closed and the property needs to be dispersed. However, we must keep in mind that the administration that God has set in place (Ephesians 1:10) does not prescribe it and God's administration (it is supported with a spiritual gift, 1 Corinthians 12:20) is suitable for the fullness of times. Therefore, there is no biblical support or accountability structure for this office, and the function of a trustee can be fulfilled through the ministry of the deacons. Additionally, some trustees are also assigned to manage the finances of the church. This process could be fulfilled by the treasurer on the elder board. This is a good fit, since elders are biblically responsible to oversee the church's finances according to 1 Timothy 5:17–18. The church accountant could be responsible for this function as a support to the treasurer of the elder board.

As we continue to look at developing proper biblical structures, we must address the upkeep of the church property or properties. A business manager, who has the gift of administration (1 Corinthians 12:28), could be appointed to oversee this area. Biblically, there is no need to develop any additional boards. This is especially important since the creation of another board adds a great deal of confusion. This is especially noted when there are two or three different boards in an organization that will require a chairperson for each one. We must remember that the church is the body of Christ, with him being the cornerstone, and the head of a carefully outlined process that functions for God's glory. Additionally, the Word of God is careful to instruct us not to establish another foundation for the church (1 Corinthians 3:10).

If a trustee board is established, it will function without biblical guidelines. Since there are no biblical guidelines, leaders function in the absence of biblical accountability. Functioning without accountability was illustrated in the Bible by the Sanhedrin. The Sanhedrin was a group of the Pharisees, Sadducees, zealots, and scribes who became extremely influential. They became so powerful that they formed a "new board." This group added three hundred new laws called the "tradition of the elders" (Matthew 15:3–9). Instead of the people becoming more committed to God, the laws established by the non-biblical board became a burden. This makes following God more religious. Instead of following Christ they denied him and crucified him because he violated their structure (John 6:39–40). As the Sanhedrin gained more power, God functionally became less influential in changing and empowering the lives of all the people (Mark 7:5–8).

The plans for a leadership structure in the church, which has been examined and explained in this chapter, is based on a biblical system prescribed by the head of the church, Christ. This is why the planning and developmental process bathed with Scripture is so crucial. Therefore, the critiquing from anyone forces an exegetical response rather than a philosophical or denominational assessment.

REFERENCES
Myra, H. L, ed. 1987. *Leaders: Learning Leadership from Some of Christianity's Best*. The Leadership Library. Vol. 12. Waco, TX: Word.

Chapter 4

LEADERSHIP PLANNING AND DEVELOPMENT IN THE MINISTRY OF THE PASTOR, ELDER, AND DEACON

Paul Cannings

L eadership planning must be done with a commitment to following the biblical guidelines, not to maintain the status quo. It must have at its core a desire to structure and organize leadership based on the prescribed biblical guidelines that are developed by way of hermeneutical principles.

Any leader that becomes satisfied with the status quo reduces the effectiveness of the group they lead because the needs of the people are constantly changing. This is what Jesus experienced while he ministered on earth. The people wanted to maintain their human made traditions and leadership structure. In doing so they ignored the commands of God and rejected Christ (John 5:39–43; Colossians 2:6–8).

> And He said to them, rightly did Isaiah prophesy of you hypocrites, as it is written: 'This people honors me with their lips, but their heart is far away from me. But in vain do they worship me, teaching as doctrines the precepts of men.' Neglecting the commandment of God, you hold to the tradition of men. He was also saying to them, "You are experts at setting aside the commandment of God in order to keep your tradition" (Mark 7:6–9).

Jay Adams (1996, 79) in the book, *Be the Leader God Calls You to Be*, states that there are three things that are essential characteristics for effective and productive leadership. They are "excellence," "initiative," and "creativity." Likewise there are three things that will allow a leader to impact those whom he or she is leading, "wholeheartedness," "singlemindedness" and "a fighting spirit." He goes on to state that

> The real test to your leadership is whether or not other leaders are developed as you lead the way. The development of Christ like character in the people for whom you are responsible is one of your prime objectives.

These characteristics are achieved when the biblical qualifications for leaders are maintained. When disciples of Christ become leaders, and these discipled leaders disciple others (2 Timothy 2:2), then the quality of leadership is constantly achieved. Disciples are challenged to love the Lord with all their hearts (John 14:15); this allows leaders to be wholehearted, to purpose in their hearts to obey Christ (John 15:1–8); this leads to singlemindedness, and the desire to serve the Lord for his glory and honor (Colossians 3:17); which creates opportunities for excellent service. Because of the diverse needs of church members, leaders' qualifications must never be diminished. Functioning within the ministry descriptions and qualifications provided in the Word, allows pastors, elders, and deacons to confidently expect results that are productive for the kingdom of God.

> Furthermore, you shall select out of all the people able men who fear God, men of truth, those who hate dishonest gain; and you shall place these over them as leaders of thousands, of hundreds, of fifties and of tens (Exodus 18:21).

It must become a sincere commitment of leaders to not choose men and or women who are not biblically qualified. It is leaders, such as this, that demonstrate a sincere desire to serve God and his people. "By this all men will know that you are My disciples, if you have love for one another" (John 13:35). This kind of leader impacts lives and creates an environment that stimulates believers to have a sincere desire to obey Christ (2 Timothy 2:2).

In order to properly plan a leadership structure, which leads to a cohesive process, it is essential that we analyze the major components before the developmental process can be properly outlined.

PASTORAL LEADERSHIP:

Pastors are required by God to lead the church. "These things speak and exhort and reprove with all authority. Let no one disregard you." (Titus 2:15) A pastor is expected to set God's structure in order even when it comes to the appointment of leaders (Titus 1:5). Timothy was required to do the same.

> I am writing these things to *you*, hoping to come *to you* before long; but in case I am delayed, I write so that *you* will know how one ought to conduct himself in the household of God, which is the church of the living God, the pillar and support of the truth (1 Timothy 3:14–15, emphasis mine).

Notice the number of times Paul says "you" in this Scripture. It seems to reiterate how God responded to Moses in Numbers 11:17. God told Moses that he would give him instruction first, and after Moses received it then he would provide direction to the other leaders.

> Then I will come down and speak with you there, and I will take of the Spirit who is upon you, and will put Him upon them; and they shall bear the burden of the people *with you*, so that you will not bear it all alone (Numbers 11:17, emphasis mine).

Pastoral leadership is essential to the strength and ability of the church to effectively implement its vision (Exodus 18:18–26; 1 Thessalonians 5:12–13).

There are many verses in the pastoral epistles that support pastoral leadership. Paul wrote the letters of 1 and 2 Timothy, along with the book of Titus to both Timothy (1:2) and Titus (1:4) respectively. He knew that these young men were appointed to provide leadership to these congregations because he had sent them there. The instructions Paul provided were to be implemented by Timothy and Titus. Paul says to Timothy "I am writing these things to you" (1 Timothy 3:14). He did not write to the elders or the deacons but to Timothy, and this was after Paul explains their qualifications. He continues this in 1 Timothy 4:6, "In pointing out these things to the brethren, you will be a good servant of Christ Jesus." Paul instructs Timothy, after outlining the qualifications for elders and deacons to "Prescribe and teach these things" (1 Timothy 4:11). He told him to not allow the members of the church to disrespect him because he is young (1 Timothy 4:12); Timothy, on the other hand must respect his elders. Timothy was obviously the main teacher (1 Timothy 4:16; 6:17; 2 Timothy 4:1–5) and was charged to study the Word (2 Timothy 2:15) because it is the inspired Word of God that made him adequate for every good work (2 Timothy 3:16–17). Considering that he is the primary teacher, he is "especially" worthy of double honor (1 Timothy 5:17). While Timothy provided oversight, the elders worked together to direct the affairs of the church (1 Timothy 5:17). In all of this, please remember that Timothy was timid and had to be encouraged to be strong in faith based on the Word of God (1 Corinthians 16:10–11; 2 Timothy 1:7).

We find this same attitude being communicated to Titus. He is told to appoint leaders (1:5), silence rebellious teachers (1:10–11) and "reprove them severely" (1:13). As stated above, Titus is told to "speak and exhort and reprove with all authority. Let no one disregard you" (2:15; 3:8). He is told to remind the people how to function in society (3:1–3). Titus is directed to let "[o]ur people... also learn to engage in good deeds to meet pressing needs, so that they will not be unfruitful" (3:14). He is obviously provided the liberty to direct the church.

A businessman was in the wool business, and he once spent the night on the Texas prairie. One night when it was pitching dark the coyote's wail pierced the air. His shepherd's dog began to growl, and his sheep start bleating pitifully. He put more wood on the fire, and as it got brighter he noticed there were hundreds of flickering reflections in the dark. He realized that in their fear the sheep kept their eyes on the shepherd, not the wailing of the coyotes. Sheep need a clear leader, and maybe this is why Hebrews 11 and 12 are written right after a list of troubled times (Hebrews 10:32–39):

> Therefore, since we have so great a cloud of witnesses surrounding us, let us also lay aside every encumbrance and the sin which so easily entangles us, and let us run with endurance the race that is set before us, fixing our eyes on Jesus, the author and perfecter of faith, who for the joy set before Him endured the cross, despising the shame, and has sat down at the right hand of the throne of God (Hebrews 12:1–2).

Despite there being God the Father, God the Son, and God the Holy Spirit, Christ is the head of the church (Ephesians 1:22–23).

LEADERSHIP ASSISTING A PASTOR WHO MAY NOT POSSESS STRONG LEADERSHIP CHARACTERISTICS

A church may have a pastor that may be a good shepherd and Bible teacher, but he may not have the gift of leadership. However, the pastor may have the ability to carve out a vision, provide strong leadership when the church experiences difficult times, and choose qualified leaders. Leadership should not try to take away the pastor's direction or influence because the pastor may not execute these responsibilities efficiently. The church leadership should seek to assist a pastor in areas of leadership but they should not seek to usurp the pastor's leadership.

It is important to remember it is in the church's best interest to have a key person that the people view as their leader. To take over the leadership role from the pastor is to change from God's intent. This is what Satan tried to convince Christ to do when he told him to turn stone into bread. In other words, Christ was told by Satan to take what God perfectly decided in making the stone what it was, and make it bread because the length of Christ's fasting created a need for food (Luke 4:1–13). But Christ even though being the very nature of God and being one with God (John 10:30) respected the leadership structure of the Godhead and left things the way God intended.

I do not support pastoral leadership because I am a pastor. I support pastoral leadership because it is outlined in Scripture, which we will now examine. An elder can desire to be an elder and if the elder meets the qualifications, the elder desires "a fine work" (1 Timothy 3:1). A deacon, who is required by God to be a person full of the Holy Spirit (Acts 6:3), can be recommended by the people and, after being trained, can serve in this position. A pastor, however, must be called by Christ (Ephesians 4:11) and must have the gift of teaching (1 Timothy 4:14; 2 Timothy 1:6). These distinctions are important, and we must respect God's structure. An example is Aaron's and Miriam's approach to Moses. Even though they had a good point, God expected them to respect Moses and defer their concerns to Moses to resolve them before God (Numbers 12).

When the pastor does not demonstrate a desire to establish the church's vision or aggressively resolve problems, a few leaders should approach the pastor respectfully and offer to work with the pastor directly. The few leaders should then enlist additional resources. These resources biblically could be a few loyal and faithful members (two able elders, two Spirit-filled deacons, four members with two of them in leadership capacities on their jobs and two that are not [Numbers 11:16–25]). Have this committee work with the pastor through the initial stages of the vision development or crisis the church may experience. Allow the pastor, who serves as the chairperson, to freely work through the recommendations. The pastor may desire the committee's help in the implementation process. The committee should work closely with the pastor so that the pastor remains involved. When all the issues have been addressed and a consensus reached, the committee should challenge the pastor to make the final decision. The committee members must continually pray for their pastor and trust God to work through his leadership. The committee must also be prepared to step back once the pastor is prepared to move forward. They must lean to the pastor's direction even though the pastor is depending on their expertise to guide the way.

THE BIBLICAL ROLE OF THE PASTOR

The pastor is instructed to function as the primary proclaimer of the Word of God (2 Timothy 4:2; Titus 2:8) and is told by Paul to preach with boldness. This is why Paul instructs Timothy to be sure to become absorbed in the Word (1 Timothy 4:15; 2 Timothy 2:15) and not argue over words (1 Timothy 6:3–5; 2 Timothy 2:14, 23–26). Additionally, Timothy is told to trust the teaching he received from his mother and grandmother (2 Timothy 1:5; 3:15) which was confirmed by the elders of the church in Derbe and Lystra (1 Timothy 4:14). It was this process that prepared him for every good work (2 Timothy 3:16–17).

A pastor must demonstrate a commitment, even a passion for the inerrancy and authority of God's Word because it is this passion for God's Word that exposes the call (Acts 6:4; 20:27). A pastor's anointing is exclusively focused on providing the pastor with knowledge and understanding (Jeremiah 3:15), for the purpose of being a pastor-teacher (Ephesians 4:11). It is this passion, a godly lifestyle, and teaching that influence believers to abide in Christ so that they demonstrate the fruit of the Holy Spirit (John 15:1–8; Hebrews 13:7). "Pay close attention to yourself and to your teaching; persevere in these things, for as you do this you will ensure salvation both for yourself and for those who hear you" (1 Timothy 4:16). A pastor's passion for the Word influences the pastor's life (John 15:3–5). It is a life of integrity, modeled by the pastor's life style and family life (1 Timothy 3:1–7) that allows the pastor to impact believers and unbelievers for the glory of God. Paul's teaching and life became so powerful and consistent that Paul could say; "The things you have learned and received and heard and seen in me, practice these things, and the God of peace will be with you" (Philippians 4:9); and "Be imitators of me, just as I also am of Christ" (1 Corinthians 11:1).

As a pastor, I am convinced that when the sermon and worship service is complete and a man and his wife come to me for counseling (especially in the case of the man); it becomes about who I am as a husband and father. The quality of my son's life, my knowledge of Scripture, and my wisdom also make a great difference to the man in the opposite chair. He knows I am called the pastor, and for the most part he understands what that means. However, the meaning of my role, my level of authority, my education, and the size of the church or its staff *do not affect a man in need.* What will and does affect this man is whether or not he believes I am qualified to give him instruction, in front of his wife, with the expectation that he is going to apply what I say. If the thing that is of most importance, which is to make disciples (Matthew 28:18–19; Colossians 1:28–29), is lost and a person no longer listens to the sermons, it is because my life, as a pastor, is not a model of Christ.

> Prescribe and teach these things. Let no one look down on your youthfulness, but rather in speech, conduct, love, faith and purity, show yourself an example of those who believe" (1 Timothy 4:11–12).

> Remember those who led you, who spoke the word of God to you; and considering the result of their conduct, imitate their faith. Jesus Christ is the same yesterday and today and forever (Hebrews 13:7–8).

The most significant qualities that a pastor must never take for granted are to know the Scriptures, teach the Scriptures, and pray and model the Scriptures (Acts 6:2, 4; 1 Timothy 5:17). A pastor must do this with confidence and boldness (Titus 2:15).

The pastor is charged to oversee the development and implementation of the church's vision (Exodus 18:19–20; Ephesians 4:12; 1 Timothy 3:15). A pastor must also appoint leaders (Titus 1:5). A pastor is given qualifications for leaders that are outlined in 1 Timothy 3:1–13 and Titus 1:5–9. A pastor must work hard to make sure that the implementation of the vision, the coordination of leadership, worship services (Acts 2:42), and the financial operations of the church (1 Timothy 5:17–19) function with decency and order (1 Corinthians 14:40; 1 Timothy 3:15).

Chapter 4

ELDERS AS LEADERS

The qualifications for elders are not much different than that of a pastor. An elder does not necessarily have to possess the gift of teaching. The elder must be "able to teach" (1 Timothy 3:2), meaning the elder has been taught how to teach. The elder does not have to be someone who is called to be an elder. This is a position one may desire (1 Timothy 3:1), and once the person meets the qualifications (1 Timothy 3:1–7) and demonstrates that they have the gift of knowledge and understanding (Jeremiah 3:15), that person may become a part of the elder's ministry when the need arises. One of his primary tasks is to guard the congregation against false doctrine (1 Timothy 4:1–8; Acts 20:27–32).

These elders must demonstrate that they have the ability to help believers resolve the minor issues in their lives using their knowledge of Scripture and wisdom to apply the Word to real life situations.

Furthermore, you shall select out of all the *people able men who fear God, men of truth*, those *who hate dishonest gain*; and you shall place these over them as leaders of *thousands*, of *hundreds*, of *fifties* and of *tens*. Let them judge the people at all times; and let it be *that every major dispute they will bring to you*, but every *minor dispute* they themselves will judge. So it will be easier for you, *and they will bear the burden with you* (Exodus 18:21–22; cf. Acts 6:3, emphasis mine).

The knowledge base of an elder must also serve to resolve doctrinal issues (Acts 15), to recognize when a wolf has come in among the saints, or when someone is seeking to rise up and split the church (Acts 20:29–30). Paul taught the elders of Ephesus the Scriptures, so that they would be able to discern when these incidents are taking place. Guarding the Word, for the health of the church, for developing disciples (Colossians 1:28–29), and helping the weak are some things elders must strive to maintain (Acts 20:35). This knowledge vividly portrays a person of integrity that can be trusted when they give their word on a matter (Titus 1:9). This is important because an elder must not be self-willed (Titus 1:7).

Elders are responsible for assisting the pastor with church discipline issues. This includes persons who are fellow elders (Matthew 16:18–19; Acts 20:29–30; 1 Timothy 5:19–21). Additionally, elders assist with overseeing the church's finances (1 Timothy 5:17–18), the formulation of the church's policies, and the distribution of the Lord's Supper so that the spiritual life of the church dominated by the application of Scripture leads every member to spiritual maturity.

DEACONS AS LEADERS

Up to this point, we have only addressed the spiritual life of the church. We have yet to care for the flock in regards to the physical needs they may have. A model for this is highlighted in the sixth chapter of Acts. Before there was a need, for service of the widows, the church was devoted to the apostles teaching, to worship, and growing in large numbers (Acts 2:42, 47). As the church grew the demands on the apostles became greater. This is the same problem Moses experienced (Exodus 18:18–23). These demands in Acts created the need for servants who were therefore labeled as deacons (this word means servant). Deacons did not become an official office until Paul planned a church in Ephesus (Acts 20:24–35). Paul sent Timothy to pastor the church at Ephesus, and he instructed Timothy to create this office (1 Timothy 3:8–13). Paul designed it this way because in a young church, as we had in Acts, the emphasis is on discipleship.

This office does not have any requirements in the area of teaching. Deacons must be "men of good reputation, full of the Spirit and of wisdom." (Acts 6:3) This is why the qualifications listed in 1 Timothy 3:8–13 is focused more on the person's character than on their function. Since they are not required to teach, God in his sovereign will does not gift them with knowledge and understanding. Wisdom seems to be an attribute deacons may pray for based on James 1:5–8, or may achieve based on their commitment to apply God's Word to their life (Philippians 1:9–11 [discernment]). The gift of service (Romans 12:7) is definitely something that God provides for his ministry so that the service is empowered by the Holy Spirit.

The deacon's main focus is to be servants functioning under the direction of the elders and the pastor. Deacons are to care for the sick, those in need of benevolence (financially weak), assist with the distribution of the Lord's Supper, deliver food to those in need, and open and close the building for church services. The dynamic that the gift of service provides is that there is no end to what a deacon may do because service is attached to the needs of the body which are always present and always changing. This is *why the gift of service must be an essential part of a deacon's life. It must be his spiritual gift.*

In Matthew 25:14–31, Jesus demonstrates for us through the master's three servants, what the heart of a servant is and is not like. This passage demonstrates the wisdom of the master because he only gave one talent to the servant who buried his talent because he was lazy (vs. 26). The master gave to the servants based on their ability (25:15), and the gifts (money) came from the masters resources (the same thing you see in Exodus 18: some leaders had thousands, others hundreds and others fifties and tens. The same when the food was being distributed from five loaves two fishes in Luke 9:14). The servants who were faithful understood what pleased their master and allowed their life to be controlled by the gift (money) that was given to them. They never complained and they worked hard with much energy ("went and traded," Matthew 25:16) understanding that everything they worked hard to achieve belonged to the master. When the master returned, he demanded that they give an account of what they did with his money. Maybe this is why Christ would say in Mark 10:43–45 that whoever wishes to do a great job as a servant must become a "slave to all." Christ modeled this for us before he demanded this characteristic; "For even the Son of Man did not come to be served, but to serve, and to give His life a ransom for many" (Mark 10:45). The heart of a servant is one whose entire focus is to please his master by serving him faithfully each and every day. A servant also understands there is a day of accountability and the master owns everything. As a result a servant is committed to be a good steward.

Before elders and deacons can be appointed, they must consistently demonstrate a commitment to attend church regularly (Hebrews 10:25), be a committed giver (Luke 12:30–34), and also have a clear understanding of their spiritual gifts (1 Peter 4:10; Ephesians 4:16). They must also have a good reputation among the members of the church (Acts 16:1–5), demonstrate faithful service, and must lead groups to successfully complete particular tasks (2 Timothy 2:1–2; Timothy and Titus completed many tasks for Paul in an effective manner). Before being considered for this position, they must have attended the church on a regular basis for at least three years (Hebrews 5:12—a possible two-year period). Last but not least, they must prove to have two of the greatest characteristics of a leader, which is "followship" (Matthew 4:19) and the attitude of a servant (Mark 10:41–44).

REFERENCES
Adams, Jay. 1996. *Be the Leader God Calls You to Be*. Wheaton, IL: Victor.

Chapter 5

THE DEVELOPMENT OF A COHESIVE PROCESS FOR PRODUCTIVE LEADERSHIP

Paul Cannings

The importance of leadership that functions in a cohesive manner cannot be emphasized enough. When there is a breakdown in leadership as in the case with Aaron and Moses, a whole nation may worship a false god. When there is a breakdown in leadership, in the case of Barnabas, John Mark, and Paul, friendships are affected. When there is a breakdown in leadership in the case of Judas and Christ, many key leaders can be crucified.

The key to developing a cohesive leadership team is a strong discipleship process coupled with a commitment to a strong vision (Philippians 2:1–2). Leaders must submit to an accountability process and have a deep commitment to take their own family development seriously. Leaders must never appoint anyone into leadership without a thorough observation process. It is not the confession a person makes that impresses Christ; it is their fruit.

> Not everyone who says to Me, "Lord, Lord," will enter the kingdom of heaven; but he who does the will of My Father who is in heaven will enter" (Matthew 7:21).

> Do not lay hands upon anyone too hastily and thus share responsibility for the sins of others; keep yourself free from sin (1 Timothy 5:22).

Paul describes for us in Philippians 2:1–5 several principles that lead to God the Father and God the Son operating in a cohesive manner, as it relates to the care of mankind. Paul states that they have the same Spirit. This means that leaders must demonstrate by the fruit of their life that they are saved. Demonstrated fruit of the spirit would be the first thing needed to create a cohesive leadership unit. A person could come to church regularly, attend Bible study, Sunday school, and extra services and still not be saved. Paul told the elders in Ephesus "that after my departure savage wolves will come in among you, not sparing the flock" (Acts 20:29). This is why Paul continues in Philippians 2:1 with the phrase, "if there is any consolation of love," because the Lord tells us we would know disciples by the way they love each other (John 13:34–35). The fruit of a heart that loves God is demonstrated by the way that person loves their neighbor (Matthew 22:37–40).

> The one who says he is in the Light and yet hates his brother is in the darkness until now. The one who loves his brother abides in the Light and there is no cause for stumbling in him. But the one who hates his brother is in the darkness and walks in the darkness, and does not know where he is going because the darkness has blinded his eyes (1 John 2:9–11).

How could we have a person who is an elder or deacon yet they walk in darkness? (What is of greater concern is a person who is in darkness is of the devil and hates the Word of God [John 3:19–21; 1 John 3:4–9]). This person does not make wise decisions, and instead of caring for God's sheep they abuse them (2 Corinthians 11:11–33). This is why Paul continues in Philippians 2:1 to describe the nature of their love as being affectionate and full of compassion. This is the kind of love Paul had for the Thessalonians.

> For we never came with flattering speech, as you know, nor with a pretext for greed—God is witness—nor did we seek glory from men, either from you or from others, even though as apostles of Christ we might have asserted our authority. But we proved to be gentle among you, as a nursing mother tenderly cares for her own children. Having so fond an affection for you, we were well-pleased to impart to you not only the gospel of God but also our own lives, because you had become very dear to us (1 Thessalonians 2:5–8).

Secondly, Paul states in Philippians 2:1–5 that believers must develop a *"fellowship of the Spirit."* There must be a strong commitment of maturing leaders in order for them to think alike, and also consistently demonstrate the characteristics of Christ.

Thirdly, leadership must be of "the same mind"—consistency is key. The discipleship process teaches: the doctrines of the church, Trinitarianism, the meaning of salvation, the nature of the church, and also how to develop a clear understanding of the leadership structure and biblical function. Having the same mind leads to the same answers when members interact with leaders encouraging a cohesive atmosphere. This prevents members from setting leaders against each other and presents a cohesive front before the church. This works powerfully in a family. When children cannot set their father and mother against each other, they are held accountable to do what they were told.

Fourthly, leaders must be committed to "one purpose" (2:2). The vision of the church must be a commitment of each leader. Leaders must be committed to see the church reach its full potential and financially support the church remembering where a man's heart is there will his treasure be (Luke 12:34). Notice that being of "the same mind" comes before being committed to "one purpose"—making it obvious that when believers are of one Spirit and one mind they will be committed to one purpose. Therefore, it is essential that we develop the first two objectives before focusing on creating a cohesive unit for vision development.

Leaders must do nothing out of "selfishness or empty conceit" and they must not look out for their own interests (Philippians 2:3). To do so leads to wisdom that is demonic.

"But if you have bitter jealousy and selfish ambition in your heart, do not be arrogant and so lie against the truth. This wisdom is not that which comes down from above, but is earthly, natural, demonic. For where jealousy and selfish ambition exist, there is disorder and every evil thing" (James 3:14–16).

It is of crucial importance that leaders demonstrate love to one another and to the church body. Lack of this attribute destroys cohesiveness and divides the body, allowing demons the opportunity to work in the church. This is why Paul states in Titus 1:7: "For the overseer must be above reproach as God's steward, not self-willed, not quick-tempered, not addicted to wine, not pugnacious, not fond of sordid gain."

The implementation of a cohesive singleminded leadership team allows the church members to view from its leadership an attitude that displays the mind of Christ (Philippians 1:5). Paul was committed to this process and said in 1 Corinthians 11:1, "Be imitators of me, just as I also am of Christ." The writer of Hebrews crystallizes this concept in a manner that raises its significance to the ultimate level when he says:

> Remember those who led you, who spoke the word of God to you; and considering the result of their conduct, imitate their faith. Jesus Christ is the same yesterday and today and forever (Hebrews 13:7–8).

It is for all the reasons provided in this introduction that a discipleship process must be established for all leaders in the church. *A leader that does not submit to this process is demonstrating that he or she lacks the humility that is required for a leader to be a true servant of Christ* (Philippians 2:3; Mark 10:41–44).

A PROCESS FOR DEVELOPING
A COHESIVE UNIT OF LEADERS

Every church needs a pastor who can provide godly advice and who will enhance their knowledge of the Scriptures, along with being courageous enough to hold them accountable for the continual development of a godly lifestyle and ministry development. This person must be someone who is respected by the pastor's spouse, the leaders of the church, and the members of the church.

The pastor must meet with the chair and vice-chair of the elder's ministry on a regular basis for prayer, Bible study, and to develop and maintain a good relationship. It is good to have an open discussion about problems the church may be experiencing, budget issues, doctrinal issues, ministry issues, and even personal issues. The pastor must not be bashful about holding these individuals accountable for their spiritual growth and personal lives. When a pastor is new to a church or there is a traditional system where the chairman is the chairman of the deacon board, the pastor must first focus on developing a relationship with this person and this person with the pastor for reasons stated in the first part of this chapter.

When Christ decided to recruit Peter to be his disciple (a person who later preached at Pentecost and led the disciples), he first went to Peter's house and healed his mother-in-law of a high fever. Next, he met Peter after he fished all night and used his boat to preach (Christ, by using Peter's boat, showed a need for Peter). He commanded Peter to go fishing again after Peter had cleaned his net and listened to Christ preach. He cast his net to the deep side of the lake, which Christ knew was the wrong side of the lake. Peter obeyed (even though he called Christ Master, not Lord. He demonstrated respect—he owed Christ this for healing his mother-in-law), and after catching lots of fish Peter was recruited (Luke 4:38–39; 5:1–11). Developing a relationship with Peter attached to his personal life (his mother-in-law was at his house) and his professional life, Christ led Peter to respect his leadership. Peter became so excited that he left his business on its best day to follow Christ.

It is good to develop a relationship with the chair and vice-chair by first demonstrating a need for their leadership, advice, assistance in understanding church issues, and their participation for developing the agenda for the meeting. Be close to them when they are going through various personal issues such as the lost of family members, loss of employment, and sickness in the family. Show concern for how things are developing on their job and provide them advice when needed.

Begin every meeting with prayer and spend some time going through a discipleship book; there are several good series in bookstores. If a pastor finds oneself in a hostile environment, it would be good to pass out the agenda first, so that the deacons will understand that the study will not take all night. In this case, try to limit the study to about twenty minutes.

Encourage discussion even if it may seem "off the wall" at first. If it *is* "off the wall," learn from this by understanding where they are and continue to refine how you teach the lesson. It would be good to have a series of lessons compiled in a small book to hand out for them to take home. In the event that any of the lessons relate to them personally, this process prevents them from legitimately viewing the lesson as a personal attack.

The pastor when meeting with the elders should approach any problem issue in the church by first leading a discussion that addresses it biblically. The elders should spend time praying over various issues or the sick list. Discussions should work toward unanimity. If this cannot be reached, then a vote must be taken (the number of elders must be an uneven number) with the understanding that whatever the decision is no one discusses the issue with anyone that is not an elder, not even their spouse (this can prove very effective when members of the church are fishing for information because what the spouses don't know they can't tell). Spouses can sometimes have such an influence that it can cause boards to be led by the elder's spouses and not the elders themselves. This very same thing can occur with the deacon board. For this very reason, I reiterate to my own elders the importance of not discussing any difficulties the church may be experiencing with non-deacons, or their spouses.

The elders, on an individual basis, must be willing to be accountable to the pastor. Timothy and Titus were held responsible for keeping things in order as explained in chapters three and four. The elders collectively can hold the pastor accountable for doctrinal issues, financial issues, church discipline, policy issues, and provide advice on the appointment of elders and deacons. Each elder has deacons below them that they are responsible for. They must work with each of their deacons to ensure that they are functioning responsibly and growing spiritually. They must be held accountable for attending Bible study, worship, Sunday school, or discipleship classes, and personal issues—especially as relationships grow closer. Elders must meet with their deacons for Bible study, prayer, and the development of godly relationships. The deacons and their elders over a period of time should become like brothers. The deacons when meeting do not need to have a chair because it is best to have just one chair in the church (chair of the elders' ministry or board). This keeps a clear leadership structure for the members and the leaders. (My book, *Making Your Vision a Reality*, has organizational charts that show an effective organizational structure.)

P. L. Tan states, "James L. Hayes, head of American Management Association, after nearly forty years in management education, gives the following hints for getting along with workers:

1. Be people-conscious. Create a climate that will lead to job satisfaction in your company or organization.

2. Tell workers exactly what you expect from them.

3. Be a good listener.

4. Have a two-way door. Encourage employees to come to your office but also get out to where people work.

5. Be patient. Realize that bringing workers along in their jobs takes time.

6. Give your employees not only problems to deal with but opportunities to grow.

7. Keep your promises. Credibility creates trust.

8. Be a problem preventer, not a problem solver.

9. Tell the truth.

10. Pass the pride along. Show prompt appreciation for good ideas and good performance."

CONCLUSION:

Have you ever gone to a store that is a part of a chain of stores (Walgreens, McDonalds, etc.) and found any of them fundamentally different from the other? The answer is, obviously, no. In most chains, when we call for information that affects all the stores, they send us to their head office. They have a policy manual, and every store operates from this manual. The church has a policy manual called the Bible and every church must operate from it. There is one headquarters and it is in heaven run by God the Father, God the Son, and God the Holy Spirit. This is why Paul says in Ephesians 1:11 "also we have obtained an inheritance, having been predestined according to His purpose who works all things after the counsel of His will." All things are organized after the counsel of the will of the Godhead.

When we plan a leadership structure, God's will must dominate how it is structured and how it is implemented. When members serve in such a structure, it becomes easy for spiritual gifts to find their place, and this powerfully allows the Holy Spirit to fit the Lord's body together fitly (Ephesians 4:16). As a result, each believer experiences the divine will of God, whether they hear it preached or experience it through the service of others or through the service they provide. Because the Bible (policy manual) controls everything, Christ functionally becomes the head of every church every where. It is through this process leaders execute the will of God for the people of God. The church moves from being an organization to a living organism.

REFERENCES

Tan, P. L. 1979. *Encyclopedia of 7700 Illustrations.* Garland, TX: Bible Communications.

Chapter 6

MOBILIZING AND MOTIVATING THE CONGREGATION FOR EFFECTIVENESS

Lloyd C. Blue

My ministry began at the Solid Rock Baptist Church in Los Angeles, California in 1962 under the leadership of the late Reverend Sidney Birdsong and has continued for more than fifty years. My objective in this chapter is to share what I have learned over the years in hope that will be of help to others.

Commitment is a necessary foundation for a healthy congregation, and nothing less than a commitment to a kingdom agenda will turn a congregation toward a healthy, aggressive ministry. Therefore, one must understand and clarify what type of congregation it is, or that it desire to be before one can mobilize and motivate it for effectiveness. In my experience I have always found five things to be absolutely necessary for effectiveness.

1. The congregation must be mission-oriented. One needs to ask and know, "what is our mission?" Jesus inaugurated the kingdom of God. Mark 1:14–15 (NKJV) states:

   > Now after John was put in prison, Jesus came to Galilee, preaching the gospel of the kingdom of God, and saying, the time is fulfilled, and the kingdom of God is at hand. Repent, and believe in the gospel.

Jesus spoke of this kingdom ruling over people and their institutions more than any other issue. Therefore, our mission must be to extend Jesus' kingdom, to carry out the will of God in this world and to proclaim and apply his gospel. We are on a redemptive mission with God to this world, and all we do must be founded on our mission.

2. One must be a service-oriented congregation. You should assume a servant attitude as Jesus did. In Mark 10:45 (NKJV), Jesus said that "the Son of Man came not to be served, but to serve and give His life a ransom for many." Thus, there needs to be more balance between "service" and "serve us." There needs to be more balance between internal ministry and external ministry. The church is to literally give itself away through concrete ministry and sacrificial service. Our calling as a church is to serve. A part of our mission is to serve and minister with and to the people of God. One must also serve and minister, so that others may be won to Christ and become a part of his body.

3. One must be a modeling congregation. People must be challenged to live by distinct Christian values. Therefore, we need to practice what we preach. We are to be salt and light. Matthew 5:13–15 (KJV) states:

> Ye are the salt of the earth; but if the salt have lost his savour, wherewith shall it be salted? It is thenceforth good for nothing, but to be cast out, and to be trodden under the foot of men. Ye are the light of the world. A city that is set on a hill cannot be hid. Neither do men light a candle, and put it under a bushel, but on a candlestick; and it giveth light unto all that are in the house.

4. One must be shapers of cultural and social values, not shaped by them. We are to be the pacesetters. One should influence the world by being like Christ, and do so consistently. One must also be holy as the Lord our God is holy. First Peter 1:14–16 (NKJV) instructs us to be

> as obedient children, not conforming yourselves to the former lusts, as in your ignorance; but as He who called you is holy, you also be holy in all your conduct, because it is written, "Be holy, for I am holy."

Lloyd C. Blue

5. A church must be a biblically based organism. Thus, the content of the congregational health is described as being a mission-oriented, service-oriented, a modeling church, and a shaper of cultural and social values, as well as a biblically based organism. The church is alive. It is dynamic. It is vital, and as one keeps what the church is all about before our eyes, we will be able to see a kingdom agenda move forward in the days ahead.

PART ONE: MOBILIZING THE CONGREGATION TO ACTION (EPHESIANS 4:11–13)

Most people wish to service God, but only in an advisory capacity. They cannot see themselves working at the grassroots level. The question is: Why are so few individuals actively involved in ministry? Well, I'm glad you asked. The answer is: Too many people are maintenance-minded instead of harvest-minded. In Matthew 9:36–38 (NKJV), it is recorded:

> But when He saw the multitudes, He was moved with compassion for them, because they were weary and scattered, like sheep having no shepherd. Then He said to His disciples, "The harvest truly is plentiful, but the laborers are few. Therefore pray the Lord of the harvest to send out laborers into His harvest."

Others are so worried about things being done right that they neglect doing the right things, or don't do anything. Very few people believe that they have what it takes to be used by God like those who are professionally trained ministers. However, God equips everyone uniquely to be his workers (see Ephesians 2:8–19). It also helps church members to get mobilized when the leadership is willing to work beside them. Let me illustrate this point.

During the American Revolution, a man in civilian clothes rode past a group of solders repairing a small defensive barrier. Their leader was shouting instructions, but making no attempt to help them. Asked why by the rider, he retorted with great dignity, "Sir, I am a corporal!" The stranger apologized, dismounted, and proceeded to help the exhausted soldiers. With the job done, he turned to the corporal and said, "My Corporal, next time you have a job like this and not enough men to do it, go to your commander-in-chief, and I will come and help you again." It was none other than George Washington ("Today in the Word," 1991).

Some church members have the spiritual maturity to assume positions of responsibilities. Yet, everyone is told to grow up into Christ in all aspects of spirituality. Others assume that witnessing is to be left to the clergy. According to Acts 1:8 (NKJV), nothing could be farther from the truth ("But you shall receive power when the Holy Spirit has come upon you; and you shall be witnesses to Me in Jerusalem, and in all Judea and Samaria, and to the end of the earth"). This applies to everyone. To be sure, there are some who do not realize that most churches were planted and grown in home family fellowships and led by lay elders (see Acts 2:41–47).

Finally, a very large segment of church members have not properly equipped themselves for the work of the ministry through training and gaining adequate ministry experiences. How can all Christians equip themselves for the work of the ministry.

They can ask God to guide them in seeking ways to discover and develop their spiritual gifts. Most churches today has some type of teaching and training to assist in discovering spiritual gifts and place people in a ministry comparable with their gifts. As part of the discovery process, believers can quietly share their faith with those around them and observe the ways that God uses them in being faithful in little things (see Luke 16:10).

I would suggest some of type tract or booklet such as the "Four Spiritual Laws" (1952). It should be something that one may simply read to a person. This is a very simple way to share the gospel.

They can serve as an apprentices under spiritual leaders who can teach them by their exemplary lifestyles. They can also ask these leaders for opportunities to teach, preach, or lead a small group.

They can be doers of the Word when they are aware of their spiritual responsibilities to worship, witness, fellowship, pray, obey God, and study the Bible. As James 1:22 (KJV), says, "be ye doers of the word, and not hearers only, deceiving your own selves." Therefore, they should bloom where they are planted. They can make prayer lists that ask God for other ways in which they can serve him through the church, and through the fulfilling of Christ's Great Commission.

How can all people do ministry?

They can share the gospel with their neighborhoods through casual visits, enlist them in Sunday school, and teach Sunday-school classes. They can get involved with small-group Bible studies that teach how to study the Bible in depth, and get with other people who are willing to pray seriously about evangelism, discipleship, and spiritual growth. They can ask their spiritual leaders for ideas to serve the Lord in areas of greatest need, and help bring people to fellowships and ministry functions that allow people to gain exposure to the Scriptures and the love of God. They may also read Christian biographies of God's men and women, and seek to follow their examples.

Finally, let's look at some results of these ministries. These type of ministries of the early church resulted in the planting of hundreds of house fellowships that were blessed by the teaching, preaching, giving of hospitality, healing, service, mercy, and prayer ministries. Non-clergy leaders are able to go to many places where clergy cannot go, because of their implied or assumed neutrality. Such workers are able to be self-supporting and are able to work in countries that are closed to missionaries and evangelists. They are able to pray more intelligently for others in their professions, because they know the everyday temptations that are faced by them, and they are humble enough to rely on the Lord rather than on their professional training.

SUMMARY OF PART ONE

- Self-righteous service comes through human effort, True service come from a relationship with the Divine Other deep inside.

- Self-righteous service is impressed with the "big deal." True service finds it almost impossible to distinguish the small from the large service.

- Self-righteous service requires external rewards. True service rests contented in hiddenness.

- Self-righteous service is highly concerned about results. True service is free of the need to calculate results.

- Self-righteous service picks and chooses whom to serve. True service is indiscriminate in its ministry.

- Self-righteous service is affected by moods and whims. True service ministers simply and faithfully, because their is a need.

- Self-righteous service is temporary. True service is a lifestyle.

- Self-righteous service is without sensitivity. It insists on meeting the need, even when to do so would be destructive. True service can withhold service as freely as perform it.

- Self-righteous service fractures community. True service, on the other hand, builds community.

PART TWO: MOBILIZING THE CONGREGATION TO ACTION (1 THESSALONIANS 5:14)

The word "mobilize" means to help make people ready, active, and equipped for service. If you wants to win and mobilize individuals to your way of thinking, throw down a challenge. Today many people need a good challenge to be and do what God wants.

Paul wrote in 1 Thessalonians 5:14 (NKJV):

Now we exhort you, brethren, warn those who are unruly, comfort the faint-hearted, uphold the weak, be patient with all.

More and more we see people slipping in to their shells of isolation, idleness, and independence. Too many indifferent, apathetic, and complacent people do not realize the damage they are inflicting on themselves and others because of their lack of active obedience. Jesus said in Matthew 5:16 (NKJV):

Let your light so shine before men, that they may see your good works and glorify your Father in heaven.

Much of idleness comes from a desire to be safe, secure, and selfishly in control at all times of our lives. Throughout the entire Bible we are urged to be strong and courageous and act, and not fear or be dismayed. Paul told Timothy,

God did not give us a spirit of timidity (of cowardice, of craven and cringing and fawning fear), but [He has given us a spirit] of power and of love and of calm and well-balanced mind and discipline and self-control. (2 Timothy 1:7 AMP).

We are to encourage others so that they can do everything God asks them to do with the help of Christ who gives them the strength and power (Philippians 4:13). We are to be exhorters of people for prayer, for service, for love and good works (Hebrews 10:24–25 NKJV).

The following is a set of guidelines for mobilizing the people you associate with for greater effectiveness, involvement and contribution to the advancement of Christ's kingdom and righteousness throughout the whole earth.

ENVISIONING: Envisioning helps people to see the possibilities for great contributions to Christ and to his kingdom through mobilization. Jesus communicated a passion for winning the lost sheep. He said, "For the Son of Man came to seek and to save the lost" (Luke 19:10 NIV). Without a clear vision and purpose people tend to drift into idleness, complacency, and apathetic mediocrity.

Our purpose should be to fulfill the Great Commission in Matthew 28:18–20, and we must always strive for excellence.

INFORMING: Ask the Lord to help you to gain greater wisdom, knowledge, and insight into the best ways to inform people about the great ways to carry out God's vision for winning, discipling, and sending people out for service. Paul wrote, "All Scripture is God-breathed and is useful for teaching, rebuking, correcting and training in righteousness" (2 Timothy 3:16 NIV). Too many times we give people information without a vision and our teaching becomes as stale and dry as unbuttered toast. It is even hard to swallow at times. We should teach so that we are not only making people aware of their biblical responsibilities but we are seeking to help them be transformed by the renewing of their minds, emotions, and behaviors.

ENLISTING: Ask the Lord to help you put out information in a way that will help in recruiting people for service assignments. The more personal, intentional, and specific we can be about the opportunities for obedience to the Lord, the better recruiters we will become. People want to know what their roles, responsibilities, and authorities will be. Help them by giving as many specifics as possible.

INVOLVING: Give people hands-on opportunities to be involved with witnessing, teaching, and serving in some ministry of the church. Often people have volunteered only to discover that they were not really used to their capacity. When people do not sense that they are really making a valuable contribution, they tend to move on to something where they can find meaning, worth, and a sense of purposeful service.

Lloyd C. Blue

ENCOURAGING: Paul wrote, "May the God who gives endurance and encouragement give you the same attitude of mind toward each other that Christ Jesus had, so that with one mind and one voice you may glorify the God and Father of our Lord Jesus Christ" (Romans 15:5–6 NIV). To encourage someone literally means we are infusing them with courage; we are instilling confidence; and we are stimulating them to action. Let our messages, attitudes, and conversation be more encouraging than discouraging. Let us focus more on what good things we can do than the problems that are in front of us.

EQUIPPING: Paul wrote, "to equip his people for works of service, so that the body of Christ may be built up" (Ephesians 4:11–12 NIV). Provide whatever supplies, resources, or spiritual inspiration that is necessary to help people accomplish what the Lord is calling them to do. Utilize the whole range of spiritual gifts and talents in the body of Christ. Do not hesitate to call in people who maybe a specialist in areas where there are weaknesses within your own group.

ENABLING: Remind people that the word of God and the Holy Spirit are at work in us both to will and to do of his good pleasure (Philippians 2:13–14 NIV). Real motivation that lasts has to come from within a person. People need a continual sense of the enabling power of the Holy Spirit so they are merely bearing the fruit of the work of Christ within them. Be like Peter when he prayed, "enable your servants to speak your word with great boldness" (Acts 4:29 NIV).

EMPOWERING: Let's ask the Lord to infuse us with his power, might, and authority to accomplish everything related to his Great Commission (Matthew 28:18–20; Acts 1:8). Let's pray, as Paul did, that the church would be "strengthened with all might, according to His glorious power, for all patience and longsuffering with joy" (Colossians1:11 NKJV).

ENTRUSTING: Paul wrote, "be strong in the grace that is in Christ Jesus. And the things you have heard me say in the presence of many witnesses, commit these to reliable men who will be able to teach others also" (2 Timothy 2:1–2 NKJV). Ask the Lord to help you be a multiplier of the grace, love and truth he has given you.

Let us listen to Jesus, the greatest mobilizer in history, "'Come, follow me,' Jesus said, 'and I will send you out to fish for people.' At once they left their nets and followed him" (Matthew 4:19–20 NIV).

Lloyd C. Blue

REFERENCES

"Four Spiritual Laws." 1952. Orlando: CRU (Campus Crusade for Christ).

"Today in the Word." 1991. Chicago: Moody Bible Institute.

PART 3
HANDLING THE PRESSURES OF LEADERSHIP

Chapter 7

BALANCING YOUR MIND AND YOUR MINISTRY[1]

Christina Dixon

L eaders—who are we? Some say we are the ones out front. Some say we are the ones with power and control. Others say we are the experts: the ones with the answers to the tough questions. Still others say that leaders are the ones who are, in a word, responsible.

Leadership involves all these things. But all these things in themselves are not leadership. They are things that those who lead do. When done effectively, with integrity, leadership provides direction and guidance that not only causes growth in those being led; it sows the seeds of replication.

The greatest leader of all time, Jesus Christ, went beyond the shallow waters of power and control to lead a group of twelve men, as he lived among them for three years. The impact of his life upon their hearts and minds caused them to replicate his teaching to the degree that it still continues to empower others some two thousand years after the fact. I have been personally impacted by his message, and it is without apology that I write this chapter from a biblical perspective. In the marathon race of life, endurance is a major component to finishing the race. For Christian leaders, life is more

---

1. This chapter was previously published in the book *HELP! for Your Leadership* (Detroit: PriorityOne Publications, 2003). Used by permission. Some editorial changes have been made.

117

like a marathon intertwined with relay races. While it is true we must endure until the end, it is also true that there will be times when the baton of leadership must be passed to others, while we rest.

It is not that the race is over. It is simply our turn to experience a time of revitalization and fellowship with our Leader (Jesus Christ), so we can arise —with renewed strength.

Too often, those in leadership attempt to run the race without balance. Hence, those observing their leadership witness stumbling. Sadly, many take pride in their stubborn determination to "never give up." It's too bad they don't realize that their decisions resemble a weakened runner's awkward, out-of-control steps.

It is in times like these that our need for renewal is that much more pronounced. Since we are leaders, the way we handle times of fatigue and stress may be replicated. Thus we are challenged to model how to regain balance when it has been lost.

When I was asked to write a chapter entitled "Balancing Your Mind and Your Ministry," I laughed like Sarah in the Bible. Will somebody, anybody tell me how to balance your mind and your ministry? Please help this sister out!

Balance is such a challenging concept to those of us whose lives often feel like the pendulum of a grandfather clock. At times our passion to be effective in our leadership roles is so overwhelming that we find ourselves working too many long hours. It seems we are unaware that in doing so we are simultaneously eliminating time for building relationships with our God, our spouses, our children, our friends, and those to whom we minister, not to mention taking care of our bodies.

That's when the pendulum swings 180 degrees, driving us to rest and to spend time with others while leaving loose ends in leadership matters that may cause those following us to feel stifled or confused.

When I think about how out of balance my life has been at times, I can almost feel the tender spots in my head from running head first into the brick wall of imbalance. Consequently, some of the knowledge I have to share has come from the University of Hard Knocks and that is putting it mildly. But we can learn from our mistakes.

In this chapter, we will look at what balance *really* is, why it seems so impossible to maintain, the desperate need we have for it, and the caution flags that can help us recognize imbalance before it does any further damage.

THE SYMPHONY OF LIFE—WHAT BALANCE REALLY IS

The Merriam-Webster Collegiate Dictionary (2009) says that balance is both a noun and a verb. It is both something we can be and do. For the purposes of this chapter, Merriam-Webster's definition in the noun category is most helpful. It says that balance is "mental and emotional steadiness."

As a verb, Merriam-Webster defines "balance" as bringing something into harmony or proportion. When talking about balance from the prospective of leadership roles, we cannot afford to look at our lives as a pie cut in equal slices, as many do. Thinking of balance in this manner causes us to live with an internal ruler that slaps us on the wrist whenever we give one aspect of our lives more time than we do another. By contrast, considering balance in terms of harmony is not merely realistic, it is crucial.

Think for a moment what it means to be *in* harmony. In a musical score, an arrangement often calls for many different instruments to play simultaneously. The melody, along with steady timing, permits instruments to play differing notes, some quietly, some loudly, some quickly, others more slowly, some consistently and still others are heard only for moments and not throughout the entire arrangement. In fact, there can be times in arrangements where the entire orchestra rests while one instrument is allowed the liberty to express itself in a moving solo. Yet, with all these variables, our ears are pleased and at times our souls are calmed by the composition.

Likewise, when we view balance as our lives being brought into harmony, we are not pressured to have each area of our lives *playing* simultaneously at the same tempo and volume, in every measure, never resting. By viewing our lives as a symphony with a limited time to be heard, we can live a life that not only pleases God, but also calms the souls of our fellow humanity.

WHY IS BALANCE SO DIFFICULT TO MAINTAIN?

I believe the main reason so many of us as leaders in the body of Christ find balance difficult to maintain is that *we* are at the center of their lives. Our agenda, our desires, our way of doing things motivate our actions.

As human beings, this is a common thing. However, as leaders who profess Christ as Lord, we are called to a standard that defers to his agenda, his desires, and his way of doing things.

In some of our minds we have convinced ourselves that everyone and everything under our leadership is required to harmonize with us. In some cases, those who choose not to *follow our lead* suffer the unloving penalties of rejection and ridicule. We think, "After all, I am the leader. If you can't do what I say, leave." There are even those in church leadership who go beyond the boundaries of Scripture and place disagreement with them on their made-up list of unpardonable sins that banishes one from "membership" in the body. Clearly this type of behavior reveals an imbalance in the way some view their role as leader.

As I write this chapter, I am compelled to draw attention to its title, "Balancing Your Mind and Your Ministry." The word "balance" may cause some to see images from their lives, but I want to emphasize that we are talking about how we as leaders think about our role.

God's word instructs us in Romans 12:3 to not think more highly of ourselves than we ought. It further says that we are to think soberly. This does not mean that we devalue the gifts and abilities God has given us by thinking of ourselves as worthless. It does mean that we have a clear view of our strengths *and* our limitations and weaknesses.

One of the first steps toward balance is to recognize where we really stand in the scheme of things. As Christian leaders we must always be mindful that we are merely instruments in the hands of the Lord. Sure, we are handy instruments. But we must never forget that we have been ordained to be so. As such, the Composer (Jesus Christ) sets the purpose for use and the time of use. Jesus said that apart from him we can do absolutely nothing (see John 15:5). Any music that soothes others can only be attributed to the Master's skill.

I can almost hear someone thinking—"I know that already!" My concern for you isn't whether you know what the Bible says about this already. My concern is, does your behavior reflect that knowledge as it relates to your leadership? Bible teacher Raymond Smith Jr. (2003, unpublished work) discusses different levels of knowledge:

> Another self-evident truism is that we cannot act upon that which we do not know. Knowledge is the foundation by which we base our thoughts and behavior. II Timothy 2:15 states: "Be diligent to present yourself approved to God as a workman who does not need to be ashamed, accurately handling the word of truth." We must recognize however that there are varying levels of "knowledge" that we tend to govern our lives by:

Level 1—Faint recognition

Level II—Ability to recall

Level III—Ability to explain, prove, and illustrate

Level IV—Active knowledge, resulting in modified behavior.

Smith goes on to emphasize additional concerns that believers struggle with in this area. Christian leaders are no different. Even though you *know* you can't do everything, do you *feel* that **you** have to oversee and or do everything? Although you are aware that God is really the One *in charge,* do you still run things by *your* agenda? Would those closest to you agree that your perception of your role as a leader is that of a servant? Would those under your leadership testify on your behalf that you do not lord it over them but, in fact, exemplify the heart of a servant of the Most High? How you *walk* before God and his people exposes the truth of how you perceive yourself as a leader.

From an individual standpoint, we have our relationship with God, with others, and with ourselves.

Every song has a melody. Without it the song is not recognizable. In the lives of those who follow after Christ, he is the melody. It is to him that every "instrument" of our lives must harmonize.

Bishop Anthony Johnson (2000) states:

In life everyone has some particular area where they provide leadership that nurtures and forms visions for men, women, children, business, and community. Whether the scale is large or small, your leadership or lack thereof has profound impact (either positive or negative)! Make no mistake about it. Your input causes growth and achievement or stagnation and eventual ruin. We must not underestimate our role of leadership within these great structures and recognize when our conduct damages rather than encourages excellence. A large part of successful leadership comes from an internal quality of heart that is communicated from God to man, and from man to man. Putting our trust in Christ to obey His word develops this heart quality.

In other words, if Christ is the melody, then we are challenged to *play* in harmony to God's word.

Take a minute or two and really think about this. Have you ever seen anyone run up to a violinist's bow and say, "Oh Mr. Bow, I am so impressed with how well you glide over the strings. You sound so beautiful"? Sounds a bit silly, doesn't it? But don't laugh; consider the implications of what I'm saying and ask yourself, have I been seeing myself as the violinist or the violin and bow?

I challenge you to examine yourself—honestly. If you are clear on the reality that you are simply an instrument, may God continue to bless you with his wisdom and empower you with his love and grace.

If you are not clear, I want to encourage you, while at the same time helping you to embrace the difficult concept of being a servant. In our minds we often think we've accepted that we are servants of Christ. Yet, in order to be effective in the work he has called us to, we must seek to follow his example. In John 10:27, he tells us that we will recognize his voice and follow him.

Sometimes in our humanness we forget that we are just instruments that he has chosen to use. What we want and what we think are foremost in our minds. As those who have been given authority over others, we find ourselves desiring control, power, and the accolades of humans. At times, we even use the influence we have to our own benefit, without once considering the needs of those he has called us to serve. We cannot always blame Satan.

As you read this chapter, you may experience moments when you are ashamed as you realize that often it has been your own pride and selfish ambition that has sought to draw you, and those you lead, away from God. Yet the Holy Spirit within us has created a yearning to be in harmony. There is a stirring deep in our souls to be consistently obedient to the tasks the Lord has assigned to us.

As you examine your own motives, the reality that you have been at the center of your life may become more apparent. If—or should I say, when—that happens, seek his forgiveness. Let Jesus Christ cleanse you from your lust for power and attention. Let the Holy Spirit develop his fruit in your heart (Galatians 5:22) so that you will be able to abandon the corrupt thought life that places your desires at the center of the life he has given you. There is no question that our self-centeredness is at war against God's way of doing things (Romans 8:6–8).

As you humble yourself under God's mighty hand and trust his wisdom and sovereignty, you will place yourself in a position to receive the grace needed to honor him in all you do.

The Holy Spirit really can be trusted to help us understand and accept God's will for our lives. And we need to *truly* place his agenda and his desires at the center of our lives.

Christina Dixon

For leaders who are reading this and are already bearing the fruit of the Spirit in your life, don't begin to feel smug. If there is any fruit in your life, it is because he has allowed you to bear it. Also remember that those who are fruitful he desires to prune so that they will bear more fruit.

Let's begin to consider various aspects of our lives that we must *harmonize* with Christ. This will require a willingness to allow the Holy Spirit to reveal whatever he chooses. The Scripture speaks clearly in Proverbs 23:7 about the importance of guarding our hearts because as a man *thinks* in his heart, so is he. No lasting change can begin outside of us. So, let's look at us.

BALANCE IN LEADING OURSELVES

In our attempts to live a balanced life, we often focus on some area of our life where going in and out is easy. Wouldn't it be simpler if we only had one or two things to juggle?

Marion Pledger (1996) in a workshop spoke to the tendencies leaders have to feel overwhelmed by the needs they see. She challenged attendees to remember that Christ, at a time when thousands were following him, did not say, "Go get 'em, boys!" Matthew 9:36–38 says that he instructed his disciples to pray that the Lord of the harvest would send forth laborers. Doesn't it seem strange that Jesus, who had the power to literally meet every single need before him, did not?

That bewilders us. Christ chose to leave us with an example that sets a precedent for all leaders to follow. In other words, don't try to do it all yourself, even when you can. Many of us fantasize about the awesome accomplishments we would have if we only had a small portion of Christ's power. Yet, we have access to Christ's power by faith, and we still fail to see the value the Lord placed on connecting with, developing, and learning to trust others.

When sending the disciples forth to minister, He didn't send them out alone. He sent them two and two (see Mark 6:7, Luke 10:1). Even Paul took at least one other person with him on missionary journeys. For many in leadership, the sin of self-sufficiency beckons us to do it all. In doing so, we isolate ourselves to the point of rejecting those God would send to come along side to help. In our minds we aren't rejecting them. To us they just aren't "ready" yet. They are too green, too zealous, or too ignorant. Maybe they are too much like we were when we started out. It's sad to say that many leaders don't have the inclination to patiently walk with others.

Too often leaders fail to see that by allowing others to walk *with* them; those under them can learn better how much we must depend on God to fulfill his will in our lives. Could it be that this is a lesson many of us have yet to learn, and so we are unable to replicate it? What better way for others to learn it than for them to see us do it, or maybe learn how together? But that would require patience, wouldn't it?

It would also require a tendency toward kindness, a good-natured and meek attitude that has the control over self that is needed when those under our leadership make mistakes. And that's not all! It also requires us to possess a sense of peace that exudes faith in God's ability to empower us with the longsuffering grace needed to love others when they are at their most mistake making, careless, insensitive, and unlovable selves.

Unfortunately, for many of us, we would rather just do things ourselves. Fewer headaches? Yes. Less trouble? Yes. Less worry? Certainly. Less godly? Absolutely!

Thanks be to God that he doesn't take that attitude with us. In spite of all his infinite ability and resources, even he has chosen to do the work he could do alone, with our help. It is wrong for us to think that we should do things alone. The first ones leaders must lead to God's way of doing things are themselves. We must recognize that his concept of leadership requires us to follow his lead, by emulating his actions.

I can hear someone in the imagination of their mind saying, "You know God punished some folk when they didn't do what he said. God doesn't coddle folk!" While it is true that he takes punitive action against his people for their disobedience, one has to completely overlook the actions that preceded punishment in order to maintain that attitude. There were warnings and calls to repentance while he was blessing them. In most cases, it was the consistent failure to obey over a period of years that caused him to bring judgment upon his people and even then he did not utterly destroy them. Let's not forget that our God is "plenteous in mercy."

Ask yourself: How patient have you been with those under your leadership? How patient and merciful are you when others under your leadership fail to "obey?" How many years have you been blessing them while they mess up? If God were to treat you the way you treat those under you, what would it look like?

I said all that, to say that if we are going to lead others in a godly way, we have to first be honest. If you are leading because you answered God's call to lead, I pray that God will give you an increase in the fruit of his Spirit, especially temperance. Truly, the fruit of the Spirit is required to consistently love as we lead—no matter what those following us are doing.

For some of us we will have to confess and repent that we don't really want to lead people because we were called by God to do so. What we really want is control and servants to do our bidding.

For others of us we will need to confess and repent about our need for attention. We didn't really want to lead anyone; we just wanted to be out front.

The sinful motivations that sometimes drive people to lead are a list much longer than the pages of this book can hold. If I haven't mentioned yours, may the Holy Spirit now reveal it to you.

Take heart! Once you come out with the truth, God is willing to provide the mercy so that your iniquity can be purged (Proverbs 16:6). Lead yourself to the throne room of grace. If there is harmony and balance with God, surely we must begin there. We can begin with a prayer.

Father, as I speak the truth to you, I repent of all the sins the Holy Spirit uncovers. Help me not to recant, if I see a season of brokenness or death on the horizon. Remind me that you, Lord, are the Healer and the Resurrection. If need be, you can heal that which is broken or speak life to the dead things in my life. Your word says that when I know the truth, it will make me free. I want to experience the liberty of heart and mind as I receive cleansing from you, Father. Deep in my heart, though my feelings may say differently, I believe that all will be well. I no longer want to walk in prideful self-sufficiency. I realize that I desperately need you. I also remember that you resist the proud, but give grace to the humble. Help me to become familiar with the humility of mind this process takes, for it is the vehicle of Your grace. Truly, I need your mercy—and your grace. I thank you now for them both. In Jesus's Name. Amen.

BALANCE IN MARRIAGE FOR LEADERS

Balance in marriage, in my view, can be summed up in one or two sentences. *First, we should assure our mates that there is no other human being we'd rather spend time with* (see 1 Corinthians 7:33–34). If this isn't true, then you may want to examine why it is that you've made a vow to God to be with someone with whom you don't want to spend time.

Now, hear me well. I'm not saying that as leaders we have to measure the amount of time we spend with our mates. What I am saying is that if we are married and we want our marriages to reflect balance, we must give ourselves to our mates with a sense of passion that affirms and reassures them of our love.

We are challenged to consistently display a tenderness of heart, kindness, and love toward our mates that exceed that which we show to any other human being.

Second, we should value our mate's opinion and recognize, that we don't have the entire picture, and that we have the capacity to deceive ourselves (see Ecclesiastes 4:9–10; Jeremiah 17:9).

Several years ago, my husband and I were on the verge of an argument. We each felt that the perspectives we had were divinely inspired. Frustrated to no end, my husband asked, "How is it that God can be telling me one thing and you something entirely different and be talking to both of us?"

Wanting to know the answer myself, I literally looked up and said, "How about that, Lord? How can that be?" The answer has since saved us from many arguments and has enhanced our ability to embrace each other's point of view. In fact, it has made a major impact on my ability to hear many other points of view, especially when all involved parties believe they are hearing from God.

Immediately following my question to the Lord, this is what I heard in my spirit. "Cover your right eye. Now look around. What can you see?" I looked around (without turning my body, only using my left eye), and to the left, I could see everything on my left and behind me just over my left shoulder. When I looked toward my right, I could only see as far right as my nose. Once again, in my spirit, I heard, "Now cover your left eye and do the same thing." After I did that I realized that the Lord indeed was speaking to both of us. We could both see the situation's outward appearance. Yet, my husband was shown an area I could not see, and I was shown an area he could not see. When we put both views together, we had a full panoramic view of the circumstances. Trust me, sisters and brothers, the wisdom of that illustration is way beyond me.

The reality is that a pair of eyes has a range of vision. At the same time, each one has a range of vision the other cannot see. This truth has the potential to begin the healing process in relationships.

For instance, does the left eye argue with the right eye about the data it sends to the brain, or vice versa? No, it doesn't. In fact, it is not either eye's responsibility to make the other eye agree with what it sees. Both are parts of the body that send their information to the brain, where the data they take in is processed.

Now, before you carry this illustration too far, I know some folks have vision that is like mine. In my case, one eye actually sees better than the other one. That's why I need glasses. But let's stay focused on the topic. Your mate is able to see things you are not just as you are able to see things your mate cannot. Therefore, all opinions should be valued.

Letting them know that you'd rather spend time with them than with any other human beings, creates the kind of security in your love that gives them the liberty to release you to lead others without fear. Valuing your mate's opinion undergirds that security and provides you as a leader with insight you might not otherwise obtain.

At a marriage workshop we facilitated, my heart warmed as my husband, Elder Michael Dixon, spoke of how a difficult truth came to him. He had sought to love me with the best of his love. He bought me gifts, took me to restaurants, all the things he thought would make me happy and make him a good husband. He spoke of how he faced the hard cold reality that his love wasn't enough to keep our marriage from trouble.

My husband went on in passionate transparency to explain that no matter how much he could have or would have tried, his best just wasn't good enough. I have even heard of spouses who unwisely spoke the words, "Your best just isn't good enough," with venomous malice that left their mates crushed to the core. When you've given all you've got and the one you love most says it's not enough, it's devastating.

I know this may be hard to accept, but the truth is, as a Christian leader, your best isn't good enough either. The prophet Isaiah (64:6) inspired by the Holy Spirit said that our righteousness is as filthy rags. Only when we admit that we can't get the job done on our own, can we willingly receive God's way of doing things. And why not do it his way? God wrote the original book on marriage. I'm a living witness that his word is true, and his ways are good and acceptable.

Talk about harmonizing with the Lord, you can't get any closer than a marriage that exemplifies his relationship with the church. What a team! Him loving us, us loving him and us together reaching out in a way that causes others to love him too! Can you hear the harmony of godliness?

Christina Dixon

BALANCE IN PARENTING FOR LEADERS

Sometimes the fact that we lack balance will show up in our relationships with our children. One of the times I realized that I lacked balance came many years ago, as I faced the reality that my relationship with my children was deteriorating. I so enjoyed ministering to those who were seeking God to find a way out of the sludge of unhealthy, sin-filled lifestyles. After all, I had been there. I knew their pain. When I cried out to God, he rescued me. I was filled with such overwhelming gratitude that I was driven to let others who were still trapped know, "There is hope! Don't give up! God really does love you!" O how I relished the affirmation that came from being instrumental in the pivotal moments of other's lives. That is why I was so devastated when the truth of how out of balance my life was came to me.

One day my youngest twin daughter, Alicea, began to take her turn in the household chore of mopping the kitchen floor. One of her siblings, who had the chore the week before her, failed to clean the mop. Not only did Alicea not clean the mop first; she proceeded to sling dirty soapy water everywhere.

Thoroughly disgusted, I began my rant about what a horrible job she was doing.

In the midst of my ranting, a voice spoke in my soul that stopped me dead in my tracks. "When did you ever take the time to teach her how to mop?"

Suddenly my mind was filled with the painful awareness that I had not been fulfilling *my* responsibility to prepare my children for life on their own. Here I had been traveling the Midwest, trying to "make a difference" in people's lives, and the lives upon which I had the most potential influence were being left untaught.

In the following days and weeks, I humbly explained my plight to my children and asked their forgiveness. My opportunities to minister, outside my home, came to what felt like a screeching halt. My role as a leader before my children had been grossly neglected. The truth is, my life became more balanced when I accepted the season of life I was in. I was a parent who had young children. As such, I needed to make time to raise my children.

Sometimes, in our pursuit to do God's work, we leave our families unattended. Oh sure, we fuss when they do things wrong. We make sure they go to church. But many of us don't give ourselves to our families like we should. If we obey the word of God and raise our children in the way they should go, we will need to spend time getting to know who they are. Our children are more than our babies. They are God's creation. He has a purpose and plan for them, just as he has one for us. We must help them to understand not only who God is, but also the call on their lives.

I can't end this segment without mentioning the need to keep concern for our reputation as leaders in its proper perspective. At times, leaders are very protective of their position and reputation. Sometimes so much so that we find we are more worried about ourselves and what others think than our priority to our children.

How many times have you heard about a child on drugs, or a teen pregnancy, and all the parent could say was, "Why did you do this to me! What will the neighbors, church members, my colleagues think?" How sad. An opportunity to show the love, mercy, and grace of the Lord to one closest to us is marred by self-centered thinking.

In times of crisis when our children make mistakes, they need to know that they are important to us. Important enough in fact for us to be more concerned about them, than our own reputations.

I remember a moment some time ago when I read the answer the late Mother Teresa of Calcutta (2011) gave when asked how world leaders could bring about world peace. She replied, "Go home and love your children." On another occasion she said, "It is easy to love the people far away. It is not always easy to love those close to us. It is easier to give a cup of rice to relieve hunger than to relieve the loneliness and pain of someone unloved in our own home. Bring love into your home for this is where our love for each other must start."

If you have already fallen short in this area, I challenge you to talk with the Lord first, and then go and talk with your children. In as much sincerity of heart as you can muster, ask their forgiveness. Give them the liberty to tell you how they really feel. You know, like God does for you. Don't make excuses. Truly listen. Learn. Then turn the results over to God as the Holy Spirit leads you how to respond, one day at a time.

BALANCE IN LEADING OTHERS

I recall attending a church where the majority of those in leadership were "thirty-something" parents with children under the age of twelve. I have lived through the havoc that excessive church activities can impose upon family life. Consequently, I was torn between rejoicing in the beauty of warmth and fellowship that I experienced there and sorrow over what I believe was too much time at church and too little time at home rearing their children.

As leaders in the church, we have a responsibility to care for the flock, which includes our own families. Humor me as I ask you to consider the following scenario:

Go to work from 9:00 a.m. to 5:00 p.m. Get home through rush hour traffic as quickly as possible. Rush to prepare something to eat (or grab fast food). Hurry through dinner to be at church on time at seven o'clock in the evening. Stay until 8:30 or 9:00. Get home around 9:30.

Now multiply these actions by Sunday morning and evening services, prayer meeting, Bible study, ministers'-training class, choir rehearsal, evangelistic outreach, food pantry, and shut-in visitation.

Now add to this the Scriptural admonition to bring up a child in the way he (she) should go. Don't forget to multiply this by the number of children in the household.

Now add to this equation frequent admonition that *everyone* participate in every event.

Now multiply that by the desire of God's people to please him. Can you hear the *dis*harmony? Too many activities equate to too much *playing* in the wrong key—loudly.

While many may disagree, I challenge you to evaluate. Do you, or those in leadership at the church you attend, have families with children still at home? If so, how often are the leaders and members required to participate in church activities? Does their participation cause the aforementioned scenario to take place in their homes more than two or three times per week? If so, you may need to truly consider the fruit of these actions. Parents have been given the God ordained responsibility to train their children. Doing this requires time.

Many of the ills of our society can be traced back to homes where parents were too busy to *be* parents. Obsessed with achievement, many in American society override the concept of simply *being*.

Too many in church leadership have sought to build great buildings for God. They long to be revered as successful. Consequently, many lose sight of what true success in the kingdom of God really is.

Sure, I believe that there are those whom God has directed to build large buildings in order to facilitate the ministry he has called them and those they lead to do this. But, I also believe that there are those in church leadership who need to evaluate their thinking in this area.

Too often there is an absence of balanced harmony in leadership due to a desire to obtain accolades from men. They want to be able to talk about how many folk joined "their" churches. They want to be like someone else that God has permitted to have megachurches. They have great visions they long to accomplish. Christ is not the melody in their plans; their desire for fame is. And so, those under their leadership end up pursuing "the vision" and not Christ. No wonder we see so many children raised in homes led by Christian leaders that don't find the Christian life appealing.

Sadly, some have not recognized that the selfish ambition and vainglory that the Scripture admonishes us against have motivated them. As Christians, we are instructed to not only look out for our own interests, but for the interest of others as well (Philippians 2:3–4).

Consider these words spoken by my husband, Elder Michael Dixon (2002):

> Religious traditions have taught us to sit and be still much in the same way our parents taught us to "sit and be still." It has taught us how to dress up or dress down but worst of all, it taught us how to "act." But, the word of God shows us and the Spirit of the Lord empowers us to be. BE of good cheer. BE not afraid. BE strong and very courageous. BE not deceived. BE faithful. BE obedient. BE lovers of God. BE trees of righteousness, the planting of the Lord. Acting deceives our hearts, hiding in shadows. But being extends from His love within....

Despite admonitions to *be* many leaders often insist on *becoming*. Sure, we should definitely *be becoming* more like Christ daily. Definitely, some of us are becoming more mature in our walk with the Lord. But balance is lacking many times when our core values are skewed. We focus on building church buildings for God instead of building up the true temples of God, mankind.

Maybe the leadership role you have isn't in church. Maybe you have a position of leadership at your job. Don't focus on building corporate structure instead of building companies that truly serve the community. As Christians we are challenged to lead in a manner that does not cause those following us to sacrifice families for the sake of dollars.

The apostle Paul understood how the Lord intended for him to use his authority. It is clear that its main purpose was not for building edifices. He said on more than one occasion that God had given him his authority for the purpose of edifying *(building up)* the body of Christ (2 Corinthians 10:8, 13:10). We would do well to follow his lead in this matter.

The Scripture says God dwells within his people (I Corinthians 3:16–17). If he has blessed church members with families (*more temples to build*) it is incumbent upon them to make certain that they aren't causing conflict between their service *for* God in the church or on their job and their responsibility *to* God to raise their children.

When the Lord gives someone a vision, he is not anxious about getting it accomplished. He is not pressed for time, short of breath, or burning out. He is fully aware of all the responsibilities of everyone involved in bringing that vision to fruition.

Let those who follow experience the liberty of *being* in the season of life they are in. Encourage them to pursue their career goals, sure. But don't cause them to neglect their families in order to pursue the goals you've set. If the vision you have is ordained of God, fine. Just make sure your efforts to accomplish that vision are being done in his time.

It behooves us as leaders to remember that our lives, and the lives of those we lead, belongs to God. Not only is every life accountable to him, every *area of life* is also accountable to him (2 Corinthians 5:10).

By applying pressure to attend the meetings and meet quotas and deadlines to the exclusion of freedom to develop their *entire* lives, we imply that only the things *we* are doing are "for God." That is not only untrue. It is wrong. Dead wrong!

As you continue reading this book, during this time of revitalization, you will find that the Lord will give you guidelines that will bring harmony to your life. As your life becomes harmonious, it is inevitable that you will impact the lives of those you lead as you model balanced leadership to others.

PRAYER

Father, here I am again. I have need of your wisdom that I may lead your people wisely. I need so much.

As I read this book, may the sword of your word cut away those things in my life that would not bring you glory. I realize that you desire for me to bring forth fruit that brings glory to your name. As I heal from the wounds of being pruned, may I receive the comfort that comes from your Holy Spirit as he leads me into your will.

Christina Dixon

Help me to refuse to dishonor those who have placed confidence in me by lying to them about my vision. Help me to only place before them the purpose and vision that you have given me.

I realize that I need to consider the needs of those who will be performing delegated tasks. I have even failed to include them in the decision making process.

Father, give me the courage to admit when I foul up. I know I can't do it all, and yet I find myself trying. I am aware that I need the body of Christ, but I recognize that I don't know it on a level where I practice it. Help me!

Help me to make sure that risks I take don't include losing my family or my integrity unwisely. Help me not to give up on people when they make mistakes or disappoint me.

I also recognize, Lord, that you don't intend for the work that you've given me to end with me. Teach me how to groom and encourage a successor by transferring from a position of authority and power to one of wisdom and grace at the appointed time. Your word says that if I don't work with you I'm working against you.

Help me to remember to give you all the praise, and honor, for you will not share your glory with another. May I immerge from these pages healed, encouraged, and empowered to lead others by your loving perspective. These things I ask of you with a heart filled with thanksgiving.

Help me not to be complacent about any of these things. As I continue to *receive help* during this overwhelming time, I rejoice that you are with me. In Jesus's name. Amen.

REFERENCES

Dixon, Michael. 2002. "The Blessor is in the House." New Hope Progressive Church, Detroit.

Johnson, Bishop Anthony. 2000. "Principles of Leadership, Lesson 1." Praise Temple Church of God Leadership Class, Detroit.

Pledger, Marion. 1996. "Pressed Out of Measure: Into the Mold of Jesus Christ." United Conference for Women, Cincinnati.

Merriam-Webster's Collegiate Dictionary, 11th Edition. 2009. Springfield, MA: Merriam-Webster.

Mother Teresa. 2011. "In Her Own Words." Mission Audio

Smith, Raymond Jr. 2003. *Balancing Act: A Guide to Developing Spiritual Discernment.*

Christina Dixon

PRACTICAL STRESS MANAGEMENT FOR LEADERS[1]

Sabrina D. Black

The words, "Too blessed, to be stressed or depressed" can be found printed on almost everything from t-shirts and bumper stickers to coffee mugs and buttons. I'm sure you have heard it said by someone or maybe even said it yourself.

Yes, we are blessed, but we don't often tell when we are stressed and depressed. Yet the reality of life for most Christians are breathless lives, lived in the margins. We overload ourselves. We are indeed "*too.*"

We are a society driven by extremes, pushing ourselves beyond the limits, constantly doing more and more.

As a ministry leader, I know that I have been guilty (whether it is because of my intense desire to make a difference in the lives of others or because I am just a type-A personality—driven, overachieving in everything).

The overloaded lifestyles we live are detrimental to our physical, emotional, spiritual, and relational well being.

Stress tends to be more pervasive, persistent, and insidious because it stems primarily from psychological rather than physical threats. Not only

---

1. This chapter was previously published in the book *HELP! for Your Leadership* (Detroit: PriorityOne Publications, 2003). Used by permission. Some editorial changes have been made.

do we deal with external and physical stresses but internal as well. The way we think about the various circumstances and situations in our life may add to our stress. The way our body responds in fight-or-flight mode is associated with ingrained and immediate reactions over which we have little or no control.

The fight-or-flight response in humans is designed to be beneficial. When our ancestors were in danger, the adrenaline flow, which produces stress, was used to fight off the aggressor or run, thus releasing the stress. It caused them to be alert and charged up. They did what they had to do. The knowledge of what to do and how to do it was instinctual.

As Christian leaders, we have a third option in addition to our natural responses in stressful situations: We can flow in the Spirit. When we recognize and flow in the sovereignty of God, realizing that he is in control of all things, we don't stress out when faced with stressful situations.

Stress, burnout, and compassion fatigue are occupational hazards that most pastors, leaders, and professional helpers encounter. Ministering to others is very rewarding; yet it can also be draining unless we follow the ministry example of Jesus. The Lord extends this invitation in Matthew 11:28 (KJV), to all those who are too blessed to be stressed or depressed, "Come unto me, all ye that labour and are heavy laden, and I will give you rest."

I urge you to be equipped, empowered, and encouraged to fulfill your calling. Providing hope, help, and healing to God's people require leaders who have mastered the art of stress management. God wants leaders who know how to prevent stress and who know that there are provisions for us in the Bible when we are stressed.

This chapter will identify and present some alternative ways of dealing with the stresses that accompany leadership. There is good news. We can lead a more stress-free life if we follow a few practical steps. These alternatives are based on biblical principles. We will explore the physical, emotional, and spiritual effects of stress; learn how to identify various stress factors that lead to being overwhelmed, overworked, and overburdened; look at Jesus's example of self-care in the midst of ministry; and learn practical techniques for rest, relaxation, and spiritual renewal.

TOO BLESSED

Oh, the joy of being in ministry, advancing the kingdom, making an impact in the earth locally and globally.

Leadership is not something that we often choose, but we are chosen. We are the elect, the ones called of God to lead his people in this generation. We are those whom the Lord has empowered and equipped to carry forth his mission by setting a vision before the people and establishing goals for carrying out the work. We are indeed blessed. We know that promotion does not come from the east or the west but that promotion comes from God (Psalms 75:6–7). We are honored to be used by him and realize that it is an honor to serve.

God opens the windows of heaven and opportunities abound. There is so much to do and seemingly so little time. The work is plentiful and the faithful laborers (who are dedicated like us) are few; so we must be about our Father's business, praying that he will raise up more faithful laborers for the harvest (Matthew 9:37–38).

TO BE STRESSED OR DEPRESSED

What is stress? Stress can be defined as a number of normal reactions in the body (physical, emotional, mental, and spiritual) designed for self-preservation. Stress is awareness that harmony and balance are being disrupted. Stress lets us know that something is out of sync. It is an indication that something needs to change (usually our attitude, approach or agenda) in order to maintain our equilibrium and a homeostatic state.

Stress is a natural part of life—and in many ways, a helpful and even pleasant part of life. Serving in the ministry, leading other people, and making life choices can produce stress, but it is very rewarding to be used by God. We consider ourselves blessed. Planning a wedding produces stress; riding a roller coaster, doing exercises, and even getting a job promotion can cause stress.

What makes stress unpleasant and harmful is the feeling that we cannot escape it or that we are in bondage to our mindset. Many of us need to change our mindset; we need to adjust our attitudes. The daily renewing of the mind, having the mind of Christ and knowing the heart of God, can reduce stress. We are not in bondage; we always have choices.

Most of the time leaders use stress to their advantage. For example, when they are faced with deadlines they become very focused, creative, and energized. This stress is referred to as *eustress*; it is positive and constructive.

Stress, in the sense of an applied pressure, is not always detrimental. Stress can motivate a leader to begin and or complete tasks. Even though this type of stress can be productive and good, we know that "too much of a good thing is not good for you." Our bodies are not designed to sustain an extreme, continually high-energy, fast-paced lifestyle.

This extreme is what most people mean by "stress." It is a sense of being "too," overwhelmed and overloaded. They feel as if their internal resistance is at a breaking point. When leaders are at a breaking point, it is due to distress, the negative destructive properties of stress. Even reading this chapter or book can be stressful if you are hurrying through it as another "to do" on your list. Let's pause.

Take a few minutes to relax and meditate on the Word of God. The King James Version of the Bible refers to distress more than thirty times. It also uses other terms such as distraught, troubled, or vexed to describe the feeling of being overwhelmed, overworked, and overloaded, which leads to stress. Let's take a look at a few of these verses. Read each verse and then pray as you consider the stresses in your life. Don't study right now, just drink deeply of the assurance from these verses. Be refreshed as you take time to savor the Scriptures below; they will encourage you as you seek to find balance in your leadership.

> We are troubled on every side, yet not distressed; we are perplexed, but not in despair; persecuted, but not forsaken; cast down but not destroyed (2 Corinthians 4:8–9 KJV).

> So for the sake of Christ, I am well pleased and take pleasure in infirmities, insults, hardships, persecutions, perplexities and distresses; for when I am weak [in human strength], then am I [truly] strong (able, powerful in divine strength) (2 Corinthians 12:10 AMP).

> Then they cried out to the Lord in their trouble, and He saved them out of their distresses. He brought them out of darkness and the shadow of death and broke apart the bonds that held them. Oh, that men would praise [and confess to] the Lord for His goodness and loving-kindness and His wonderful works to the children of men (Psalm 107:13–15 AMP).

> In my distress I called to the LORD I cried to my God for help. From his temple he heard my voice; my cry came before him, into his ears (Psalm 18:6 NIV).

Sabrina D. Black

Answer me when I call, O God of my righteousness (uprightness, justice, and right standing with You)! You have freed me when I was hemmed in and enlarged me when I was in distress; have mercy upon me and hear my prayer (Psalm 4:1 AMP).

Who shall separate us from the love of Christ? Shall trouble or hardship or persecution or famine or nakedness or danger or sword? As it is written: "For your sake we face death all day long; we are considered as sheep to be slaughtered." No, in all these things we are more than conquerors through him who loved us (Romans 8:35–37 NIV).

Leaders encounter problems when there are too many stress producers in their lives and little or no time to relax. This is known as hyperstress. When thinking of stress many often refer to the proverbial "straw that broke the camel's back." We know that it wasn't the straw; it was all the other things that he had carried and the straw was just one more thing that the camel couldn't bear. This is similar to stress in ministry. Leaders are usually stressed to the limit yet we add more. It's not that someone asks you to make another phone call that stresses you out; it's that you have been making phone calls, coordinating meetings, preparing for messages, handling problems and there is just not room for anything else.

When conducting workshops on stress management, there is an object lesson that I like to use that you can participate in even now: Pick up a rubber band and stretch it as far as you can. Now, stretch the rubber band again and again each time you think of all the many roles and responsibilities you have.

At some point people will begin to frown and make faces while stretching the rubber band, but I encourage them to keep stretching. Many will respond "but it will break"; "I don't want it to pop"; "It might hurt me or someone else if it snaps." And they are absolutely right. Yet we rarely consider that we are stretching ourselves far beyond our capacity to function at optimal levels. And we may soon reach our breaking point, snap, and hurt someone.

You may really need a break (stress relief) before you have a breakdown.

Many Christians have found themselves at the breaking point at some time in their ministry. This need for stress relief often becomes the justification for choices that are made in an altered state of mind.

Sabrina D. Black   139

When we are stressed, we function on self-preservation. We operate in survival mode: How will I ever get all of this done? Why do I have to do everything? How can I make it through this? When we are stressed we stop looking up at God, or out to others, but look primarily at ourselves.

Stress is *extra* pressure or strain beyond the daily routine. Each individual has a capacity for stress, but the key word here is *extra*, which can be defined as "additional, more, excess, over."

Take for example a mother of five. She can handle cleaning house, changing diapers, children making noise as they play, cooking dinner, and many other tasks without much stress. This would be a normal day for her. But a single woman who is not used to handling this level of activity may be stressed by spending an afternoon in her environment. This same woman may be a corporate executive, supervising a staff of sixty, making million-dollar decisions, and be very capable and competent. Yet, when faced with something different or additional, she may become overwhelmed.

Each person is created uniquely, and people have different capacities. Everyone cannot handle the same amount of activity. Some people can manage five projects. Others can manage only one or two at a time. When we are handling more than we were designed to do, we become stressed.

We need to look at how God has formed and fashioned us and not compare ourselves to others. God made you very unique. He is a God of diversity. Why try to be like someone else? God already has an original; do you really want to be a copy? Leaders often cause stress for themselves when they make unfair comparisons with other ministries and corporations. The stress of comparisons often leads to jealousy, envy, and discouragement.

Stress is a *multifaceted* response that includes changes in perception, emotions, behavior, and physical functioning. When we are under stress for extended periods of time, it impacts our ability to think appropriately. We may take things out of context and find ourselves overly sensitive, misreading the actions and intentions of others. Our normal ability to process and make decisions is impacted by the work that needs to be done. Yes, I've also been guilty of this response as well.

I went through three administrators in a fourteen-month period before I realized that it was not them. It was me.

As a leader, I provided what many would consider ideal working conditions: a flexible schedule, great pay, opportunities for creativity and input, and other things that lead to job satisfaction.

What I didn't see was that the pressure of constant deadlines for my many ministry projects, my perfectionist tendency toward attention to detail, and unrealistic expectations for timeframes made the work environment very stressful.

As each administrator was replaced, I simply told myself that the others were not as dedicated as I was. So I perceived that they couldn't see the awesome things that God was doing. I did not see that I was so driven that I was driving them away. Busy people rarely slow down. They try to flurry everyone else along. Everything is not as urgent as we would like to believe. We drive ourselves and those around us to stress.

Stress may be a *warning sign* that we need to examine our *myths* and/or our *motives*.

When you begin to feel tense and overwhelmed, stop what you're doing and try to look at your situation from a fresh perspective. Ask yourself, "Why am I feeling this way? If this task doesn't get done, what's the worst thing that can happen? What is the absolute minimum that I need to do to complete this task?" Be realistic. Every assignment does not have to be perfect. If your assignment isn't perfect, is it really the end of the world? A year from now, will it be important? When we are striving for excellence, we are doing the best that we can do without stretching ourselves to the limit and popping like the rubber band.

Too often we get stressed over everyday inconsequential things. Try to look at the 'big picture." Who said you have to do this? Can it be delegated to someone else? Is your way the only way? What are you trying to prove? Who are you trying to prove it to? We have too many "lone rangers" in ministry trying to do things themselves. So many of our leaders wear an "S" on their chests. However it does not stand for "super"—it stands for "stretched" to the point of "stressed."

We will need to let go of the myths surrounding three areas—boundaries, perfectionism and "super syndrome"—that often entrap spiritual leaders. What has God called you to do? What is your purpose? What is your destiny? What is your charge to fulfill? Are you carrying out your responsibility and the responsibilities of others? You may have twenty great projects but they may not all be for you to do (even if you have an administrator).

We can avoid stress by serving in the areas where God has called us versus doing what everyone else wants us to do, or doing what is popular to be involved with at the time.

Sabrina D. Black

We can reduce stress by not comparing our ministry with that of other leaders. We can also reduce stress by not trying to keep up with where our friends and or colleagues are serving.

Stress will usually occur when we are caught up in ourselves. When we are focused on what we want to accomplish instead of what God wants to do in and through the ministry, it will cause stress.

The Word reminds us that we can be in perfect peace when our mind is stayed on the Lord (Isaiah 26:3). When we focus on doing things God's way in His timing, and acknowledging his sovereignty, we have more than enough time to do the things he has called us to do. He is the source and the resource. Put another way: He is the one that fills and refills. We need to call on God to revive us, renew us, and refresh us. If you are feeling stressed, you are usually at the end of me, my, and I. It's not about you. Don't wait until all of your resources have been depleted to cry out to God in prayer.

STRESS FACTORS

There are certain factors that determine the intensity of our level of stress: the environment, the magnitude of the event, personal aggravators, and personal fitness.

The environment is the space in which a person functions and carries out day-to-day activities. Close your eyes for a moment and picture the area in which you work. Is it cluttered or clear? Can you actually put your hands on the tools and resources you need to be productive? Is it a noisy or quiet place? What are the sounds that you hear? An effective way to reduce stress for some leaders is to modify or completely change their work environment. Dr. Jordan would often conduct business calls to his patients from the office he had at the hospital, as well as his library at home. Each location had a certain feel and provided a different mood. Minister McGhee found that trying to work at home in the den was not a good idea because it was his family space. Items were often used and moved by other family members, which would lead to additional frustration. What are the things that you can change in your environment?

The magnitude of an event can also cause stress. There is a major difference in stress when you are planning a women's tea versus a weekend women's retreat, a company picnic versus an executive board meeting. The more value, importance, or significance placed on an event, the more stressful it is likely to be. The more components, details, and nuances that are included, the more stressful the event. The magnitude refers to the size or vastness of the project.

For many leaders they create the magnitude. Let me explain.

There are many leaders like myself, who tend to make things grow. We are visionaries. God has gifted me with the ability to call forth greatness in others. I see the possibilities. God gives me vision to see beyond where we are to where we can be.

Whereas, this is very exciting and exhilarating, it can also be exhausting for the leader and those around them as simple projects get bigger and bigger. Thank God for his instructions in Habakkuk 2:2 to write the vision down so that a herald may run with it.

As leaders reduce stress, the many plans and activities need to be written down and realistically scheduled within the existing schedule. If the vision seems to linger or take longer than you anticipated, wait for it. Don't try to do everything now. It will certainly come to pass, if it is God's will.

Aggravators are the emotional, spiritual, and cognitive factors that make stressful events worse than they need to be. Some people are eternal optimists; they see the glass half full while others see it as half empty. How you see it has to do with your general disposition in life. Both people are right, but they function based on their perception. Those who see the glass as half full believe that whatever the project, they are almost there; they can see the end. Those who see it as half empty believe they are a long way from completion. When your glass is half full, you tend to have faith to do the impossible; when it is perceived as half empty, you tend to doubt whether change will occur.

Your level of fitness also impacts your perception, and your fitness influences your spiritual, behavioral, and emotional ability to deal with stressful circumstances. Total body fitness is crucial for effectively dealing with stressful situations. As you answer these few questions, you will be able to determine a few things about your level of fitness:

- How many hours of sleep do you get each night?
- Do you eat regular balanced meals each day?
- Do you have a regular exercise program?
- Do you spend time in quiet mediation?
- Do you make time to enjoy fun and fellowship?

I'm sure that it is no surprise that leaders need to get sleep, eat balanced meals, exercise, and experience the enjoyment of fellowship. You can't live stress-free long term on three or four hours of sleep, fast food, candy bars, potato chips, soda, and coffee. When our body is worn out, we are susceptible to disease. We are also lethargic, have memory lapses, are forgetful and have slow reaction time. Taking care of your body is important for preventing stress.

RECOGNIZING THE SIGNS AND EFFECTS OF STRESS

As a leader, you know when you're stressed, right? Sometimes we don't, although the signs may be clear to others around us. Just remember that the signs are more pervasive than you think!

Usually when we think of stress symptoms we think of high blood pressure, elevated heart rate, overeating, and sweating too much. Signs of stress also include irritability, insomnia, anxiety, headaches, indigestion, muscle tension, and much more.

Signs of stress fall into three categories: physical, emotional, and spiritual.

Review the items list in Table 8.1 and identify the ways in which stress may be affecting you and the leaders around you. Circle each of the responses that you have experienced in the past thirty days. You may wish to ask someone who works closely with you to also complete the assessment regarding what he or she has observed through his or her interaction with you.

TABLE 8.1. SIGNS OF STRESS

PHYSICAL	EMOTIONAL	SPIRITUAL
Fatigue	Depression	Compromise
Sleeping	Anger	Loss of faith
Edginess	Defensiveness	Joyless
Indigestion	Nervous	Guilt/condemnation
Grooming	Anxiety	Blame-shifting
Body pain	Cynicism/sarcasm	Hopelessness
Disease	Impatience	Loss of purpose

Too Overwhelmed

Dr. Stella Budrikis, in her article on "Christians and Stress" (2005), identified eight reasons that we as the people of God find ourselves pressed to the limit: busy-ness, technological speed, information overload, false expectations, social isolation, the burden of possession, the shrinking of time, and change. I've added some commentary to Dr. Budrikis's list to help you understand what she means by each of the eight reasons for stress that she identifies. As you read through this section, think about your own life and the lives of the people around you that impact you.

Busy-ness. Being busy has become a way of life. I have learned to keep things moving. And Christians are certainly not immune to busy-ness, as they try to fit church commitments, Bible study, and prayer into their already busy lives of work and family responsibilities.

Now, picture the life of the leader in all these activities. It's tiring just thinking about it. Most leaders realize that they are "too busy," but deciding what activity to cut back is not easy.

Several years ago I counseled with a pastor who was having a difficult time reducing his activities. His wife and children were feeling neglected and had become cynical about what he referred to as his "servant leadership." His family felt that his priorities were not balanced and that his "service in the ministry" was destroying him and his household. When I challenged him about his schedule and the need to seek balance, he insisted that it would be detrimental to try to change things and that his family would just have to understand God's call on his life. He was right about one thing. It was detrimental—he later suffered a heart attack.

Technological Speed. Modern conveniences have increased our sense of urgency. We want everything done right away. If our activities were limited to those we could carry out without technology, most of us would have much quieter lives. Telephones, fax machines, computers, and email add to the speed of life. Handwritten correspondence is passé, outdated. Trains, plane, and automobiles have also added to our stress levels. The anxiety of travel, dealing with traffic, and troubleshooting bad attitudes (of people who are required to wait) is enough to keep anyone stress out. The use of technology also limits our interaction with other human beings.

Information overload. Most people in the past relied on word of mouth for their information. Today we are bombarded with so much information that sometimes it is difficult to sort out relevant and helpful information. The effective leader's goal is to remove nonessential information so that he or she may improve the flow and efficacy of ministry. There is so much to remember and recall that there doesn't seem to be room for mediation on the Word of God. We have so much information but very little inspiration or revelation.

False expectations. Setting goals goes with effective leadership, but you must be realistic in your expectation of yourself and others. You must also be realistic about your expectations of the clock-plan ahead, but be flexible. False expectations of people or time can only add to your stress level. Effective project planning includes documentation on who will do what by when. The plan is reviewed by the parties involved and modified as needed. When expectations are not met, both parties are usually disappointed and may respond in a negative way.

Social isolation. We may be able to communicate instantly with almost anyone in the world, but we often have little time to spend with people with whom we minister. Many of our interactions, even with those closest to us, are superficial. "How are you?" "Oh, I'm blessed. Pray for me," become sounding brass. Then when we're feeling stressed, we have few people to support us, and those who do often feel overloaded themselves. Many leaders seek counsel because they are not in relationships where they feel close enough to be real about the issues in their life. They have created a public image that does not accommodate the reality of stress.

The burden of possessions. When we have learned to therewith be content (Philippians 4:11), we avoid the constant pursuit of more and more. The acquisition of goods, materials, and resources can be burdensome when we just collect and don't distribute to those in need. Every purchase we make adds an extra demand on our time to maintain it. And the more expensive the item, the more likely we are to be anxious about it being stolen or broken, thus our purchases bring stress instead of enjoyment and relaxation to our lives.

The shrinking of time. We see time as something with a reality of its own—already subdivided into milliseconds and waiting for us to fill it. This puts us under constant pressure to keep up with the clock. The quest for increased productivity has added to this pressure. We are always trying to add one more thing in the margin. Be realistic about what you can do in an hour, as well as what you expect others to be able to accomplish.

Change. Constant change has been a key feature of the twenty-first century. Some changes are superficial and others are more profound. For many, the lack of certainty created by change is stressful. That's interesting, considering that changes are one of few things that are certain. Before we become accustomed to something, it changes. There is always something new to learn and implement. People often talk about getting back to basics, the way things used to be. Even that will require change. In this instance, however, it is change that we need to embrace.

Too Overloaded

Dr. Burdrikus's list is similar to the list provided by Richard A. Swenson, a medical doctor and the author of several books, including *Margin* (2004). He believes that we are stressed because we are overloaded and live lives without margins. A margin is the space that exists between who we are and what we are capable of doing or our limits. Because we so often stretch ourselves, many leaders are not aware of their natural limit. Overload has become their way of life.

In his book, Dr. Swenson focuses on overload and the need to create balance in our lives. He identifies at least twenty-three areas where we may be overloaded. I've taken the liberty to convert these areas into a table that you can use to identify some of the stresses in your life. As you read them, check off the ones that apply to you. You may even wish to list specific items in each area on the line provided. This may take some time to do. Don't stress. Give careful consideration to each area so that you can make the necessary changes to alleviate some of the stress in your life.

TABLE 8.2. OVERLOADED	
Are You Overloaded?	
Activity Overload	Media Overload
Change Overload	Ministry Overload
Choice Overload	Noise Overload
Commitment Overload	People Overload
Competition Overload	Pollution Overload
Debt Overload	Possession Overload
Decision Overload	Problem Overload
Education Overload	Technology Overload
Expectation Overload	Traffic Overload
Fatigue Overload	Waste Overload
Hurry Overload	Work Overload
Information Overload	

Even when we are overloaded, overwhelmed, and feeling stressed, there is hope. When leaders have functioned under stress for extended periods of time, the desire for escape is greater than you can imagine. Maybe you know how close to the edge a person can come when they have lost their sense of balance and are making decisions in an altered state of mind. I have encountered numerous leaders who now regret the choices they made under stress. If you are an overloaded leader, pause, and thank God for the relief that he provides. Praise God for this book, for the upcoming conferences and the authors who are available to minister to you at your point of need. Be encouraged by the word in 1 Corinthians 10:13 (NIV):

> No temptation has overtaken you except what is common to mankind. And God is faithful; he will not let you be tempted beyond what you can bear. But when you are tempted, he will also provide a way out so that you can endure it.

Leaders who are overloaded need to establish appropriate boundaries, set loving limits, learn to say *no* (even to other leaders), and be realistic about what they are able to accomplish. This can be challenging, but remember we can't do everything, and God only expects us to do those things he has called us to do. Leaders must learn to discern the voice of God. Has he really called you to be involved in every project that is on your agenda? When you take on a new project, you may need to let two to three other things go. Leaders must discern between better and best.

Even as I worked on this book project, I had to adjust my life to accommodate for time needed to spend with God about what he would have me to say to his overloaded leaders. Then I needed time in my schedule to write.

As the deadline approached for completing this chapter, there was still too much to do in too little time. There were also other great offers to work on various books. I wanted to participate, but there was no room on my agenda. I could feel myself becoming overwhelmed. I thought, "Wait a minute, there is something wrong with this picture." I realized that I couldn't be and I would not be stressed out as I wrote about stress. So I requested an extension. Okay, I asked for two extensions. I did what any effective leader would do to avoid stress: I acknowledged my limitations, asked for help, and got the job done.

EQUIPPED, EMPOWERED, AND ENCOURAGED

"Whew! I didn't realize how exhausted I was until I stopped moving. And when I stopped, the world seemed to be spinning around me. Everything seemed like too much. I couldn't imagine how I even kept the pace at which I was moving."

These words are often the testimony of many leaders whom I counsel regarding stress. It was also my story several years ago. Granted, God's grace was sufficient for me in that season of life. But that season had passed and now God was doing a new thing. The Word tells us in Psalm 23:2–3 (KJV) that "He maketh me to lie down in green pastures: he leadeth me besides the still waters. He restoreth my soul." Praise God for times of refreshing. There is no stress by the still waters as he restores me.

When God calls you to leadership, he does indeed equip you for the work of the ministry. He also raises up others around you to help bear the burden of leading the people. Read the story of Moses in Exodus 18. There are probably many gifted and capable men and women around you. If they are given an opportunity to serve and utilize their gifts for the work of the ministry, it can help to reduce the stress on you as the leader.

God also empowers you with wisdom, knowledge, grace, and balance. God encourages you and sends those with the gift of encouragement to help edify you and build you up. When we find ourselves stressed, it is an indication that we need to reexamine our focus, our purpose, and our destiny.

Now that I have stopped moving so fast I am able to enjoy in the moment what God is doing in me and through me for the building of his kingdom. Here are some simple things you can do *today* to control, reduce or prevent stress.

This list of stress reducers is compiled from interviews with leaders and followers. Many of the ideas were repeated. As you read through the items listed in Table 8.3, circle five to seven items that you can implement today that will help you reduce your stress.

TABLE 8.3. STRESS REDUCTION SIMPLE THINGS YOU CAN DO TODAY

Simplify and unclutter your life.	Spend time in prayer and mediation.
Pamper yourself (rest, body massage, facial, manicure, make-over, etc.).	Get away from your daily stresses with group sports, social events, and hobbies.
Obey God.	Pray continually.
Practice the presence of God.	Listen to soft, soothing music.
Exercise (run, walk, bike, swim, tennis, golf, garden, etc.).	Just say no to projects that won't fit into your schedule.
Fellowship with the body of Christ.	Memorize and meditate on Scripture.

TABLE 8.3. STRESS REDUCTION
SIMPLE THINGS YOU CAN DO TODAY

Get organized so everything has its place.	Keep a folder of favorite Scriptures on hand.
Maintain accountability.	Praise and worship.
Have backups—an extra car key in your wallet, an extra house key buried in the garden, extra stamps, etc.	When you are not able to K.I.S.S. (Keep It Sweet and Simple), then K.M.S. (Keep Mouth Shut).
Sit on your ego. It's about you, but it's not about you.	Do something for the kid in you everyday.
Go to bed on time.	Get enough exercise.
Get up on time so you can start the day.	Carry a Bible with you to read while waiting in line.
Encourage yourself with spiritual readings.	Be kind to unkind people (they probably need it the most).
Listen to songs of praise and worship.	Give, share, or help someone else.
Pace yourself. Spread out big changes and difficult projects over time; don't lump the hard things all together.	Remember that the shortest bridge between despair and hope is often a good "Thank You, Lord!"
Delegate tasks to capable others.	Laugh and laugh some more!
Allow extra time to do things and to get to places.	Take your work seriously, but yourself not at all.
Less is more. (Although one is often not enough, two are often too many.)	Develop a forgiving attitude (most people are doing the best they can).
Pray.	Eat right.
Take one day at a time.	Slow down.
Learn the Serenity Prayer.	Talk less; listen more.
Live within your budget; don't use credit cards for ordinary purchases.	Have fun and laugh out loud (a merry heart doeth good like medicine).
Breathe slowly and deeply. Before reacting to the next stressful occurrence, take three deep breaths and release them slowly.	Choose one simple thing you have been putting off (e.g., returning a phone call, making a doctor's appointment) and do it immediately.
Listen to a tape while driving that can help improve your quality of life.	Get outdoors for a brief break. There is healing power in the air.
Write thoughts and inspirations down.	Talk out loud to a friend/counselor.
Plan something rewarding for the end of your stressful day, even if only a relaxing bath or half an hour with a good book.	Do a quick posture check. Hold your head and shoulders upright and avoid stooping or slumping.
Having problems? Talk to God and get counsel.	Don't worry about things you can't control, like the weather.

TABLE 8.3. STRESS REDUCTION SIMPLE THINGS YOU CAN DO TODAY	
Make friends with godly people.	Sleep and have periods of relaxation.
Every night before bed, think of things you're grateful for.	Don't be a procrastinator or perfectionist.
Every day, find time to be alone.	Develop an action/contingency plan.
Remind yourself that you are not the general manager of the universe.	Identify the worst-case scenario, but trust the sovereignty of God.
Do something about the things you can control.	Try to look at change as a positive challenge, not a threat.
Do not allow yourself to waste thought and energy where it isn't deserved.	Prepare to the best of your ability for events you know may be stressful.
Remember God has a way of turning things around for you.	Make a conscious choice not to become angry or upset.
Ask for help from friends, family, or professionals.	Work to resolve conflicts with other people.
Set realistic goals at home and at work.	Read a book of lyrics, prose, or poetry.
Whenever you feel overwhelmed by stress, practice speaking more slowly than usual.	Watch for the next instance in which you find yourself becoming annoyed or angry at something—let it go.

It is important to remember your relationship with God. When you are stressed, you need to remember that you are not alone, and that God's love for you is constant. If people are pressuring you, or the ministry seems overwhelming, it may be hard to sense the reality of God's love. When you feel yourself getting stressed, simply stop whatever you are doing, take a deep breath and remind yourself of the truth in God's word. Let's do that even now. Breathe deep, then say out loud the Scriptures listed below:

I will lift up mine eyes to the hills, from whence cometh my help, My help cometh from the LORD (Psalm 121:1–2 KJV).

God is our refuge and strength, a very present help in [times of] trouble (Psalm 46:1 KJV).

From the end of the earth will I cry unto thee, when my heart is overwhelmed: lead me to the rock that is higher than I (Psalm 61:2 KJV).

Sabrina D. Black

Fear thou not; for I am with thee: be not dismayed; for I am thy God: I will strengthen thee: yea, I will help thee; yea, I will uphold thee with the right hand of my righteousness (Isaiah 41:10 KJV).

Faithful is he that calleth you, who also will do it (1 Thessalonians 5:24 KJV).

The Bible reflects the truth about God and his faithfulness to you. Learn helpful tips from Jesus Christ, our example for holy, stress-free living. Look at Jesus's ministry as an example.

JESUS, OUR EXAMPLE

Jesus had only one focus in life: the kingdom of God, for the glory of God. He called his followers to be equally single-minded. "But seek first (God's) kingdom and his righteousness, and all these things (i.e., material needs) will be given you as well" (Matthew 6:33 NIV).

Consider the ministry of Jesus as evidenced in each of the Scriptures listed below. I've noted three things that you can glean from each text. Read each Scripture, and pray that God will give you additional insight and revelation.

Matthew 14:13–23

A leader must have compassion for others, even when they are themselves in need of compassion.

Little is much in the Master's hand.

Get along and pray.

Mark 1:32–37

Jesus healed many but not all. You can't do it all.

Find a quiet place alone to pray.

Get up early and redeem the time.

Mark 6:30–32

Get away from the crowd.

Rest, work, rest, work. Get the idea.

There will always be one more thing to do.

The words, "too blessed to be stressed or depressed" can indeed become a reality in the lives of leaders as we allow the Word of God to work in us. The Word of God can soothe our stress like the balm of Gilead. It is more necessary than our daily bread. Like manna from heaven, it revives and refreshes. It is a light unto our feet and a lamp unto our path. It is a source of comfort and strength. We truly are blessed. God has given us everything that pertains to life and godliness. Don't be stressed. Enjoy your role as a leader in the work of the ministry.

PRAYER

Father God, I know your plans for my life are plans of peace, to give me a hope and future, an expected end. I recognize that in some ways I have lived my life on the edge, full of stress and anxiety.

I come seeking your forgiveness, as well as your directions, asking the Holy Spirit to lead, guide, and instruct me in the way I should go in all the affairs of life. I desire to be a leader who is effectively able to overcome emotional stress, discouragement, and avoid burnout.

I long to please you, Lord, as I go before your people. Help me to see the leadership principles of Jesus; to take charge of my health, better manage my time, and worry less about the work of the ministry.

Help me learn to rest in you and renew my mind with your words of counsel. To fellowship with you as I hear your voice to make the best decisions in the work of the ministry.

Give me insight to make the best decisions for my family and myself while I perform the role of leader.

I pray your perfect will be done in me. I cast all my cares, anxieties, stresses, and worry over on you. I choose to trust your plan and timing for me and my ministry. In Jesus's name. Amen.

REFERENCES

Budrikis, Stella. 2005. "Christians and Stress."

Collins, Gary R. 1998. *Breathless: Transform Your Time-Starved Days Into a Life Well Lived.* Wheaton, IL: Tyndale House.

Emery, Gary, and James Campbell. 1986. *Rapid Relief from Emotional Distress.* New York: Rawson Associates.

Komor, Christian R. 1991. *The Power of Being: For People Who Do Too Much!* Grand Rapids, MI: Renegade House Productions.

McCutcheon, M. 2010. *Roget's Super Thesaurus.* Fourth Edition. Cincinnati, OH: Writer's Digest Books.

Minirth, Frank, Paul Meier, D. Hawkins, and Richard Flournoy. 1986. *How to Beat Burnout: Help for Men and Women.* Chicago: Moody Press.

Peck, M. Scott. 1993. *Further Along the Road Less Traveled.* New York: Walker and Company.

Spera, Stefanie and Sandra Lanto. 1995. *Beat Stress with Strength: Achieving Wellness at Work and in Life.* New York: Drake, Beam Morin, Inc.

Stress. 1996. *Prevention Magazine.*

Swenson, R. A. 2004. *Margin: Restoring Emotional, Physical, Financial, and Time Reserves to Overloaded Lives.* Revised edition. Colorado Springs, CO: NavPress.

Chapter 9

LEADERSHIP IN CRISIS[1]

Pamela J. Hudson

"Why art thou cast down, O my soul?" (Psalm 42:5 KJV). It is widely reported that the symptoms and causes of depression are as prevalent in our neighborhood homes, city council offices, corporate offices, as they are in the church.

Depression knows no boundaries. Depression does not discriminate based on gender, race, income, or position. The statistics are mind-boggling. It is "estimated that 20 million adults in the U.S. alone suffer from depression each year." In further breaking down of these statistics, it is estimated that "25% of women and 12% of men in the U.S. will experience an episode of major depression," and that "1 out of 6 Americans adults have depression during their lifetimes" ("Understanding Depression," 2001).

In a broadcast of Focus on the Family, the program "Ministering to Pastors" claimed that more than fifty-two percent of pastors suffer with depression. Since this impacts the family and the ministry, both will suffer when the pastor is hurting in this manner.

In yet another Focus on the Family program, "Pastor to Pastor—Overcoming Weariness," a number of pastors stated they have been discouraged in ministry in the past *six months* at an alarming rate of ninety to ninety-five percent.

---

1. This chapter was previously published in the book *HELP! for Your Leadership*. 2003. Detroit: PriorityOne Publications. Used by permission. Some editorial changes have been made.

Another fifty percent are experiencing burnout, and another twenty-five percent were battling depression while actively serving in ministry. Wow!

It goes without saying, but I will, that this is a real problem that is creating a crisis in leadership as we find our pulpits and study groups lacking competent leadership as leaders are tired and hurting.

What are the signs of the walking wounded in the ministry? The term "depression," according to Pfizer Research, is described as follows (Understanding depression, 2001): Depression is a persistent sad mood and/or loss of interest or pleasure in most activities and is accompanied by some of the following symptoms:

- Changes in appetite or weight

- Changes in sleep patterns

- Restlessness or decreased activity that is noticeable to others

- Loss of energy, or feeling tired all the time

- Difficulty in concentrating or making decisions

- Feeling worthlessness or inappropriate guilt

- Recurrent thoughts of death or suicide

The Bible also describes depression in Psalm 42. What we can derive from looking at Psalm 42 is some spiritual maladies that contribute to depression. We see feelings of guilt, sinfulness, sense of being unworthy, and feeling very much apart or separated from God.

CAUSES OF DEPRESSION

Life is filled with challenges on all fronts. How much more for the man or women who has committed their lives to be of service to others? The work of the ministry is stressful. Some experts attribute depression to any stressful event in a person's life.

The height of depressed moods and a sense of worthlessness may be apparent when the ministry leadership forgets that God is the real healer, helper, and problem-solver, and takes on more than they are assigned instead of setting boundaries.

Another cause of depression is when a leader attempts to handle problems of their congregation based on their intellect, degrees, position or power, which is a precursor to depression and stress. It becomes so important to always remember that men and women in ministry are vessels/instruments yielded to serve the Lord first and his people.

Leadership's dependency should be upon the greater One within—the Holy Spirit of God. It is he who will work through leadership to meet the needs of the people. Once we have ministered the Word of God, and provided a framework or pattern for parishioners to put into practice, we as counselors and pastors must release ourselves to the Lord and not take the matter home at the end of the day.

WHAT PREVENTS CHURCH LEADERS
FROM SEEKING PERSONAL HELP

What is it that prevents ministers and others in church leadership from seeking help for themselves? Does pride, position, fear of being human, or feelings of inadequacy hinder church leaders from calling out for help? Can the wounded bring substantial hope and healing to others in the body of Christ?

Some church leaders prefer to suffer in silence while being the therapist and counselors to others. How can leaders serve their congregation if they themselves don't know where to go for help? Christian leadership can be effective when they are incapable of handling their own matters of the heart and mind. This creates havoc instead of peace.

Let's try to address these questions by taking a look at some real people who were confronted with the depression, despair, and discouragement to catch sight of what they did to overcome and how they remained effective in the service of the Lord.

According to experts, there is a consensus that everyone has short periods with feelings of sadness and helplessness. According to Bobb Biehl, the author of *30 Days to Confident Leadership* (1998, 81–83), "hopelessness, helplessness or sad(ness) makes it extremely difficult to lead."

The acceptable response to depression is to identify the root causes as quickly and efficiently as possible. Don't allow it to fester!

Bobb offers some very good questions that can be asked to ascertain the root causes:

"Am I Angry at Anyone?"

The act of forgiveness will bolster the healing process for "anger-caused depression." The Word of God admonishes us:

Do not let the sun go down while you are still angry (Ephesians 4:26 NIV).

It is acknowledged that anger is a natural human emotion; yet, the Bible tells us we have the ability to control our anger.

When we look at Proverbs 15:1 (NIV), we find our answer:

A gentle answer turns away wrath, but a harsh word stirs up anger.

"Is This Depression Caused by Physical or Mental Fatigue?"

Oftentimes leadership performs their tasks with little or no sleep. Therefore, sleep deprivation could be a contributor to depressed mood swings and the Achilles heel in making poor decisions. God offers peace and sweet sleep to the believer. Doctors urge all of us to get plenty of rest, allowing our bodies to renew and recharge to keep our immune system strong. Even God rested on the seventh day.

In peace I will lie down and sleep, for you alone, LORD, make me dwell in safety (Psalm 4:8 NIV).

When you lie down, you will not be afraid; when you lie down, your sleep will be sweet (Proverbs 3:24 NIV).

"Have I Been Experiencing Too Much Change Too Fast?"

The work of the ministry requires much work with major planning. Sometimes expansion or growth, changeover, betrayals, funding issues, and building matters can be overwhelming for one person. It can be more than one can digest. The "disorientation in the middle of constant, hard driven change" is a key determinant in leadership's bout with depression (Biehl, 1998, 4). The Bible says:

Cast all your anxiety on him because he cares for you (1 Peter 5:7 NIV).

Some leaders have taken on burdens and anxieties of leadership and forgotten that they are in partnership with the Lord Jesus Christ, having internalized the problems and taken on the role of burden-bearer. This can be remedied when they spend more time in prayer, getting a clearer understanding of what they are assigned to do.

Clearly, God has not called anyone to the role of leader without fully equipping him or her to successfully fulfill his or her role. We must examine what leadership entails and how best to serve God, the people and the community without losing our perspective or becoming overwrought.

INTRODUCTION TO LEADERSHIP

There are many definitions of a business leader. The one that sticks out for me covers someone who has general management, administrative skills, solid interpersonal skills, diplomacy and personal skills with a willingness to take on risks. This leader is a change agent. Qualified leaders are persons who take into consideration all of their resources (technology, people, and processes) to help define what and how to guide successfully the organization.

A good leader promotes a positive outlook, sets goals to deliver solid service, is conscious of cost, has a vision, and encourages cooperation and honesty.

Leaders make sure plans and purposes are clearly written, attainable and measurable.

Write down the revelation and make it plain on tablets so that a herald may run with it (Habakkuk 2:2 NIV).

The focused leader promotes planning and seeks multiple ways to attain success by establishing goals based on performance driven initiatives. Looking at corporate America, we see the description of a successful organization as one that makes improvements visible and makes sure they are well communicated throughout the organization. This is just as important in the front office of the church as it is in corporations.

The defining and performing of core competencies within a ministry drive successes and explain failures. The attentive leader must handle church business to the glory of God in all they do, as well as uphold honor to the whole church.

Leadership must bring character, integrity, and dignity to their position. They should always regard the congregation with an attitude that they are valuable to God first and to the ministry second, while building a community of true fellowship and suppressing internal conflict.

> May integrity and uprightness protect me, because my hope, LORD, is in you (Psalm 25:21 NIV).

All organizations deserve to be managed by competent and well-trained leaders. Those who know what their purpose is can carry out the organizational program to meet the established goals, not with fear or intimidation, but with cooperation and sincerity. Those in positions of leadership must know within themselves they are called by God and answerable to God for their ministry, recognizing that God gets all the glory. They are instruments, God's workmanship created for good works; keepers of the vision of God.

> My feet stand on level ground; in the great congregation I will praise the LORD (Psalm 26:12 NIV).

All in positions of leadership should realize they are to mentor or disciple others by modeling behavior that pleases God and by giving future leaders an example to aspire to in becoming a servant of the Most High God. Developing, sharing, and training others to service will in time reap a harvest of godly leaders who also fear and honor God with their lives and ministry.

> Be very careful, then, how you live—not as unwise but as wise, making the most of every opportunity, because the days are evil" (Ephesians 5:15–16 NIV).

Because leaders are the ones who go before the people, their leadership or leading by example should reflect the following traits:

- Open communications
- Unity among the brethren (attitude)
- Flexibility toward change
- Respect for authority
- Reasoning and zeal with knowledge

All future leadership development must promote effective communication, submission to God, and foster change within organizations to meet the needs and demands of the people. Leaders must enable the people by empowering them with the Word of God to build confidence, to motivate, to bring enthusiasm for truth and victory, and to face any challenge with boldness.

In the pages to follow, we will read of some powerful leaders whose leadership by example was less than stellar, nonetheless, leaders who come to realize the all-sufficiency of God's grace, mercy, and trustworthiness.

THE HELP OF MY COUNTENANCE

Why art thou cast down, O my soul? and why art thou disquieted within me? hope thou in God: for I shall yet praise him, who is the health of my countenance, and my God (Psalm 42:11 KJV).

I recall an article that depicted the distinctions between the role of a manager and a leader. Interestingly, the key words that peaked my interest were, "to motivate, inspire, lead, and do the right thing."

What impressed me was the fact that whoever is in leadership is the catalyst behind any organization predetermining the tone or imprint for the success or defeat of an organization.

In the body of Christ, men and women who have answered the call to serve are also expected to be motivators, inspirational, and upright in their attitude and actions.

Yet, there is an alarming epidemic in the Christian community that, if it continues to be left unattended, will scatter the flock and possibly destroy ministries.

What I am alluding to is the outrageous figures that show that more than seventy percent of ministry leadership is battling depression, and that more than fifty percent of wives of ministers are battling with the same disease.

By all accounts, the word "depression" is as upsetting or scary as "cancer." Its growth among leaders is astronomical, creating a leadership gap in many congregations. Who does the minister go to when he/she needs help? How can the one who gives out so much, replenish their lives to keep on going?

Many would ask, "How can men of God be able to advise me on standing on the Word of God, when they are not able to handle the day-to-day operations of ministry and family? Did they miss their calling? Are they operating in sin?"

Oftentimes, those with ministry gifts (pastors, teachers, apostle, evangelist, prophets) have lost sight of who they serve and are depending upon their own intelligence, spirituality, wit or interpersonal skills to facilitate the operational, tactical, and strategic business of ministry.

They are possibly holding to what worked last year, last month, or last Sunday to carry them through the year. Failing to refuel their spiritual tank with a fresh anointing from the Holy Spirit is probably a core indicator why so many are burning out.

Furthermore, they are becoming self-absorbed and feeling self-important, believing that what has excelled within their ministry was based on their mental agility. They are allowing their self-image to be exalted and looking at success and refusing to attribute all to the Lord.

> For by the grace given me I say to every one of you: Do not think of yourself more highly than you ought (Romans 12:3 NIV).

We have a perfect example of a depressed leader in the book of Daniel. This great leader was the overseer of a great nation, the political and spiritual figure of the day. He was so lifted up in pride; he failed to acknowledge that all he had was by the hand of the Lord God Almighty. He blew his own horn, kept referring to what he had accomplished with his victories over his enemies and the great wealth accumulated in the nation's coffers. He was a rich man and the nation was blessed.

Then one day the man of God interpreted the king's dream of the great tree. (Daniel 4:24–27). The man of God warned the king:

> [B]reak off thy sins by righteousness, and thine iniquities by shewing mercy to the poor, if it may be a *lengthening of thy tranquility*" (Daniel 4:27 KJV, emphasis added).

Notice the term "lengthening of thy tranquility," for the sake of the king's own peace, was told to be merciful and acknowledge the Lord God of the universe. But the king came in the next day into the palace and opened his mouth to declare:

> Is not this the great Babylon I have built for the house of the kingdom by the might of my power, and for the honour of my majesty? (Daniel 4:30 KJV).

No sooner were these words spoken out of the king's mouth, did the "tranquility" leave him. The Spirit of the Lord spoke to King Nebuchadnezzar and declared the interpretation of the dream to be fulfilled at that time. The king found himself driven from the presence among men to the nature of the animals and beast, eating grass with his body wet with dew, his hair growing wild on his person likened to feathers and his nails becoming like animal claws (Daniel 4:31–33).

No doubt this man experienced a great depression that transformed him into another person. Notice the impact of his words, which we recognize to be powerful seeds. When the king spoke, he did not speak glory to God, nor acknowledge that without God's help he would have absolutely nothing. Man does not have absolute power. Power belongs to God.

This depressed and down trodden leader experienced the lowest level of abasement that anyone could experience. He was outside of himself, wallowing in his sinful nature, separated from God, the Giver of life.

He had to come to the place in his mind, that he understood that he was nothing without God. He could do nothing except by God. And he had nothing except for what God had given him the ability, skills, and understanding to have. That is when King Nebuchadnezzar, lifted up his eyes and said these words:

Then I praised the Most High; I honored and glorified him who lives forever" (Daniel 4:34 NIV).

Not until he believed in his heart and declared this newfound truth out of his mouth, did his tranquility return. The weight of depression and the sense of helplessness were lifted. He now understood the importance of maintaining an ongoing relationship with Almighty God. He now comprehended the awesomeness of the creator of heaven and earth, coming to the conclusion that without God he could do nothing. This realization will spark your mental and spiritual focus to shift away from self toward God.

Selfishness leaves no room for God. You must become more God conscious and less self-conscious:

Yes, my soul, find rest in God; my hope comes from him (Psalm 62:5 NIV).

Depression knows no ranks or limits. Wherever the spirit of depression can find a willing, empty, or unfocused target, Satan will set all his attack weapons against that person to deceive them, while moving them away from fellowship and peace with God and self.

Regardless of your station in life, when you forget to "[i]n all thy ways acknowledge him (God)" (Proverbs 3:6 KJV), you are leaving yourself open to the attack of your stout enemy—an enemy who would love to give you (especially leaders) such guilt and pain (physically and emotionally) that you become ineffective, inefficient, lacking in your ability to carry out your duties for others. Know this:

> Your enemy the devil prowls around like a roaring lion looking for someone
> to devour (1 Peter 5:8 NIV).

Rather than leaders operating with assurance, they will begin to "suffer from neurotic depression because of their high expectation and the low realities, perpetuating low self-image, self-worth, alienation and guilt." (Moyes, G., 1998)

What about the person who feels inferior or questions their anointing or ministry gift? What about the one who in their soul (mind, will, and emotions) feels "bowed down" or inadequate? This is another leader who would be vulnerable to feelings of depression.

When individuals fails to fully comprehend who they are in Christ, they will question themselves, allow others to define who they are as they battle negative feelings, apprehension, and whether they truly make a difference.

Such leaders will not find peace or relief because they are trying to please others. This type of depressed mind is motivated by fear, not faith.

This sense of loss and oppression is the result of losing sight of who they are in Christ and forgetting that Christ died on the cross to redeem them from the stronghold of death, disease, and depression.

Deliverance then comes to these leaders as they are reminded of how the Lord, "lifts up those who are bowed down" (Psalm 146:8 NIV). Their hope rests in loving the Lord who is a preserver of the faithful: "Be strong and take heart, all you who hope in the LORD" (Psalm 31:24 NIV). The assurance comes in knowing that the Lord has "never forsaken those who seek" him (Psalm 9:10 NIV). Faith will be built up when leaders recognize Jesus and the work he did on Golgotha. When they understand how much Jesus loves them, this will be the healing that will take them from fear to faith, to confidence, to boldness, and renewed assurance in yourself.

Pamela J. Hudson

Recognizing that "God will come ... with vengeance; with divine retribution he will come to save you" (Isaiah 35:4 NIV) is enough to build your confidence and invigorate your spirit man to a newness of life.

Don't forget who you are and who you serve. Be quick to humble yourself and allow the perfect will of God to be your goal or objective in all of your life.

POWER OF CONFESSION TO RELIEVE A DEPRESSED MIND

> Therefore, holy brothers and sisters, who share in the heavenly calling, fix
> your thoughts on Jesus, whom we acknowledge as our apostle and high
> priest (Hebrews 3:1 NIV).

The power of your confession from sin is another answer to depression. The Word of God is plain in 1 John 1:9 (NIV), "If we confess our sins, he (God) is faithful and just and will forgive us our sins and purify us from all unrighteousness."

Note that the act of confession is the responsibility of the individual. The obligation is for you to acknowledge you have missed the "mark of the high call in Christ," to ask God for forgiveness, and make a decision to turn 180 degrees in the opposite direction.

What all individuals in leadership should realize is that our words, which are seeds, are serious business, and it is our responsibility to gain information on how best to use our words.

The battleground as we know is the mind and our mouths. To use the Word of God when Satan attacks your ministry or you personally, you would wield tremendous power to "cast him down" in the situation and gain victory.

Leaders like the rest of us too often call those things that be as they are. We confess the negative, or "telling it like it is." Instead of saying what God says about our challenges as leaders, about our congregations, about our financial situation, we speak from our feelings or emotions. This can lead to defeat and a downward spiral into depression.

Our words when mixed with faith are powerful, transforming, and miracle working medicine for an overcoming life in leadership. We overcome "by the blood of the Lamb and by the word of [our] testimony" (Revelation 12:11 NIV).

A MAN AFTER GOD'S OWN HEART—LIFTED BY PRAISE

The presence and power of a praise lifestyle is one of the key antidotes for depression. David, the king of Israel, prophet and poet, had times when he dealt with bouts of depression while on the run from King Saul. His promise through Samuel was that he would be king. His position at the time was on the run from King Saul who would rather have him dead. The promise of God, the anointing of oil by the prophet Samuel, did not make his belief in the Lord's promise to be leader over Israel easy.

David served a man who hated him. David lost his possessions, friends, and a wife. This would be enough to make any man feel depressed and distressed. Yet, in the midst of all these traumatic experiences, David found the will to focus his strength on God acknowledging his desire for God like a thirsty man desiring water (see Psalm 42). The feeling of abandonment was very real to David. Look at verse nine of Psalm 42 (NIV), where we read, "Why must I go about mourning, oppressed by the enemy?"

The sense of isolation, the fear of eminent death all around, the uncertainty of the next meal or place of shelter and safety, were all too real to David on a daily basis. He eventually held an important leadership position in government, had oversight of millions of people, was wealthy, handsome, and a gifted musician, a great orator, and a military hero. He had beautiful children, a most beautiful wife, yet he asked the penetrating question, "Why so disturbed within me?"

This may sound like the headlines of today, but it applies to a great man of the past, a most picturesque king—King David of Israel. By all standards he should have been the most blessed and empowered person. Yet, when you look closer, you see the symptoms that led to his solemn question.

How David handled depression with the word of God is the positive way to overcome leadership tests and trials—through praise. What a leader does when confronted by difficulties will spread throughout their congregation. How the leader expresses his or her confidence in the Word of God in the midst of challenges, will minister to the body while preparing it to be bold and "blameless and pure, 'children of God without fault in a warped and crooked generation'" (Philippians 2:15, NIV).

The power of praise cannot be overlooked. King David found his solace and power when he "lift[ed] up his eyes to the mountains" and recognized that his "help [came] from the LORD" (Psalm 121:1–2, NIV). Not until David gave over his tongue to magnify the goodness of the Lord in the midst of his confusion did he receive deliverance and healing from fear, futility, and the hurt of betrayal by a friend.

Opening your mouth to speak words of honor and praise while acknowledging who and what the Lord has done for you, will transform your heart from discouragement to hope.

Lifting your voice in praise will support your increase in strength and confidence toward God in the face of the depression. The power of praise will renew the presence of the Spirit and transform your mind as you turn back the attack of the enemy against your ministry and leadership.

> Through Jesus, therefore, let us continually offer to God a sacrifice of praise—the fruit of lips that openly profess his name (Hebrews 13:15 NIV).

DEPRESSION ROOTED IN DISOBEDIENCE—KING SAUL

> Whoever sows to please their flesh, from the flesh will reap destruction (Galatians 6:8 NIV).

Hunt (1998) states:

> Day by day the darkness pervades your soul with an inescapable sense of loss—a loss of what was held dear. This loss is not just grief. It could represent loss of leadership power, position, loss in relationships, authority, dreams, hope, lost goals, programs objective lost. These can cause chronic grief that can lead to depression.

This description is the temperament and mindset that was King Saul's downfall. Here is a leader who experienced wide mood swings, difficulty sleeping, agitation, delusion, and indecisiveness, to name a few. Each is a symptom affecting a leader dealing with chronic depression.

King Saul acted out his depression by forsaking God and seeking advice from a witch or psychic. With jealousy and rage as adrenaline, he sought to kill his protégé, quarreled with his son, and led a nation into moral chaos and a poorly planned war that ultimately caused his death and that of his son.

King Saul had a love-hate relationship with David. He was holding on to his position when he understood that David would replace him as king. Instead of releasing the "choices that could lead to depression," King Saul held on to the problems and with his hurting rage, along with the "depression, he made bad choices" (Conner 1995, 7).

The loss of the people's admiration (1 Samuel 18:7–8) spurred his anger and he turned against everyone who did not go along with his bitterness. He was a classic example of a leader expressing symptoms of "grief with the sudden change in his life," all because he failed to process all the changes in light of the word of God, instead he "triggered a depressive episode" (Graves 1999, 1).

Normally this time of loss would pass, yet, Saul held on to his displeasure, creating havoc and chronic disorder as his self-image spiraled into the abyss. He was drowning in his depression, losing control of his leadership abilities, destroying a nation and alienating himself from family, friends, and loved ones.

Because of his poor decisions, he used the nation's resources (manpower, military might, legislative, and administrative) to hunt down one man, David, who he labeled as his nemesis.

As in King Saul's example, "the loss he held on to and internalized covered people, profitability, position and power" (Conner 1995, 101). Rather than turning to God for help and comfort, King Saul sought the advice of a witch or psychic, contrary to the word of God. This is a perfect example of "faulty decision" by a distraught and unfocused leader (Connor 1995, 107).

David and King Saul represent two parallels of how leadership should and should not respond to circumstances. One of the best visual aids I have found to display vividly the steps toward depression are offered by People to People Ministries of Dallas, Texas.

This table labels each step toward deep depression and the positive alternative to deliverance.

As you can see, the road to depression requires you to make a decision how you receive, process, and react to life's test. James gives us a way to face life:

Consider it pure joy, my brothers and sisters, whenever you face trials of many kinds, because you know that the testing of your faith develops perseverance (James 1:2–3 NIV).

Pamela J. Hudson

TABLE 9.1. DEPRESSION OR DELIVERANCE?

How Does One Become Depressed?
↓
Improper Thinking Patterns
↓
Insult/Injury Rejection
↓
Disappointment
↙   ↘

Fear/Anger	Thanksgiving
Self Pity	Peace
Depression	
Despair	

Source: People to People Ministries; table used by permission.

ELIJAH'S RECOVERY FROM DEPRESSION

Let's look again at the definition of depression as described by the National Institute of Mental Health, They state that "depressive disorder as whole-body illness, involving your body, mood, and thoughts. It affects the way you eat and sleep, the way you feel about yourself, and the way you think about life" (Graves 1999, 1).

This describes what the great prophet Elijah was dealing with when he "succumbed to mental and spiritual exhaustion after a remarkable season of prophetic ministry" (Ibid, 1). Leaders, who have had or are having bouts with depression, appear to have had a great time of ministry, leading and serving the people. The leader has committed to do all that is asked of him and then hits the wall, having set goals so high that he or she is unable to fulfill the task, resulting in feelings of isolation. Or the leader physically exhausts his or her body to the place where responsibilities cannot be mentally executed.

The depressed leader is like Elijah. He had poured so much of himself into his work that there is no time for refreshing. He was experiencing a loss. For Elijah, it was the feeling of worthlessness, helplessness, with thought of suicide. This is a major call for help. What we see is that Elijah did nothing wrong, except boldly speak the uncompromised word of God. Nor was there some moral failure attributed to his ministry. He was just battling some personal weakness and was not able to "pull himself together." (Ibid, 1)

With all leaders, God had enough understanding and love to believe that each of his chosen leaders would overcome their adversity when they fixed their "eyes on Jesus, the pioneer and perfecter of faith" (Hebrews 12:2 NIV).

It is in the recovery that God offers his greatest help to keep the flow of his power by offering some ideas to "pass over the rugged emotional terrain" (Ibid, 3). Here is a great list with hope for all that are confronted with depression:

- God views depression as a problem you have, not a problem you are. He discerns between you and it and stands with you against it.

- Set goals and take on responsibilities that are in portion to your physical and emotional energy level. This means guarding against unrealistic expectations, which will only increase feeling of failure if you fall short.

- Do not make major life decisions at this point in time.

- Do what you can as you can. The choice is not between inertia and activity. It is a question of progressively and proportionally reengaging life

- Do not criticize yourself if you don't simply snap out it. All things being equal, slow, steady improvement is the most common and reliable route to recovery.

- Don't withdraw from the company of caring Christian friends and fellowship. The community of faith is a "hospital" you go to while you are "bleeding," not after you've stopped bleeding. Avoid complete isolation (Ibid, 3).

Don't you see Elijah in each of the listed recovery stages? Originally, he was seeing his life and ministry as a problem and blaming all his failure, after the big show down with the prophet of Baal, on himself. He had stretched his limited resources to the limit. He felt that because of what he just ministered he should not be in a state of panic from the threats of Jezebel. He just wanted to run away and hide, cry, and die. He was willing to make the big decision about life and death in his agitated condition.

He felt alone, the only remaining prophet of God. He withdrew into the desert, even refusing to eat or help himself. God had to send a raven and the angels to wait on him to renew his physical strength. It was a progressive recovery, little by little. Don't you recall the church family coming to your aid when a life crisis occurred, giving you nourishment, words of comfort and encouragement, and letting you know that you could call on them for prayer when you have need?

God moved Elijah from one place to another, sharing life revelations and intimacy that Elijah had never been exposed to before. Elijah was drawing closer to God, as God was healing his mental, physical, and emotional mind. What an awesome and caring God we serve:

> "Because he loves me," says the LORD, "I will rescue him; I will protect him, for he acknowledges my name" (Psalm 91:14 NIV).

We have biblical examples that give us a clear picture on how to overcome tests and temptations, how to keep our eye on the prize in Christ Jesus. Let us never forget the redemptive work of the cross and remember how much God loves us all.

THE WORD PROMISES TO COMBAT DEPRESSION

> Who among you fears the LORD and obeys the word of his servant? Let the one who walks in the dark, who has no light, trust in the name of the Lord and rely on their God (Isaiah 50:10 NIV).

> You will keep in perfect peace those whose minds are steadfast, because they trust in you (Isaiah 26:3 NIV).

> Peace I leave with you; my peace I give you. I do not give to you as the world gives. Do not let your hearts be troubled and do not be afraid (John 14:27 NIV).

> Submit yourselves, then, to God. Resist the devil, and he will flee from you (James 4:7 NIV).

Pamela J. Hudson

This is an ongoing task. You have to be obedient to God, submitted to his Word and willing to follow his way of doing things. This will release you spiritually, mentally, and emotionally from the bondage the devil would try to pressure you with in all areas of your life.

The Word is of the utmost importance in directing your mind away from tests and trials, discouragement, oppression, and fear:

"Who has known the mind of the LORD, so as to instruct him?" But we have the mind of Christ (1 Corinthians 2:16 NIV).

[H]ave the same mindset as Christ Jesus (Philippians 2:5 NIV).

For men and women in leadership, the battleground is the mind and one way to defeat yourself is to question your calling—whether you are worthy of the call to minister, disagreeing with your assignment by turning your back on that task or doing it your way without seeking the help of the Spirit of God. The only outcome will be fear, agony, and eventual burnout.

As one anointed, appointed, and qualified by the Spirit of God, you cannot afford to be rebellious by excluding God in your ministry, personal life, and leadership style.

A careless manner toward God and his Word will infect negatively the message you impart over the pulpit or in the counseling office. Indifference will lead to the weakening of your ministry and eventually distraction from the perfect will of God.

The Lord Jesus has placed leaders to oversee the people for whom he laid down his life on the cross at Calvary. Fulfilling the leadership role with the help of the Holy Spirit, teaching the uncompromised Word of God with boldness and conviction, and refusing to abandon your commitment to truth and righteousness will lead to success. It was he who

gave the apostles, the prophets, the evangelists, the pastors and teachers, to equip his people for works of service, so that the body of Christ may be built up until we all reach unity in the faith and in the knowledge of the Son of God and become mature, attaining to the whole measure of the fullness of Christ (Ephesians 4:11–13 NIV).

Leaders, who are doing everything heartily as to the Lord and not to humans, will not burnout or become depressed in their task. Such self-assured leaders will fight the good fight of faith, holding fast to their love of God, and the life-changing power of the Word of God:

> You did not choose me, but I chose you and appointed you so that you might go and bear fruit—fruit that will last—and so that whatever you ask in my name the Father will give you (John 15:16 NIV).

PRAYER

Father God, in the name of your precious Son Jesus, I come boldly to the throne of grace asking for forgiveness in anything that I have done to disrupt, destroy, or even create confusion to those I lead. Seeking your guidance to oversee your people with skill, sensitivity, and sincerity. To walk in a manner pleasing to you while I uphold your standard of peace, love, and joy in the Anointed and his anointing.

Dear Lord, let my time of service be a beacon of light and hope to others. May I show the highest level of godly leadership to all. I want to walk before You in the land of the living, not in ignorance, or as a fool, but as wise. May I properly redeem my time in leading your people to that place where they may grow, develop, and become men and women of maturity, confidence, and power. Create in me a clean heart, that I may serve you, not myself, in the power of your Holy Spirit. In Jesus's Name. Amen.

REFERENCES

Biehl, Bobb. 1998. *30 Days to Confident Leadership*. Nashville, TN: Broadman & Holman.

Conner, Clint. 1995. *Cures from the Counselor*. Springdale, PA: Whitaker House.

Graves, Cliff, D. 2002. "Depression." http://rpeurifoy.com/

Hunt, June. "Key Collections—Decision Making." http://www.hopefortheheart.org.

Pamela J. Hudson

www.mentalhelp.net.

Mitchell, Steve. 2002. "Depression Screen Suggested for Adults."

Moyes, Gordon. 2000. "Coping with Depression." Sunday Night Live Sermons. http://www.wesleymission.org.au/Christian_Life/

Moyes, Gordon. 1998. "Dealing with Life's Flat Times." Sunday Night Live Sermons. http://www.wesleymission.org.au/Christian_Life/

Nemade, Rashmi, Natalie Staats Reiss, and Mark Dombeck. "Major Depression and Other Unipolar Depressions." http://www.mentalhelp. net/

"Understanding Depression." 2001. http://www.zoloft.com

Chapter 10

LEAVING THE LONE-RANGER MENTALITY—ALONE[1]

Brenda A. Jenkins

"People grow through experience if they meet life honestly and courageously" (Eleanor Roosevelt). I have heard people say, "I do not need people; as long I have God, I am okay." Others may feel they are self-sufficient within themselves and in need of no one. The latter is what has been called the lone-ranger mentality. Neither perspective is in line with God's purpose for his creation.

When you come into difficult relationships in your daily life, do you examine yourself? Does what you are doing match God's standards of relating to his people? When you are being obedient to God's Word, this leads to fellowship with him and with others. You are part of a bigger purpose. God wants you to work together with others, using your skills and gifts.

Being a lone ranger disconnects you from God's purpose for you, and it disconnects you from others. There is your way, the other person's way, and God's way. Does your way match God's way? Does it glorify him?

---

1. This chapter was previously published in the book *HELP! for Your Leadership* (Detroit: PriorityOne Publications, 2003). Used by permission. Some editorial changes have been made.

As a prisoner for the Lord, then, I urge you to live a life worthy of the calling you have received. Be completely humble and gentle; be patient, bearing with one another in love. Make every effort to keep the unity of the Spirit through the bond of peace. There is one body and one Spirit—just as you were called to one hope when you were called—one Lord, one faith, one baptism; one God and Father of all, who is over all and through all and in all. But to each one of us grace has been given as Christ apportioned it (Ephesians 4: 1–7 NIV).

It is because of grace and mercy that God accepts you. God loves you just as you are. Ask yourself, "Am I showing grace and mercy to all people?" When confusion appears, know that confusion is not of God. Because of Jesus Christ, you are victorious over Satan.

When you begin to look at people as God does, you may see them differently. When you love God with all your being, you will obey Him. Through obedience to God, who is love, you will love others.

This chapter will be devoted to fellowship, both vertical and horizontal. I will discuss God's original design of man and how fellowship, both with God and others will bring a more fruitful fulfillment in life. I will look at trust, individual responsibility, crossing our boundaries, accountability, plus sharing of self, forgiveness, and reconciliation.

If you are willing to put off sinful ways, renew your mind, and put on righteousness (Ephesians 4:22–24), you will be able to have the more fulfilled life that God intended for you to have. Be honest with yourself and know that it is a continuous process that you will experience as long as you are in the flesh.

Also included will be two biblical examples about forgiveness and reconciliation. I will discuss possible scenarios a person may have in a relationships with others and provide some suggestions for targeted areas for change.

CURRENT CONDITION

In the introduction of Dr. Tony Evans's book (1999, 56), *The Kingdom Agenda*, he discusses a world off target—one where there is chaos starting from individuals extending to the world problems. He states, "The refusal of people to take personal responsibility for their actions has become a national epidemic. Everyone is playing the blame game." Take a good look at yourself and ask these questions:

- Who am I?
- What is my purpose?
- Do I take responsibility for the areas in which I am responsible?

With all the technological advancements, spending time with neighbors has been limited. With attached garages, working people rarely see their neighbors. Many homes have decks on the back of their homes with bushes or trees for privacy, and many homes are built without front porches. When you call a company, you get a voice mail, not a human being to talk with. Many take care of banking business through electronic funds transfer or automated teller machines. Even at the gas station, you can get gas without talking with a human being. Despite all the time management theories and gadgets, little time is left over for others. Where and when is the fellowship taking place? Some even schedule time with God.

I read Dr. Michael A. Proud Jr.'s (2002) sermon on "Worship: A Picture with God: Part 2." Dr. Proud discussed how freedom is a double-edged sword that must be kept in check or it will destroy believers. He states:

> Living in a free society as we do, that concept of freedom and independence can evade every part of our lives, even our spiritual lives. It can create in our minds a Lone Ranger mentality of life, that is, I don't need anyone and I can live as I like.

As we grow closer to God and depend on him, doing things our way is not an option. To do things our way puts us out of fellowship with God and one another. Dr. Proud (2002) states, "Yet, our love affair with independence can hinder our willingness to depend upon God and on others."

What a lonely life this can be. God made us to be relational beings. He created Adam for Himself, and then he created Eve for Adam.

In the very beginning, it was to be that vertical relationship with God and that horizontal relationship with Eve. He commanded Adam and Eve to populate the earth. That was their purpose. So, together as man and wife, they began populating the earth (Genesis). Man and woman were created in God's own image. Woman was also created as a helpmate for man. All of humanity comes from Adam and Eve. Our relationship is with God and each other.

GOD'S DIRECTIVE

All through Scripture we are told to love one another. If you love God, you will love others.

> If anyone says, "I love God," yet hates his brother, he is a liar. For anyone who does not love his brother, whom he has seen, cannot love God, whom he has not seen (1 John 4:20 NIV 1984)

"The Daily Walk Bible Calendar," on December 18, 1993, stated: Fellowship is a shared conviction, a shared commitment, a shared compassion. It is two people walking the same road, bearing the same load. Fellowship involves a vertical dimension with the Father and a horizontal dimension with fellow Christians.

> That which was from the beginning, which we have heard, which we have seen with our eyes, which we have looked at and our hands have touched—this we proclaim concerning the Word of life. The life appeared; we have seen it and testify to it, and we proclaim to you the eternal life, which was with the Father and has appeared to us. We proclaim to you what we have seen and heard, so that you also may have fellowship with us. And our fellowship is with the Father and with his Son, Jesus Christ. We write this to make our joy complete. This is the message we have heard from him and declare to you: God is light; in him there is no darkness at all (1 John 1:1–5 NIV)

All of us belong to God. Only God knows each of us totally. True love puts an end to anger, resentment, and bitterness. We must replace our reactions to people with God's reaction.

This is truly a testing time for us Christians. Because of the pain many of us have endured in our lives, the sinful nature attempts to protect us from those who created pain for us, and those who are different from us. The test comes when we don't agree. It's very easy to practice love with those who have the same values as we do.

Think about the S-word (submission). True submission is when you disagree but submit to the person in authority based on God's Word.

Do many of you become solo to prevent yourselves from submitting? Do you become solo so you don't have to love? How many people (and this could be those in leadership) want things done their way?

My question would be, "Is your way God's way?" The love affair you are commanded to have with God requires you to die to self, love your enemies, and pray for those who curse you.

Loving one another in this sinful world hurts. Remember the cost that our Lord paid for His relationship with us.

> A new command I give to you: Love one another. As I have loved you, so you must love one another. By this all men will know you are my disciples, if you love one another (John 13:34–35 NIV).

> If you obey my commands, you will remain in my love, just as I have obeyed my Father's commands and remain in his love. I have told you this so that my joy may be in you and that your joy may be complete. My command is this: Love each other as I have loved you (John 15:10–12 NIV 1984).

Jesus calls us his friends because of the knowledge he passed on to us in his word. Everything he learned from his Father is passed on to us (John 15:15). Do we share what we learn with others (family, coworkers, ministry team workers, friends, etc.)?

A PATH TO FELLOWSHIP

There is a path you can use to develop fellowship with God and man by obeying Jesus's greatest commandments (Matthew 22:37, 39). Love the Lord your God with all your heart, and with all your soul and with all your strength and with all of your mind. Psalm 63 (KJV) does an excellent job of explaining our fellowship with God.

God's Presence

> O God, thou art my God; early will I seek thee: my soul thirsteth for thee, my flesh longeth for thee in a dry and thirsty land, where no water is (v. 1).

> To see thy power and thy glory, so as I have seen thee in the sanctuary (v. 2).

God's Love

> Because thy lovingkindness is better than life, my lips shall praise thee (v. 3).

Thus will I bless thee while I live: I will lift up my hands in thy name (v. 4).

My soul shall be satisfied as with marrow and fatness; and my mouth shall praise thee with joyful lips (v. 5).

God's Knowledge of You

When I remember thee upon my bed, and meditate on thee in the night watches (v. 6)

Because thou hast been my help, therefore in the shadow of thy wings will I rejoice (v. 7).

My soul followeth hard after thee: thy right hand upholdeth me (v. 8).

But those that seek my soul, to destroy it, shall go into the lower parts of the earth (v. 9).

They shall fall by the sword: they shall be a portion for foxes (v. 10).

But the king shall rejoice in God; every one that sweareth by him shall glory: but the mouth of them that speak lies shall be stopped (v. 11).

In Psalm 103:11, 17, we see the heights and depth of God's love toward us, and in Psalm 139:1–10 God knows and accepts us. He is with us through our every situation. He is everywhere. Fellowship with God is the foundation of your fellowship with man, so likewise "love your neighbor as yourself."

You ask the question, "How do I love my neighbor? I know the Scripture, but how do I do that? I can't stand the pain."

You cannot do it by yourself. It is vital that you get the knowledge of God's Word and pray for wisdom to apply the Word in your everyday life. You can't do it by yourself. It is crucial that you understand redemption. You ask, "How do I get started?" The answer is to first seek the kingdom of heaven (Matthew 6:33). Your mind is to be on God's desires, heavenly things (Philippians 4:8).

In John 14:6 (KJV), Jesus said, "I am the way, the truth, and the life." Our most important relationship is the relationship we have with God

Brenda A. Jenkins

through His son Jesus Christ. Our makeup is unique—no human can completely satisfy us.

As we grow in the Lord, we must do more than share what God has done for us. We must direct people to God's Word.

As Christians, we have God's grace. We must remember the sacrifice (Jesus) that permitted us to be united back with our Creator in perfect union. It is through grace and mercy that we are saved. Let Jesus be Lord of your life. He provides peace and joy in our lives.

POSSIBLE BARRIERS TO FELLOWSHIP

In the name of Jesus, we have power to overcome sin. Why are we allowing sin to continue to separate us from God and our fellow man? We were born in sin, but Jesus paid the price for us. We must accept Jesus as our Lord and Savior. We must die to self.

Do we know what our responsibilities are, and what God's responsibilities are? Doing the responsibilities of others can create a barrier in the relationship. The following table may assist you in determining your responsibilities. Remember Jesus saves. The Holy Spirit clears my mind so that I won't get confused, unless I am trying to figure out something that I need to leave in God's capable hands.

Shown below are some responsibilities of the "five Rs," sorted by God versus man.

TABLE 10.1. FIVE RS

GOD—Father, Son, and the Holy Spirit	MAN
Responsibility • Creator and Finisher (Alpha and Omega) • Gives grace • Provides promises	**Responsibility** • Make your bodies a living sacrifice (Rom. 12:1) • Make Jesus Lord of your life, be obedient to God's Word
Redemption • God sent his only begotten son, Jesus Christ, to pay the price for our sins • He died on the Cross, rose, and sits on the right hand of God. God's *Word* gives the revelation of redemption	**Redemption** • We must be in agreement with God's verdict on sin in the cross of Jesus Christ • We must have a conscious experience of salvation in our lives

Brenda A. Jenkins

181

TABLE 10.1. FIVE RS	
GOD—Father, Son, and the Holy Spirit	MAN
Reconciliation • Reconciliation between God and man • God brings us back to himself by blotting out our sins and making us righteous • He reestablished relationship between God and man	**Reconciliation** • Ministry of reconciliation (2 Cor. 5:18–19) • Reconciliation between man and man—"Therefore if thou bring thy gift to the altar, and there rememberest that thy brother hath aught against thee; leave there thy gift before the altar, and go thy way; first be reconciled to thy brother, and then come and offer thy gift" (Matt 5:23–24 KJV). • Our relationship with each other affects our relationship with God
Regeneration • Jesus sent the Holy Spirit to be with us until his return (strength)	**Regeneration** • Let the Holy Spirit control your life
Restoration • Second coming, new earth, Bible begins with the majestic story of creation of the universe, and it concludes with the creation of a new heaven and earth (Rev. 21:1–5)	**Restoration** • Knowledge of God's Word (Rom. 15:14; Col. 3:16) • Know the word and how to apply it (Gal 6:1) • Restore others • Remember, love one another • Glorify God • First teach yourself, then teach others
© 2000 Brenda A. Jenkins	

Another barrier that may interfere with relationships with one another is trust. What makes a person appear to not be trustworthy? Are you a trustworthy person? Trust can break down if someone:

- Is a backstabber
- Exploits you
- Consistently breaks promises
- Misleads you in some way
- Gossips about you
- Rejects you
- Breaks an agreement or contract

Brenda A. Jenkins

- Withholds important information from you
- Takes credit for your work
- Criticizes you unfairly

We all know that the only person we can change is ourselves. We are uniquely made. It is possible for someone to have a different interpretation of words and actions based on their makeup (physical, mental, and moral). God's Word is the same yesterday, today, and tomorrow. Perfection is only in God. We are connected through Jesus Christ. God's Word will help lead us when it comes to dealing with others. The following table has some possible instructions for dealing with trust issues both within you and with others.

Remember that "trust is the highest form of human motivation. It brings out the very best in people" (Covey 2004).

TABLE 10.2. TRUTH SCRIPTURES BASED ON YOURS AND OTHERS' ACTIONS

Your Actions	Possible Impact on Others	God's Word	Others' Actions	What God's Word Tells You to Do
Backstab others	May feel like you have been stabbed	Ephesians 4:25 Proverbs 12:17 Proverbs 25:18	Backstab you	Hebrews 12:2 Proverbs 12:6, 13
Exploit others	Person may feel used	Proverbs 16:11 Proverbs 20:10	Exploit you	Proverbs 15:3
Consistently breaks promises	May feel let down	Genesis 4:7	Fails to keep promises	Proverbs 12:22
Mislead someone	May feel let down	Proverbs 14:25 Ephesians 4:29	Misleads you in some way	James 1:19
Gossip about others	May feel excluded	Proverbs 13:3	Gossip about you	1 Peter 5:8–9
Rejects someone	Person may feel unwanted	1 Peter 3:11 Romans 16:17	Rejects you	Proverbs 12:16 Proverbs 19:11
Break agreement or contract	Person may feel disappointed	Genesis 3:15 Genesis 15:12–21; 17:1–4; Hebrews 8:16–13	Breaks an agreement or contract	Proverbs 22:20

TABLE 10.2. TRUTH SCRIPTURES BASED ON YOURS AND OTHERS' ACTIONS

Your Actions	Possible Impact on Others	God's Word	Others' Actions	What God's Word Tells You to Do
Do not provide important information	May feel setup to look bad, or to fail	John 15:15	Withholds important information from you	Proverbs 8:23–24
Takes credit for someone else's work	May feel betrayed	Proverbs 21:3	Takes credit for your work	Philippians 4:13
Criticizes someone else unfairly	Closeness may be broken when judging and criticizing begin	John 8:7	Criticizes you unfairly	James 2:13 Proverbs 9:7–9
© 2003 Brenda A. Jenkins				

God's Word supplies many Scriptures. These are ones that helped me. You may have to search for others to help you. Let the Holy Spirit lead you. Meditate on Psalm 37.

This is a time for us to be humble. We know we are nothing. We must thank the Father for living within us. This is a time of healing. Let God love us and pamper us; he is truly the only One that can totally satisfy and understand us. We thank him, for he is truly worthy. Spending time with God is a prerequisite for anything we do.

Relationships with one another are what Jesus commanded us to do in love. If we miss that fellowship, we don't operate efficiently (to full capacity).

Two Biblical Characters Being Advised by Paul to Be Reconciled

Philemon

Paul appeals to Philemon to forgive his runaway slave, Onesimus, and to accept him as a brother in the faith. He asked him not to punish him but to forgive and restore him as a new Christian brother.

Christian relationships must be full of forgiveness and acceptance. Can we forgive those who have wronged us? We need to get pass barriers that work to separate us and be courteous and respectful, loving one another as God loves us.

Two Women

At the Philippian church two women were having relationship problems. They had been working for years for Christ in the church. Their broken relationship was no small matter.

Because many had become believers through their efforts, there was no excuse for remaining unreconciled. Paul encouraged them to become reconciled.

Are you in a broken relationship? Look in God's Word. It is specific on how we are to reconcile with others. Remember, all have sinned. Treat others as God has treated you. You may say some people don't deserve your forgiveness, or they sinned against you. Get in the presence of God. Now, ask yourselves, do you deserve his forgiveness and have you sinned?

Scenarios

Scenario 1: Problem

What if you are a loner and you do not have someone you can be intimate with? You associate with people, but there is no one to help you when you are down. You may or may not have an intimate relationship with God.

Scenario 1: Suggestions

First, it is important that you know the difference between being alone and being lonely. Being alone involves physical separation from others. Many times that is what we desire. It could be for rest, to get our thoughts together, communicating with God, or just a time to be alone

Being lonely includes both physical and psychological isolation. If the situation is that you are truly lonely, you have two choices. The lonely person can rise above the loneliness, or stay in it, suffering the consequences. We were not created to be alone.

As you read the pages of this chapter, I pray you will realize it is because of you that these words are written. You are more than conquerors with Jesus. The intent is to help leaders recognize that they are not alone. Being alone is a choice. Meditate on the following Scriptures.

Brenda A. Jenkins

- John 15:15—Jesus is your friend.
- Hebrews 13:5—God will never let you down.
- Hebrews 12:2—Stay focused on Jesus, your Guide and Savior.

In addition to meditating on Scripture, read a work like "Lonely But Never Alone" by J. Oswald Sanders.

Scenario 2: Problem

Those very close to you are in pain because of sin in their lives. Because of your love for them, you also feel pain. You may be able on some level to relate to the pain they are going through. You see their mistakes. You feel helpless because you can't help them. You don't want to fall with your loved one, as you have done in the past. Being an overachiever (survivor) you know how to get back up when you fall. You get back in the race. You are broken once more.

The question is, "What do you do?" Do you get as far away from them as possible? What if it this is your spouse, parent, child, brother, or sister?

Scenario 2: Suggestions

Pray and ask God for guidance. Know yourself. Know your boundaries. Know what you are responsible for. This is a good time to write out what your role is with this person. Have you crossed boundaries and taken on their responsibilities? Have you detached yourself from this person? Detachment is not separation. It is easy to lose yourself in close relationships.

Ask yourself, what would Jesus do? Do not throw the relationship away. God did not throw you away. Love is the most potent weapon in this universe. Love the person as God has loved you. This is a time for intercessory prayer. In Hebrews 4:15 Jesus interceded for you as your High Priest.

Galatians 6:1b warns believers to be careful lest they fall. You can tell the person you love them, and God loves them more. If this is an unsaved person, this is your opportunity to tell them about Jesus. Tell them what Jesus has done for you. Tell them how they can also be saved. You should apply reconciliation Scriptures.

Salvation Scriptures to Share. Many study Bibles have salvation Scriptures that you can use for yourself and share with others. To be effective in sharing with someone, it is important that you believe the Scriptures in your heart and show others by your example. To read them in the following order (left to right) makes an awesome impact.

TABLE 10.3. SALVATION SCRIPTURES TO SHARE	
John 3:16	John 10:10
Romans 3:23	Romans 5:8
1 Corinthians 15:3–6	John 14:5
John 1:12	Ephesians 2:8–9
John 3:1–8	Revelation 3:20

Christian to Christian. If Christians are in right standing, confessing their sins, asking for forgiveness, and working on living in righteousness (1 John 1:9), use reconciliation Scriptures such as the following:

> Therefore if thou bring thy gift to the altar, and there rememberest that thy brother hath aught against thee; Lleave there thy gift before the altar, and go thy way; first be reconciled to thy brother, and then come and offer thy gift (Matthew 5:23–24 KJV).

Scenario 3: Problem

How do you deal with someone who criticizes you? The critical person does not take responsibility for anything that happens. From your frame of reference, that person is taking on the role of a victim. When you are around the person, the two of you clash. You are very different. The two of you create pain for each other.

Scenario 3: Suggestions

Recognize that this person may have internal issues with relationships. You have to ask yourself, "Why am I reacting to this person?" If you are feeling pain, there may be some unresolved issues within yourself. People, who are hurting, hurt other people.

Talk with God about your feelings. Ask for help and healing from whatever is within you that makes you react. Pain is a sign that something needs to be changed. As far as the other person is concerned, love him or her like God told you to love another person. You may need to work on developing a relationship with this person.

Ask yourself, "What do I know about this person? Do I trust the person?"

You may want to do the self-assessment on trust. Make changes in light of the Word. The situation you have may be two people with issues. You are responsible for yours. To paraphrase Ephesians 4:22–24, do put on and put off those things you are responsible for.

Also, become an intercessory prayer warrior for the other person. The Bible says that reconciliation is your ministry (Matthew 5:23–24). Trust God that all things will work together for those who love him (Romans 8:28). Look at what improvements can be done in your life and be at peace with all men

SUMMARY

Once I had at a meeting in my home with a couple of my girlfriends. I am always trying to get as much done as possible on the days I have at home.

This particular Saturday morning I decided to have the refrigerator repairman repair the icemaker, and the washer and dryer repairman come out for these two appliances. After all, I was going to be at home.

I scheduled two meetings at my home that day: my writer's group (girlfriends) meeting and my family reunion committee meeting later that day.

The repairman for the washer and dryer came at 9:00 a.m. Hallelujah! He was done before my 10:00 a.m. meeting with my girlfriends.

The repairman for the refrigerator came in the middle of our meeting. It was okay because we were in the dining room. The dining room is adjacent to the kitchen. Any information he needed from me, I could give him and still continue with my meeting.

When he completed the repair of the refrigerator, I had to go over to the refrigerator so he could explain what he fixed. When I looked behind the refrigerator and saw all the mess behind it, there was no way I could let him return the refrigerator to its original place without doing some major clean up. I had to do more than just sweep.

I told the repairman to leave the refrigerator where it was, and I would move it back after I cleaned the area behind the refrigerator. He left, and I returned to my meeting.

My girlfriend said, "I know you are going to write about that?" My response was, "What do you mean?" She said, "After you saw the mess behind the refrigerator, you said it must be cleaned. Think about that when it comes to God showing you things."

My question for you to ponder is, "Has there been some mess identified in your life that needs to be cleaned up before you can move back to your original place with God, or are you going to cover it up, deep within your

Brenda A. Jenkins

heart, thinking it won't affect anything? Won't it start smelling after a while and affect other things?"

We all need the loving connection of God. Living in this world we are going to experience pain. Being connected to God through Jesus with the help of the Holy Spirit is what protects us when we experience pain. Being obedient means to deny self and depend totally on him. God is love, and we must give love to one another. In this way, we will receive love.

Remember to ask God for help (James 4:6). Know what you are responsible for, and turn those other things over to God. You can't save anyone. Jesus saves. Cast your worries on Him (1 Peter 5:7). Take one day at a time. Do not worry about tomorrow (Matthew 6:34). but "turn from evil and do good… seek peace and pursue it" (1 Peter 3:11 NIV).

PRAYER

Heavenly Father, I praise you and thank you for loving me. I thank you for your Son who died on the cross for my transgressions. I thank you for the Holy Spirit that dwells within me. Continue your work in me, for Lord, I know I am a work in process. Help me to stay focused on you and to do your will in all areas of my life. Help me to be obedient to your Word and be in fellowship with you and my fellow man. In the name of Jesus. Amen.

REFERENCES

Cloud, H. and J. Townsend. 1995. *Safe People.* Grand Rapids, MI: Zondervan.

Covey, S. R. 2004. *Seven Habits of Highly Effective People.* New York: Free Press.

Evans, Tony. 1999. *The Kingdom Agenda: What a Way to Live.* Nashville, TN: Word.

Jenkins, Brenda A. 2000. "Accepting Your Spiritual Heritage." Midwest Biblical Counseling Conference, Detroit.

Proud, Michael A. 2003. "Worship: A Picture of Intimacy with God: Part 2." http://www.thetrinitytouch.com/

Sanders, Oswald J. 1991. *Lonely But Never Alone*. Grand Rapids, MI: Radio Bible Class.

"The Daily Walk Calendar." 1993. Wheaton, IL: Tyndale Calendars.

PART 4
SOME SPECIAL ASPECTS
OF LEADERSHIP

YOUTH LEADERSHIP DEVELOPMENT IN THE BLACK CHURCH

Michael and Maria Westbrook

"Don't let anyone look down on you because you are young, but set an example for the believers in speech, in conduct, in love, in faith and in purity. Until I come, devote yourself to the public reading of Scripture, to preaching and to teaching. Do not neglect your gift, which was given you through prophecy when the body of elders laid their hands on you. Be diligent in these matters; give yourself wholly to them, so that everyone may see your progress. Watch your life and doctrine closely. Persevere in them, because if you do, you will save both yourself and your hearers" (1 Timothy 4:12–16 NIV).

INTRODUCTION AND FOCUS

We hope you will be inspired to look at your own experience—to reflect on the impact the Black church, or any church, has made in your life if, in fact, the church has been part of it. There were some tremendous examples that we were privileged to have, and many principles that we learned are being used in our own lives as we train others. Leadership development doesn't end once one is no longer a youth. The rite of passage(s) that we go through are reflected at constant stages of development. Youth leadership inspires our young when we refuse to forget what it felt like to be young... to celebrate them while shaping them into the people God has created them to be, just like someone did for us.

After all of the positions we've been privileged to serve in the Black church over the years, we can truly say that our hearts lean toward the youth within the church, along with outreach to the streets, to bring more into the church. Thanks, in advance, for taking this journey with us as we share what we've learned thus far—our "best practices" to encourage and inspire you to learn more about effective youth leadership development in order to accomplish God's mandate. For some, this may be a refresher course, while others it may be the first time you've heard some of this. No matter where this chapter finds you, *thank you* from the bottom of our hearts for allowing God to strengthen your youth leader development model in the Black church.

MICHAEL'S STORY

It was a Sunday morning in June: Youth Sunday at a local Baptist church. It was also the Sunday that the church celebrated Boy Scout Sunday. The youth were given various responsibilities in the church. After the opening, one of the scouts was responsible for one of the readings in the worship service. This seventeen-year-old scout, dressed in full uniform, stepped up to the lectern and delivered his reading. There was a little nervousness on his part, but he completed his task. As he went back to his seat to sit down, the pastor stood up in the pulpit and remarked to the congregation, "That was very good. One day that boy is going to be a preacher!" As my pastor, Rev. Hugh Jones, said those words, I remember thinking and chuckling to myself, "Not me!"

That event took place in 1975, almost forty years ago. Now here I stand as an ordained minister for over twenty years, having served in various ministry assignments, including as a vice-president of an international youth ministry, cofounding pastor of a mission-style church fellowship, and president/CEO/cofounder of a faith-based youth, family and community organization. It is apparent that those prophetic words of Rev. Jones were true.

As I look back over the journey that got me to the place I am at right now, I realized that it was my local church that prepared and equipped me for my life journey. It was that local Black Baptist church, through its formal and informal youth leadership development program, that paved the way for me to move to my next level of leadership.

MARIA'S STORY

What can be said about a little girl who believed in Jesus from the time she can remember? She loved Jesus, and enjoyed Sunday school, Bible study, the choir, and the preacher! Her mother sang like an angel, which inspired her to sing as well. There were several occasions that the church offered for youth to participate in Sunday evening youth services. This was a natural venue for this little girl to read Scriptures and sing in duets and choirs.

Through the years, her pastor and youth minister encouraged her to continue to "fall in love with Jesus" in word and in song. The example of leadership in the church inspired her, taught her, and walked alongside her. This little girl became a teenager and was taught to reach others through soul-winning classes and intentional outreach events and activities in order to develop as a leader and peer mentor. By now, surely you, the reader, realize that it was me! I was offered the greatest leadership development that anyone can ask for.

The Black church took what I learned and prepared me for public school: educationally and spiritually. It was the church who first taught me to read. It was the church that taught me to speak. It was the church that encouraged my gifts, talents, and abilities. It was the church where I saw leadership development and implementation as an intentional and deliberate process. Many did not even know just how much they were accomplishing, just how much they were inspiring me.

Now, I too, am a preacher of over twenty years, copastor and vice-president of administration and finance/cofounder, along with my awesome husband, who was hand-picked just for me! Besides preaching alongside him, I am also privileged to be a professional singer and performer. Thanks to the Black church for being faithful to God!

WHAT DOES YOUR CHURCH LOOK LIKE?

In order to impact youth the way we were impacted, there are a couple of questions that have to be addressed. Where do your youth come from? Do they come from the neighborhood or is it a commuter/regional church with youth coming from communities other than where your church is located? Assessing this determines how to most effectively operate your youth ministry, such as days and times of programming, along with leadership allocation and availability.

What types of youth do you have coming into your church? Are they youth who have grown up in the church all of their lives or are they "street kids" who are recent converts to Christ and have recently joined your ministry? Or have you been blessed with a ministry that has a mixture of all types of young people?

Henrietta Mears, Christian education director of the Hollywood Presbyterian Church and founder of Gospel Light Publications, started her amazing ministry teaching eleven eighteen-year-old girls in a small church in Minneapolis. The group of girls called themselves the snobs. Because of her dynamic teaching, the class soon grew to five hundred. After moving to California and to the Hollywood Presbyterian Church, her ministry influenced hundreds directly, and thousands indirectly, including Bill Bright of Campus Crusade for Christ and evangelist Billy Graham. This one person shaped the lives of future leaders of the church by staying true to her calling.

Whatever the group of youth you may be privileged to have, God has uniquely called you to be the one to train and equip them for His service. Just think within your group are future pastors, elders, deacons, leaders that will take their place in the church, society and the world.

WHERE ARE YOUR YOUTH TODAY?

All one has to do today is pick up a newspaper or listen to a news report on TV, and, unfortunately, there is article after article that involves African American young people in a negative situation. We also recognize the media tends to report the negative and the sensational, but, for some of us, it's not just what we read or hear, but what we have experienced as well—whether as a victim, or as the parent, or the loved one involved in negative behavior.

As chaplains for our local police department, we've have been privileged to ride in a radio car, which has included that saddening component of responding to homicide calls. We also have the opportunity to speak to a group of youth who are incarcerated at the county juvenile detention center. When first introduced to speak, there is always some talking and murmuring among the teenagers. On one occasion, we could just see on their faces that they were probably thinking, "Oh no! Here comes the sermon!" Noticing that, God had us go in a different direction. One of us started off saying, "I am a minister and sometimes ride in a police car." That draws an even louder response of "ooh!"s Going on, one of us would say, "Sometimes I am called to the scene of a homicide." That drew a bigger and louder response, with high-fives and snickering. Continuing on, we would say, "When I arrive on the scene, the body is still on the street." At this point there were even more responses from the young men and women. Speaking a little louder, the next thing said was, "I was not there for the victim lying on the street. In fact my job is to comfort that mother, those children, wife, girlfriend, and others, who are over on the side of the body crying uncontrollably because their loved one is lying over there with a sheet pulled up over them!" Now, at this point, it's so quiet you can hear a pin drop. It is obvious that we have struck a nerve because very few of them ever give thought about those that are left behind. It is at this point that they come face to face with a decision about their own destiny choices—hopefully life, and life in Christ—not in jail!

With this said, we realize that many kids today are trapped emotionally, socially, and psychologically. They are in what we call "survival mode." They live in a fast-paced, massive, and seemingly hopeless world. They feel insignificant, lonely, frustrated, and powerless. With crime, incarceration, poor education, and with unemployment rates way above the national average, for many of them it seems that there is no hope and the only answers lie in the streets. In addition, our youth have to contend with the tremendous negative influences of music, movies, television, the internet, and so-called friends. With all of this, they enter our churches, and God chooses us to reach, teach, and disciple them while He transforms them into new creations.

WHAT YOUTH NEED

As followers of Christ there are many things we bring to the table, including culture, language, baggage, fear, tension, and yes, prejudices. In light of this, we can offer the life-changing message of Jesus Christ as we accomplish ministry through relationship and lifestyle. Borgman (2004, 32) states that:

> Today we need holy youth ministers tested in the waters of contemporary culture. Many young people want to be heard and need to be appreciated. They will open up only to those who have come into their world. They will hear from only those who are present, learn only from those who love them. And the pain they feel!

Michael and Maria Westbrook

SOLUTION: YOU!

Webster's Dictionary (1987, 176) defines to "lead "as "to guide or con- duct by going first… to guide by influence… to act as a guide or director." Our youth need leaders that are committed, that are willing to enter their world, that will go the extra mile to overcome all types of obstacles to fulfill their mission. As has been stated (Westbrook 1998, 39–40):

> With all the news coming out in the media about our youth, even though somewhat depressing, there is no greater challenge for the church than to go out and reclaim our young people.

In addition, we have to do it with all the urgency we can muster. The kind of fervor I'm advocating can be found in the Gospels in the story of the paralytic. Just as those four men did not let anything stop them from bringing their paralyzed friend to the feet of Jesus, we, too, should have that desire for our young people who are caught in the negative forces of society.

EIGHT CHARACTERISTICS OF A YOUTH LEADER

In today's world, in spite of the constant barrage of negative behavior among leadership, the challenge is greater, now, more than ever before, to challenge leadership to biblical standards. In order to model Christlikeness before young people, these are some basic characteristics that we've identified.

TABLE 11.1. CHARACTERISTICS OF A YOUTH LEADER

Characteristic	Scripture	Result
Spirituality	2 Peter 3:18	Growing in the grace and knowledge of Jesus
Evangelism	Matthew 28:19–20	Intentional outreach
Respect for Authority	Hebrews 13:17	Obedience, submission, and accountability
Moral Purity	Ephesians 5:3	Free from immorality and sexual impurity
Physical Purity	1 Corinthians 3:16–17	Respecting the temple of God
Propriety	Romans 12:17	Respecting others
Responsibility	Ephesians 5:15	Walking in wisdom
Relational	Matthew 22:36–40	Love God, love kids

TEAM BUILDING AND REPRODUCING LEADERS

To have a strong, stable, and long-term leadership model within the context of the Black church that can effectively reach youth of today, there are four necessary steps that must be accomplished intentionally:

Choose Your Team

Jesus chose his disciples. While we should keep biblical standards in mind, it is important to remember that our disciples may not look like we expect. Remember what was said of David's followers in 1 Samuel 22:2 (KJV):

> And every one that was in distress, and every one that was in debt, and every one that was discontented, gathered themselves unto him; and he became a captain over them: and there were with him about four hundred men.

Motivate Your Team

Develop a relationship with leaders and potential leaders. Furthermore, it is critical to give them a vision or help them understand the task at hand.

Equip Your Team

One of the best things we can offer leadership is a model of healthy mentoring and modeling of the example we are challenging them to follow. Matthew 10:1–20 records the words of Jesus, teaching his disciples how to navigate various situations, and instructing them on how to respond to different circumstances and people they would come across in life. In order to effectively impact youth of today, we must empower leadership to be able to effectively do God's work.

Reproduce Others Like Yourself (Incarnation)

Order your life so you can produce a life in Christ in others (Galatians 4:19). Possess Christian character, fruit of the Spirit (Galatians 5:25). David produced mighty men of valor and Paul produced Timothy. So must we. We must allow the Holy Spirit to lead and sensitize our hearts continuously to be able to love youth, even when they are sometimes unlovable and don't smell so well or look so appealing. And we must not forget: Except for the grace of God, go we.

Michael and Maria Westbrook

ELEMENTS OF A GOOD YOUTH MINISTRY

In order to be most effective, the elements of a good youth ministry must consist of evangelism/outreach, worship, teaching/discipleship, fellowship, and service.

Necessary components should include incarnational agape love, servant leadership, development, and outcomes to make disciples!

Incarnational Ministry

The incarnational approach (based on John 1:1–5; 10–17 and John 4:1–10) is represented in John 4:4 (NIV), which is one of our favorite passages:

Now [Jesus] had to go through Samaria.

Just as Jesus purposed himself to go through Samaria, we made up our minds to go where young people congregated. We became visible on basketball courts and various streets in our target community where our church exists.

We must be willing to enter the world of a youth. It takes a lot of courage to do this, but the greatest examples are found in the life of Jesus. Time and time again, he went where people were to really make a difference with those who were considered outcasts in society, as many of our youth feel today. We are compelled by Christ to be light in a very dark world. Therefore, we can witness how to encourage and inspire youth to surrender their lives to Christ by our own example of outreach and to inspire them to also allow the light of Christ to shine in, and through, their lives. Furthermore, just as Jesus went through Samaria, we are compelled also to enter the world of youth in order to bring them "the living water."

Contact Work

There are various stages that the Black church can follow that will enhance the church's outreach component. We follow the example of the Great Commission (Matthew 28:19–20). Then we enter the world of a youth and/or parent. From there it is critical to listen to youth while earning and winning the right to be heard.

As the process of intentionalization takes place, we are able to reach what we call, "street kids, church kids, good kids, and bad kids." When we are present in their lives, we are able to "enflesh" Jesus to them. One of the greatest advantages that exist within the Black church is the opportunity to *serve* youth. It is an art that has been lost over the years, yet has the greatest opportunity to be reestablished! This is always a challenge for the congregation and other leadership to "wrap its arms around." Effective outreach and presentation of the gospel resulting in youth accepting Christ into their lives as Savior and as Lord, we have found produces youth that inspire others with the realness of their lifestyle turnaround. It is also at this point that we see the love, comfort, and guidance that the Holy Spirit gives us for them, offering the breakthrough that makes a difference in life choices and purpose for them and us.

Worship/Club/Program Event

In order to keep youth in the church, the focus must become more youth oriented. Youth must feel that there is a positive environment for them. Also, student involvement is essential in the planning and implementation of youth programs.

A serious presentation of the gospel should include an element of fun. For example, an icebreaker/skit/run-on is a good way to reach youth and draw them in a fun way to be prepared to receive the message. Also, music has always been a great way to present the gospel in song, encouraging reinforcement of God's Word.

Finally, it is important to offer a time of commitment for youth to formally accept Jesus into their heart and to allow Christ to have lordship in their lives.

ROLE OF THE BLACK CHURCH

In addition to strong leaders that pour their lives into youth, there is also a need for strong institutions to provide the support, training, and modeling that is needed by African American youth. We have read where many of our contemporaries have been critical of the Black church regarding its retention and seemingly disinterest in the plight of our youth. It is true that when you look at a large number of African American congregations, you will find young people over the age of fifteen, especially black males, missing in action. In fact, the National Black Church Initiative, which is a consortium of denominations, has made reaching out and retaining black males a national priority for the next five years as of this writing (http://www.naltblackchurch.com/mentochurch.html).

Michael and Maria Westbrook

As advocates of the Black church, and as products of its ministry that was stated earlier in this chapter by both us, while reaching out we also know that the Black church needs to "go back to the old landmark" and use the principles of yesteryear to raise this current group of up-and-coming African American youth.

The Black church has always been a major source of leadership development for our communities. Many of our leaders in all walks of life, whether business, education, the sciences, government, or even religion, can trace their development back to the Black church. All of those individuals, including ourselves, were taught some of the same basic principles. For example, we learned:

- Power of Influence, Discipleship/Mentoring/Apprenticeship
- Vision-Casting
- Public Speaking
- Sacrifice and Service to Others
- Perseverance in Extreme Situations
- Financial Stewardship and Education
- Problem Solving
- Character Development
- Relational Skills
- Fulfilling Responsibilities

All of the above principles have been important, and still are, for the development of African American young people to help them reach the next level in life. It also helps them navigate life's difficult challenges as African American people. For example, when Michael was first elevated to a national position in a large international youth ministry, he was asked to attend a reception for new board members. There were current board members present that were considered to be very important individuals in attendance. After a time of informal mingling and small talk, the formal portion of the afternoon was about to begin, and at the beginning, there was an expectation of the new people around the table, which included new board members and those appointed to new positions, to introduce themselves and speak briefly about who they were and where they had come from. Prior to the session beginning, a subordinate of the chief executive pulled Michael to the side and advised him to only say his name and introduce the person next to him, who happened to be a Latino brother. What this person was indirectly saying was that he didn't think Michael had the ability to speak publicly. Michael didn't know where he got that idea because up to that point they had not spent any length of time together.

As God would have it, when the introductions began, the chief executive decided to have introductions begin in an opposite direction to the expectation of the subordinate. This meant that the person originally intended to be introduced spoke *before* Michael. He hesitated and stumbled in his attempt to address the group. When it was Michael's turn, he was able to spend the next five minutes allotted not only speaking about himself, but also addressing a number of the board members that Michael and Maria personally knew from previous contacts. At the conclusion of the event, the same subordinate rushed up to Michael and asked, "Where did you learn to speak so well?" Michael flippantly remarked, "At church!" And walked away, savoring his victory.

Unbeknownst to this gentleman, Michael had a foundation of many hours of Easter speeches that had been memorized and presented over many years, the Youth Sundays where he had been asked to stand up and publicly carry out some portion of the service, the times in Sunday school when he was read to and had to read out loud himself, or those Sunday-school teachers as they taught us lessons from the Bible. All of those things Michael learned from youth in his African American congregation are what made the board meeting moment possible, along with numerous others.

Another example is reflected by an experience that Maria had in college. One time, when Michael was asked to preach his first sermon for a chapel service (the first Black man to preach in the pulpit of the chapel at our college in Iowa in 1981), he asked Maria to sing a solo prior to his message. The service was a normally established sequence of events, from the prayer, to Scripture reading, to choir singing, etc. Many did not know that Maria had the ability to not only sing, but also to present herself well on stage, including a new professor. She had arrived one month prior at the college to specialize in training vocalists professionally, and soon after Maria excitedly approached her for personal voice lessons! This professor looked at Maria and assumed that she couldn't sing. You see, Maria had just overcome laryngitis. The professor brushed her off and went about her business. Since Maria had been singing since childhood, under the tremendous leadership of great musicians and choir directors at her Black church, she was taught well as an African

American how to care for her voice and quickly overcome laryngitis. So soon after speaking to this professor, she was at peak performance!

The day approached for her to sing for Michael's chapel service, and she sang "It Is Well with My Soul" like an angel, as Michael later stated. Well, this same professor who had ignored Maria's request just weeks prior, "leaped over the pews" as Michael put it, and not only complimented Maria on her singing, but also asked her to come to her office the following morning, where she offered her free singing lessons (tuition free!). Of course, the professor asked, "where did you learn to sing like that?" Maria humbly responded, "at church," and walked away praising God!

As you can see, the principles that were taught to both of us as youth through the Black church, served us well later in life. Here are the ministries that were used to help teach us, and many others, the principles that propelled us forward:

- Sunday school—gave a foundation in the Word of God, with opportunities to read it out loud

- Easter speeches—learned memorization and public speaking

- Youth choir—taught that everyone had something to contribute, regardless of ability

- Junior officers—assumed leadership roles and were mentored by adults

- Soul-winning class—learned to convey God's love to others

- Youth Bible Study—learned how to apply the word of God to our lives

- Youth/young adult group—learned to socialize as Christians with one another

CONCLUSION

When it comes to the Black church, few have ever been able to effectively, consistently, intentionally, professionally, and with longevity, produce more quality leaders while instilling life-changing principles. Yet one of the greatest challenges in the twenty-first century is the neglect of youth by the Black church.

It is our hope that this overview has inspired and encouraged a new, and or, renewed vigor to step up our youth development and youth leadership development. Yes, we must do it intentionally, all the while remembering that we need to "go back to the old landmarks" and refresh ourselves on the principles of what worked "back then" and simply bring those principles into a "current state of mind," which is the premise of what we do in our own Black church, and attempted to communicate in this writing.

Therefore, both the older and younger members of the church will experience a much more effective and impactful outcome!

Our youth are waiting on us—let's allow them opportunities to learn and grow so that we may tell them just like our pastors and youth leaders did, "One day you are going to be a preacher!" "You are going to fall in love with Jesus." And we both did!

REFERENCES

Borgman, D. 2004. *When Kumbaya is Not Enough: A Practical Theology for Youth Ministry*. Peabody, MA: Hendrickson Publishers.

National Baptist Action Network, http://www.naltblackchurch.com/mento-church.html.

New Concise Webster's Dictionary. Revised Edition. 1987. New York: Modern Publishing.

Westbook, M. T. 1998. "Reaching and Nurturing African American Youth. "Chapter 4 in Parker, M. and Seals, E., *Planting Seeds of Hope: How to Reach a New Generation of African Americans with the Gospel*. Chicago/Detroit: Moody Press/Institute of Black Family Development 39–51.

Chapter 12

CONSECRATED WOMEN: FREEDOM TO LEAD BY FAITH

Patricia Robinson Williams and Shirley Spencer June

The concept of God's creative purpose for women has been a perplexing issue in the Christian community, in general; and this issue has also been of particular concern in the African American community. This is evident by the numerous books that have been written on this general topic, even in recent years (see, for example, Grenz and Kjesbo 1995; Sumner 2003; Gundry and Beck 2005; Kostenberger and Schreiner 2005; and Boyd and Eddy 2009, chapter 15). Within the African American community, several books and chapters have also addressed this topic, some of which are referenced later.

What really was God's intention when he, by wisdom, created humankind? How did he design this intent to be modeled in the earth? And what is God's proposed blueprint for the use of women in the causes of his kingdom? Issues relative to each of these questions can initiate an endless debate. Since there is so much variance in thought concerning this topic, the discussion that follows seeks clarity from the Word of God. As such, the chapter proceeds by opening the canon of the Word of God, examining key passages on the topic of women in spiritual leadership and unveiling examples of women in functional roles as leaders in the biblical record. During the latter survey, biblical presentation and analysis, attention is devoted to God's particular use of women in leadership within the progressive unfolding and manifestation of his salvation plan and the origination of the church. This survey serves as a means of uncovering God's divinely directed and openly orchestrated leadership profiles for women. The profiles, in turn, present a foundational perspective toward discussion of God's design and purposeful use of women in leadership. Pursuant to the biblical/historical survey and analysis, the experiences and perspectives of African American women are presented, with special emphasis on anecdotal information from the authors of this chapter, both of whom serve in spiritual leadership roles. Without doubt, this discussion does not resolve the controversy surrounding God's divine plan, purpose, and permission for the role of women in Christian leadership, but it proposes to offer substantive information for reflection and further examination.

Accordingly, the intent of this work is to glorify God, to provide a tool to foster spiritual reflection and growth, promote unity in the body of Christ, and move toward eliminating roadblocks that hinder effectiveness, personal growth, character formation, and responsible stewardship to and in the body of Christ and her calling to the world.

Admittedly, the underlying question/problem that makes a project like this necessary is that there is a deep divide around the issues of spiritual leadership, mostly on questions of headship and order. While it is not the intent and purpose of this work to try to resolve those issues, it does purport to acknowledge some of the attendant contentions. The primary intent of the work, however, is to stay focused on "What does authentic, God-ordained leadership look like, and how do women proceed, recognizing gifts and callings, and reflecting God's image in the world?"

THE CONSECRATED CREATION

"In the beginning God...." Genesis 1:1 (NIV) opens the written record of God's self-revelation—His divine power and mighty acts, his righteous character, and His ways. In these opening words of the written record of God's revelation, one thing is evident: God exists, and in the words that follow, God establishes claim to all else that exists, all creation, a claim made throughout Scripture, as in Psalm 24:1 or the Nehemiah passage included below. It might seem an unlikely place to start an analysis of the development of women in leadership, but is fitting because of the integral part it has in God's overall plan for humanity and the world. God claims leadership and ownership over

Patricia Robinson Williams and Shirley Spencer June

everything—from before the first Adam to and through the work and reign of the last Adam, the Lord Jesus Christ. God, in his sovereignty, goodness, and love, acts in power, order, authority, and purpose.

	TABLE 12.1. CREATION—WHAT GOD DID					
God's Creation Activity				**God's Creation Activity**		
1:1	God created	P1		1:18	God saw	A
1:2	Spirit of God moved	P1		1:20	God said	A
1:3	God said	A		1:21	God created…God saw	A
1:6	God saw…God separated…God called…He called	A	"Blessed be your glorious name, and may it be exalted above all blessing and praise. You alone are the LORD, You made the heavens, even the highest heavens, and all their starry host, the earth and all that is in it, the seas and all that is in them, You give life to everything and the multitudes in heaven worship You." Nehemiah 9:5c–6 (NIV)	1:22	God blessed	A/P2
1:7	God made	A/O		1:24	God said	A/P2
1:8	God called	A/O		1:25	God made…God saw	P1
1:9	God said	A/O		1:26	God said	P1/P2
1:10	God called…He called	A		1:27	God created…He created…He created	P1/P2
1:11	God said	A/P2		1:28	God blessed…God said	P1/P2
1:12	God saw	O/P2		1:29	God said	P1/P2
1:14	God said	A/O		1:30	I have given	P2
1:16	God made…He made	P1		1:31	God saw/He had made	O
1:17	God set	A/O				
A=Authority; O=Order; P1=Power; P2=Purpose						

Patricia Robinson Williams and Shirley Spencer June

The specific focus of this discussion is God's creative purpose for humankind. What really was God's intention when he, by wisdom, created humankind? God created humankind, male and female, based on a principle of unity; and it appears with unified purposes. An examination of the passages in the Creation narrative reveals this claim. Focusing on Genesis 1:27 (NIV), the Word of God states:

> So God created man in his own image, in the image of God he created them; male and female he created them.

Divine causation is the obvious force in the stated act in the text; God himself causes humankind to exist. The movement of thought in the text demonstrates three outcomes in the creative process. Through his power, God causes mankind to exist; and by design God implants his blueprint in humankind. Then, God further specifies his creation by decreeing two types of the same kind. Furthermore, the grammar of the action in the verb tense, as presented in the New International Version (2011), signifies an act completed [perfected] with the permission of an eternally present God:

> Let us make mankind in our image, in our likeness, so that they may rule over the fish in the sea and the birds in the sky, over the livestock and all the wild animals, and over all the creatures that move along the ground (Genesis 1:26, NIV).

This original decree unfolds the will of God in the eternal present and invites further examination with respect to the immutability and unchangeableness of God. That is, God is and always has been; and he is unchangeable. Consequently, the eternal, unchangeableness of God is essential to an understanding of his will, intent, and creative purposes for humankind, generally, and for women particularly. For purposes of the exegetical examination of Scripture, therefore, the "grammar" of the claims asserted as actions will constitute declarative points. God does not change; and "He is exalted above the processes of history and the determinative compulsions of the human race" (Daane 1991, 943). Thus, the first thought for consideration is that God assigned both genders of humankind to jointly rule or govern his creation, which is certainly a command that requires unity. It seems that he decides that both are capable of this stewardship responsibility.

Subsequently, God intentionally and purposefully "blessed" them and said to them:

> Be fruitful and increase in number; fill the earth and subdue it. Rule over the fish in the sea and the birds in the sky and over every living creature that moves on the ground (Genesis 1:28 NIV).

Again, the movement in the grammar of the action in the text follows a pattern—from the causation or completion of action to the habitual permission. When God creates humankind, it is his eternal intention to assign stewardship of perpetuating His image through them—"Be fruitful and increase in number." This is a second part of God's unification plan for humankind in his world. Again, God expresses his intent in the habitual, ongoing form of the verb—"Be fruitful," not they *were fruitful* and *multiplied.*

From these unification concepts of humanity, God creates a covenant provision that unites them in flesh and spirit. Again, God's action reflects His immutability; that is, he establishes that which will not change.

> The Lord God said, "It is not good for the man to be alone. I will make a helper suitable for him" (Genesis 2:18 NIV).

God establishes the fact that man requires a suitable helper, but that helper is one that God creates from him. Moreover, how God creates the helper further confirms His unity principle, for the helper is created from the man and, by God's wisdom, is of the same created matter as he. Following this action, God pronounces the marriage covenant:

> For this reason [she was taken out of man; thus, she is *of* him] a man will leave [separate from] his father and mother and be united to his wife, and they will become one flesh" (Genesis 2:24 NIV 1984).

Conclusively, God ordains another unity principle, covenant union, with this declaration. The unchangeable God decrees joint stewardship of his creation to male and female with his divine command for them to increase in number, create humankind and with his will for them to become one flesh in marriage or, as the prophet Malachi queries: "Has not [the LORD] made them one?" (Malachi 2:15a NIV 1984). These principles of unity suggest God's creative design and unification of function for male and female over his creation, with respect to perpetuation of his image in procreation and with respect to relational unity in marriage. The question that is implied in some considerations of the contemporary positions on God-intended roles for humankind is whether there is a shift after the fall of humankind.

Following the fall of humankind, the eating of the forbidden fruit, God provides a pronouncement of judgment due to the sin of disobedience. His judgment sentences Adam to painful toil (Genesis 3:17) and Eve to painful childbearing (Genesis 3:16). Again, the concept is centered in the sense of the declaration in the verb tense. These actions are acts of God's will. The New International Version uses "will" four times in verse sixteen as God addresses Eve; and "will" is used five times in verses seventeen through nineteen as God addresses Adam. Eve is also warned that she will "war" with her husband, as her desire shall be for him [his functional role as leader] (verse 16); and Adam is sentenced to a life of endless labor (verse 19). It is important to note that God is free to assume whatever characteristics he desires. In other words, he can establish circumstances that affect in ways that are not habitually his nature. One scholar suggests that "God is free to become the Creator. In becoming so, he does not cease to be the eternal God; his act of creating mankind and the world neither violates nor compromises his nature as the eternal unchangeable God" (Daane 1991, 943). This means essentially that God, the preexistent One, decides to reenact that which he had already brought into being. This creative reenactment and intervention in behalf of his righteousness and holiness, instead, was necessary to remediate man's sin state. If God had chosen to remain aloof to the disobedience, then humankind would still be lost in sin.

Essentially, it is God's plan to save humankind that redeems and restores all Adams and Eves. And how does this holy design reflect God's original intent for the functional role of women in his plans and purposes for humanity in the earth? Since leading and ruling ("he will rule over you") are associated concepts, a differentiation needs to be made between the meanings of the two. "Rule" is normally used to indicate one's power over another, while "lead" indicates one's guidance of another. Both roles require subjugation to the one who is serving in the "head" position. There is yet another attendant concept, which is generally accepted as inclusive of all the redeemed. This is the concept, "reign." The Word of God declares that "if we endure, we will also reign with him" (2 Timothy 2:12a NIV). "Reign with" is a two-part verb and signifies co-rule or to jointly have power over. In salvation, then, it appears that all are rulers, regardless of gender. Thus, the declaration in God's Word proposes a kingdom reality that certainly reflects how Jesus taught his disciples to pray: "your kingdom come, your will be done, on earth as it is in heaven" (Matthew 6:10 NIV). If it is God's desire for all to reign with him in heaven, then the sentence of the husband's functioning as ruler in the marriage covenant does not preclude God's holding to his salvific posture and allowing all to lead in the earth. God's salvific posture is a benefit that comes through faith. Most assuredly, there is evidence that when repentance, through faith, and obedience exist, God sets aside his punitive decision, as he did with the Ninevites (see Jonah 3:10). Could it be, then, that women of redemptive grace and faith, stand free of the penalty of a fallen Eve and are restored to God's original stewardship charge in leadership?—"Rule over the fish of the sea and the birds of the air...." (Genesis 1:28c NIV 1984).

THE TEMPTING TESTS

How, then, does the concept—"to rule"—fit with New Testament teaching and the role of women in Christian leadership? Two of the significant expositions on the topic of functional leadership roles of women, which also expose temptations and tests, are examined for reflections in response to this question. The first of these is 1 Corinthians 11:3–12, and the second is 1 Timothy 2:11–15.

Rules of discourse analysis are chosen to dissect the content in these passages. The 1 Corinthians passage is concerning propriety, the positional and functional roles of humankind, and how these apply in worship. The main point is the "order," decorum in worship. Causation in creation defines positional role, but not necessarily exclusivity in functional role. This point commences in the headship hierarchy as it is prescribed in verse three, but it also alludes to the temptation God proposes would be Eve's test (Genesis 3:16)

> Now I want you to realize that the head of every man is Christ, and the head of the woman is man, and the head of Christ is God (1 Corinthians 11:3 NIV 1984).

God permitted the Incarnate Word (Jesus) to enter the world; Jesus, who was among the "let us" in creation, created man; and woman receives her material existence from man. Consequently, the positional hierarchy, in correspondence with order of creation for earthly existence, begins with God in the topmost position; then Christ, the Incarnate Word; followed by man and, finally, woman. These positional statuses, however, do not negate shared spiritual leadership for men and woman in the worship assembly. Each can pray and prophesy; that is, each can serve in roles of spiritual leadership in worship (1 Corinthians 11:4–5). The concern in this passage seems to focus the propriety or appropriateness in representation of the position in Christ [faith status] and the image of God in created order. The evidence in the pericope supports this idea, for verse seven indicates that "A man ought not to cover his head, since he is the image and glory of God; but woman is the glory of man" (1 Corinthians 11:7 NIV). This is profoundly revealing of the order of creation: man being the initial representation of humanity carries the totality of the *imago Dei*; and woman is formed from him, so that she is the fruit from man, also of the *imago Dei*. Man, however, is her covering, and she is his [man's] glory. These thoughts support the concept of appropriate representation of God's created order and, accordingly, serve as a foundation for presentation of oneself in spiritual leadership. Since God created humankind to hold joint stewardship over all he spoke into existence and since he is immutable (unchangeable), it is unlikely that he would revoke his intentions, except in instances of a lack of penitence. Accordingly, it seems that penitent women, who are, indeed, women of faith, still have the privilege of God's original purpose. The test, however, is the temptation to compete by attempting to mimic the presentation and representation of the male.

Likewise, the 1 Timothy 2 passage addresses propriety. This pericope is often viewed as problematic, and women sometimes find it offensive. Careful observation of the structure and terms in this passage, however, proves fruitful.

> A woman should learn in quietness and full submission. I do not permit a woman to teach or to have authority over a man; she must be silent. For Adam was formed first, then Eve. And Adam was not the one deceived; it was the woman who was deceived and became a sinner. But women will be saved through childbearing—if they continue in faith, love and holiness with propriety (1 Timothy 2:11–15 NIV 1984).

Patricia Robinson Williams and Shirley Spencer June

An examination of the meanings of "quietness/silent" (verses 11–12); "teach" and "authority" (verse 12) proves useful. God knows explicitly the nature of his people, and he is aware of customs, traditions, and mores prior to their manifestations. It is therefore wise to view his Word as a representation of essential principles that reflect his holiness, his love, and his justice. The passage in 1 Timothy 2:11–15 is no less reflective of God's character.

The term translated "quiet/silent" (*hesūchia*) means "stillness," "keeping one's seat," "desistance from bustle," which is excited and noisy activity (Strong 1996, and Thomas 1981). From these same sources, "authority" (*authenteo*) means to act in accordance with one's own permission or to govern. The most curious of these terms is "teach," for there are a number of words in the Greek language for this term. The term used in 1 Timothy 2:12 is *didaskō*, which means "to instruct in the law." Granted, the Law constitutes a portion of God's Word; but the reference here is to specialized teaching relegated to those who were among the learned, which in itself excluded women of the first-century church.

Looking at the structure of the 1 Timothy 2 passage, a significant point culminates the passage—women are to continue in faith, love, and holiness with propriety (verse 15b). Furthermore, the thoughts in this passage suggest that God, in his righteousness, is providing protective guidelines for the women of the early church, a shield from the harm of temptation. He does not deny them their privilege, however, to reflect qualities of spiritual leadership in their deportment—penitence and reverence, consistent focus and purpose, as they continue in faith, love, and holiness. The latter three behaviors illustrate the leadership of the Holy Spirit and demonstrate human character as reflective of the image of God and appropriate for leadership.

Thus far, observations have been unveiled concerning key canonical periscopes concerning God's creation of woman, with attempts to provide observations on created position and consecrated function. To further examine these observations, a survey of the actual use of women in spiritual leadership, as found in the Word of God, with respect to the progressive unfolding and manifestation of the salvation plan follows.

THE DIVINE DEVELOPMENT: GOD'S USE OF WOMEN

Fish and fowl had assignments upon their creation: to be fruitful, to multiply, and to fill their domains (Genesis 1:22). Humans, however, received a more extensive mandate (Genesis 1:26–28). As image bearers of God, they were to "be fruitful, multiply, replenish the earth, and subdue it, and have dominion" over the rest of God's creation.

Not only did God ascribe joint responsibility, along with the male, to the female; but, also, in salvation history, God has strategically used women, along with men, at critical times to maintain and carry out his plans and purposes for humanity, nations, and peoples. In these interactions can be seen something of the character, plan, purpose, provision, and protection of God. These acts of God are moreover apparent in the birth of humanity, in the birth and preservation of a people through whom God would bless the whole world, and in the establishment and growth of the early church. In interactions involving and surrounding these leaders, more evidence surfaces of the character, ways, and dealings of God, and his unfolding plan of salvation for all of humanity.

SPIRITUAL LEADERSHIP ROLES OF WOMEN

Utilizing classic biblical concepts of leadership found in the table below, the observations that follow provide an analysis of God's use of women in consecrated leadership roles in the progressive unfolding of his salvation plan. Formed from ideas of Nehemiah's leadership skills in the Old Testament canon, the table aims to define qualities and attributes of the spiritual leader.

TABLE 12.2. BIBLICAL CONCEPTS OF LEADERSHIP

Types	Traits	Scripture—Nehemiah
Leadership 1	Penitent and Reverent	1:5–11; 5:15c
Leadership 2	Consistently Prays	1:4–11; 2:4b; 4:4–5, 9; 6:9c, 14
Leadership 3	Discrete	2:12–16
Leadership 4	Tenacious in the Face of Opposition	2:18–19
Leadership 5	Constantly Depends on God	4:14b, 20
Leadership 6	Wise and Discerning	6:8–9, 11–12
Leadership 7	Focused and Purposeful	2:8b; 5:16; 6:3–4

With these attributes from the table above as a conceptual framework, we note the spiritual roles of women in the progressive unfolding of God's salvation plan. Such analysis encompasses the involvement of women in the unveiling of plans for the divine revelation, incarnation, crucifixion, resurrection, and redemption.

First Woman

Eve. This is the third name given to the first woman.

When she was created and brought to the first man, he named her "woman" to indicate that she was taken from man, made of the same bone and flesh, and therefore able to become his partner, and to become one flesh with him (Genesis 2:23). This was her second name.

Her first name was given to her by God. It is the same name given to the first man. Together they are called '$\bar{a}d\bar{a}m$ ("man," "mankind"), created by God in his own image, to be fruitful, to fill the earth, and to rule over all living creatures (Genesis 1:26–28).

Together, male and female, in God's image (Genesis 1:27), they were blessed and told to multiply, fill the earth, subdue it, and have dominion over the rest of God's creatures on earth (Genesis 1:28). Eve misappropriated the leadership quality—tenacity—and thereby created a sin factor that opposed God's divinely ordained plan for all humanity (Rienstra 1992, 204–5).

Preservation of a People

The Israelites were enduring cruel bondage as slaves in Egypt. God engineers their entrance there as refuge from the famine in Canaan by sending Joseph ahead of them, who becomes second in command to Pharaoh. Valuing the Hebrews as a labor force, the Pharaoh seeks to devise plans to ensure their continued enslavement and render them incapable of defense. Thusly, he orders Hebrew midwives to destroy male infants at birth, but to allow the daughters to live.

During this perilous time for a nation, God's strategic use of women in the continued preservation of a nation is seen through the decisive action of two Hebrew midwives, Shiphrah and Puah, as they courageously defy the orders of Pharaoh, in order to save the lives of Hebrew boys against the sinister plot to ravage a nation by destroying the newborn males (Exodus 1:15–21). It is because of their reverential fear of God (Exodus 1:17, 21), characteristic of consecrated spiritual leadership, and their tenacity in the face of opposition, that the midwives are able to make the right decision and stay focused on the goal of preserving the babies' lives. Because they feared and honored God, he rewarded them by giving them their own families.

A second plot to kill all the Hebrew boys, by discarding them in the Nile River, emerges. Again, God has a different plan, which preserves the life of Moses whom God uses in delivering the Israelites as he had promised Abram he would do. Moses' sister, Miriam, is one of those God uses as he preserves Moses's life, and later during their wilderness journey after leaving Egypt. As a young girl, Miriam follows her mother Jochebed's instructions and helps execute the plans to save Moses's life. Discreet in interactions with Pharaoh's daughter, she is able to arrange for Moses's mother to care for him for Pharaoh's daughter. In Hebrews 11, Moses (v. 24–29) and his parents (v. 23) are commended for their faith and responses to God. Admittedly, Miriam's critical attitude regarding Moses's wife reflects thinking that results in negative leadership.

Deborah, noted in Judges 4:4, is recorded as a prophetess, wife, and a judge. As a prophetess, Deborah listens to the voice of God and does what God says. Therefore, a great victory is accomplished on behalf of the people of God. Deborah is involved in at least three different realms in the life of Israel: the religious life (as a prophetess); the social/familial life (as a wife); and in the civic/political life (as a judge of Israel). A typical role for a woman? Perhaps not. Her courage shines in the midst of difficulty, not in midst of ease. Specific references to Deborah in Scripture occur in Judges 4–5. Chapter 4 records the context of the story, while chapter 5 includes the song of victory sung by Barak and Deborah after the Lord had given them great triumph over their enemies in battle, primarily utilizing Deborah's wise and discerning leadership in following God's directive.

Another example of God's preservation of his chosen people through women in spiritual leadership is seen through the contributions of Esther during the time of the Persian Empire, when there was a plot to annihilate all Jews in an area that extended from India to Ethiopia, and included 127 provinces (Esther 1:1). Mordecai, a Jewish man from the tribe of Benjamin is exiled to Babylon by Nebuchadnezzar, along with the Judean king and others. Mordecai rears his young cousin, Esther. Esther is a beautiful young Jewish girl who comes to the throne through unusual circumstances. She is one of several young women brought to the palace of Susa to be groomed and prepared for the King Xerxes to select to become his bride and the queen. Esther is chosen from among all the other young women and selected to become queen, replacing Queen Vashti who had been removed from the throne. In the meantime, the day comes when Esther has to risk all she has, in the interest of saving her people from slaughter. Her resolute determination to intervene on behalf of her people is shown in her plea for a three-day fast, accompanied by consistent prayer, and her promise and pronouncement:

> When this is done, I will go to the king, even though it is against the law.
> And if I perish, I perish (Esther 4:16 NIV).

God honors Esther's prayerful reverence and penitent attitude and grants the safety of her people. She leads through modeling prayer and reverence for God.

The Family through Whom Messiah Would Be Born

Another illustration of spiritual leadership is found in the choice of a family through whom God would bring the Messiah. Naomi and Ruth, two women who lived during the same period as the judges (Ruth 1:1), both experience personal tragedy and loss of husbands, and face new and major life challenges. Naomi leaves her home in Bethlehem in Judah, which is experiencing a famine, with her husband and two sons, and journeys to the country of Moab, in search of food, expecting no doubt better living circumstances than those in Bethlehem. Some years later, after the death of her husband and sons in Moab, she learns of God's blessing his people in her home country by "giving them food." Naomi decides to return and is accompanied by devoted daughter-in-law Ruth, of the land and people of Moab. Naomi considers it inappropriate for her daughter-in-law to follow her in this uncertain venture:

> But Ruth replied. "Don't urge me to leave you or turn back from you. Where you go I will go, and where you stay I will stay. Your people will be my people and your God my God. Where you die I will die and there I will be buried" (Ruth 1:16–17a NIV).

Ruth makes a lifelong choice to accept, follow, and depend on Naomi's God, people, and land. She is focused and purposeful. This story is largely recorded in the book of Ruth, though Ruth also appears in the New Testament, in the genealogy of the Lord Jesus Christ (Matthew 1).

Birth of the Savior and Deliverer

Further revelation of God's use of women in the progressive unfolding of His salvation plan is disclosed in the use of Mary as the birth mother of the Christ child. The prophet Isaiah declares:

> Therefore the Lord himself will give you a sign: The virgin will conceive
> and give birth to a son, and will call him Immanuel (Isaiah 7:14 NIV).

Mary, a young virgin maiden, is pledged to be married to Joseph. Meanwhile she is found to be pregnant through the Spirit's power and grace. The virgin, not only gives birth, but she gives birth to a male child. Mary's willingness to reverently obey God positions her as a spiritual role model, leader, in his plan to save all humankind.

Life and Growth of the Early Church

The contributions of women in the life of the early church also demonstrate God's divine appointment and use of them in leadership. Women like the Samaritan woman, Lydia, Priscilla, and Phoebe are prime examples.

Lydia is mentioned in Acts 16:14 as a dealer in purple cloth from the city of Thyatira, one who worshipped God, whose heart God has opened such that she listens and receives the gospel Paul preaches. She and members of her household are baptized. As a "seller of purple," she is perhaps a woman of means since she is a trader of expensive goods, and has sufficient housing to host the Apostle Paul during his campaign in the region. Lydia takes the initiative to invite him to lodge at her home. Ben Witherington (1992, 423) notes Lydia's pioneering role:

> While Lydia could not be a founding member of a Jewish synagogue, she
> can be and is, the first European convert to Christendom, and in fact is the
> founding member of the Christian community which begins to meet in her
> household.

God is the real initiator. He opens Lydia's heart to receive the truth to build on what she already knows and to show acts of love and hospitality to the apostles. With Lydia, as with us, this is a powerful reminder that salvation and the works that follow issue from God's goodness, grace, and love. God could have used anyone. In his providence, wisdom, and love, he chooses to use this woman Lydia from Thyatira to model reverence for him; thereby she serves as a leader in the salvation of her entire household.

In the closing part of his letter to the Romans, the Apostle Paul writes:

> I commend to you our sister Phoebe, a servant of the church at Cenchrea. I ask you to receive her in the Lord in a way worthy of the saints and to give her any help she may need from you, for she has been a great help to many people, including me (Romans 16:1–2 NIV 1984).

It is believed that Phoebe was the carrier for the letter to the Romans from Paul. He asks that she receive accommodation and assistance in whatever way she might need. That Phoebe was a prominent figure in the church at Cenchrea seems not to be at issue. Her valuable service and obvious reverence for God is expressed in Paul's testimony about her work and service to the church and to himself as well. What seems to be the matter of debate is the nature of her role.

Gillman notes that Paul described Phoebe using three titles: *adelphē,* "sister"; *diakonos,* "deacon"; and *prostatis,* "patroness" (1992, 348). He takes issue with describing, as some do, Phoebe's role as less than that of male counterparts who helped Paul in the gospel ministry.

Still another example of God's use of women as servant leaders in the early church is found in the role of Priscilla. She and her husband, Aquila, hosted a church in their home (Acts 16:19). Paul acknowledged them as his fellow workers in Christ who had endangered their lives in service to the gospel and him, for which all the Gentile churches were grateful. In the Acts 18 account, Aquila and Priscilla enlightened Apollos, one "eloquent and mighty" in the Scriptures, instructing him more completely in the gospel of Christ. One of the spiritual gifts for the teacher is wisdom. Could it be that Priscilla was also a woman of wisdom?

Several other New Testament women may not have been named, or may not have been written about extensively, but their contributions are critical in the spread of the gospel. The Samaritan woman, for example, in John 4, responds to Jesus's revelation to her of his identity as Messiah, spreads news of Jesus to the Samaritans, and urges others to come see Jesus, with report of her encounter with the one who "told me everything I ever did," questioning "Could this be the Christ?" John the gospel writer notes the overwhelming response by Samaritans (John 4:29 NIV 1984).

In the letter to the church at Philippi, Euodia and Syntyche are noted by Paul as helpers with Paul in the gospel ministry, though later they seem in conflict with each other. Paul pleads with them to do what it is possible for them to do: "be of the same mind in the Lord" (Philippians 4:2 NKJV). Eunice and Lois instruct Timothy in the Scriptures (2 Timothy 1:5; 3:15). Because of their leadership in focused, purposeful godly instruction in the home, Paul is able to remind Timothy that he has learned these vital truths from them as a young child. Paul later directs Timothy to teach faithful men what he (Paul) has taught him that the gospel might continue to spread and produce fruit (2 Timothy: 2:2).

The leadership traits the foregoing women display are listed in the table that follows. Without doubt, what keeps these women focused is their reverence for God, their focus in the face of opposition, their trust, their faith in God, and their consistent reliance on God demonstrated in their willingness to wait for God's plan to manifest. Sarah (Hebrews 11:11) and Rahab (Hebrews 11:31) are recorded among those specifically acclaimed for their faith. Anna, a prophetess who constantly prays and fasts, is rewarded as she witnesses the coming of the Christ (Luke 2:36). When there are grave errors in functions as leaders, a lack of reverence for God, and disobedience to his plan and purpose, these should be good starting points for examination. Eve's and Adam's rebellion and Miriam's personal claim of authority equal to that allotted to Moses reflect a refusal to honor God's known will, choosing rather to follow a personal and deviant agenda and plan. Paul's urging Euodia and Syntyche to "be of the same mind in the Lord" implies that these women, at that time, were also not letting the Spirit control their work and service. It is the intent of the latter sections of this work to demonstrate that God's proclaimed plan is to generate purposeful privileges for all who choose the way of unrelenting faith in him.

For further reflection on women in different roles, see such sources as Lockyer (1995) and del Mastro (2004). For a more African-centered approach to the Bible, including the role of women, see Adeyemo (2006).

THE PROCLAIMED PLAN

Edwards (1991, 1095) cites Galatians 3:25–29 as "the Magna Carta of humanity." This passage, beginning with verse 23, however, is even more valuable contextually.

TABLE 12.3. LEADERSHIP SKILLS OF GOD'S CHOSEN WOMEN		
Leadership L1 – L7	Women in Scripture	Scriptural Principles and Questions to Consider as Leaders
Penitent and Reverent	Sarah Rahab Esther Ruth Mary, mother of Jesus Samaritan woman at well Lydia Phoebe	Who gets the glory for what I am about to do? Whom am I seeking to advance? Will God's kingdom and the cause of Christ be helped or hindered if this action is taken, in the manner planned? Have I come before God for him to search my heart regarding this matter, and yielded my will to what he has already revealed in his Word regarding this?
Consistently Prays	Esther Anna	Have I sought God's will, directions, and timing for this matter? What has God said in his Word about this? Am I thanking God for what he has already done or will be doing regarding this? Do I need to just wait in thanksgiving until the appointed time, based on his Word?
Discrete	Young Miriam Deborah	Considering Jesus's instructions in Matthew 10:16, what is the best way to proceed?
Tenacious in the Face of Opposition	Jochebed Shiphrah and Puah Deborah	How must I stand in this situation? Are there examples in God's Word to instruct me?
Constantly Dependent on God	Naomi Ruth	How would God have me proceed? What really represents him in choices before me?
Wise and Discerning	Deborah Naomi Anna Priscilla	Have I sought, and am I seeking to follow God's wisdom?
Focused and Purposeful	Miriam Ruth Esther Eunice and Lois Phoebe	How can I find God's way in this circumstance? How must I seek him to receive direction?

Before this faith came, we were held prisoners by the law, locked up until faith should be revealed. So the law was put in charge to lead us to Christ that we might be justified by faith. Now that faith has come, we are no longer under the supervision of the law. You are all sons of God through faith in Christ Jesus, for all of you who were baptized into Christ have clothed yourselves with Christ. There is neither Jew nor Greek, slave nor free, male nor female, for you are all one in Christ Jesus. If you belong to Christ, then you are Abraham's seed, and heirs according to the promise (Galatians 3:23–29 NIV 1984).

The law exposes humankind's sin and, thereby, establishes the need for liberation from the bondage therein. The sacrificial death on the cross pays this penalty and all humanity is set free in Christ because "if the Son sets you free, you will be free indeed" (John 8:36 NIV). The unity that all believers share in Christ eliminates the lines of demarcation in cultural origin, "Jew nor Greek"; social status, "slave nor free"; and gender designation, "male nor female." Women, however, have not fully realized their consecrated position in Christ, for all the redeemed have been set aside, consecrated, for God's purposes. Women who are surrendered to God are experiencing perpetual sanctification as they seek to walk by the guidance of God's Spirit through faith. Accordingly, all the redeemed may stand in self-assurance, "being confident of this, that he who began a good work in you will carry it on to completion until the day of Christ Jesus" (Philippians 1:6 NIV). As such, redeemed women are being progressively positioned in complete consecration, by faith.

Along the journey, however, at least three barriers seem to exist with respect to the functional role of women in spiritual leadership. These are tradition, limitation, and validation. These three factors become more complex as the circumstances of African American women are examined, for African American women often commence the journey to leadership status with indigenous deficits. These include, but are not limited to, cultural stereotyping, sociopolitical marginalization, and substratum socialization. As members of a minority cultural group, "difference" becomes definitive of unwanted shift in tradition, of automatic designation of limitation, and of acceptable denial of validation. While these minority group membership realities hold revealing observations, it is helpful to hear the voices of women who are experiencing the reality of the struggle in positions of spiritual leadership, as the following section of this chapter attempts to provide.

THE CONTEMPORARY CHALLENGES

Bishop Vashti Murphy McKenzie, the first woman elected bishop in the African American Episcopal Church, in the book *Strength in the Struggle* (2001, 1) indicates that "leaders who happen to be women had to transform negative barriers into stepping-stones of success." This is the precise reason that the experiences of the women are presented, so that they will serve as reflections for transforming negative barriers into opportunities to realize complete consecration in God-given assignments in spiritual leadership.

With respect to the barrier of tradition, breaking the mold for well-established leadership representation (i.e., "men hold these positions") can be wearying and hurtful. The scrutiny a woman endures who is a "first" in certain roles can be intimidating and threatening to her effectiveness. Since there are no female models to establish precedence, the woman has to define how to function in the role with "propriety" at the point of origination. The authors of this chapter have personally experienced such events. On several occasions, they have been the "first" woman to preach to a certain denominational congregation. One of these was the inauguration of a shift in a well-established tradition: A male pastor had always delivered the Annual Women's Day sermon in this congregation. While the "type" of messenger shifted, certain proprieties surrounding the role remained traditional. The message could not be delivered from the main pulpit podium. Instead, the female messenger had to stand at a small lectern in a "side" location away from the pulpit. This was awkward for addressing the entire audience, and there was barely enough room on the lectern to place Bible and notes. Admittedly, the pulpit podium is a symbol of power and authority, both of which present issues with respect to ascription to women. Nonetheless, the author's experience reflects that creating an issue around "difference" compromises the consecrated use by God, for she found herself more focused on the special arrangements than on the assignment to rightly divide the Word of Truth.

In the biblical tradition, what really is the precedence for appropriate use of women as messengers to God's people? The First Corinthians passage cited earlier in this chapter permits women to pray and prophesy in the same manner as the men, with one exceptional expectation. The women are admonished to demonstrate their divine position by adorning their heads in a manner appropriate for women, hair or a veil. The Scripture definitely suggests that women are not called to mimic men in their presentation. This is a key behavioral issue. Women are not denied the spiritual leadership in offering prayer and prophesy, but they are encouraged to present themselves in these consecrated roles in their created representation.

Citing Luke 8:1, Dr. Renita Weems also substantiates God's impartial inclusion of women functioning in His ministry as members of the leadership team: "Mary Magdalene, Joanna, Susanna, and other female traveling evangelists made up the band of female workers who surrendered and sacrificed everything to follow Jesus" (1988, 87) . Dr. Weems further asserts that Mary Magdalene is a leader, due to her "first mentioned" status in many of the biblical accounts. If this is so, this woman, Mary Magdalene, is a prime example of the next barrier to women realizing their potential as spiritual leaders—limitation. Prior to the healing of Mary Magdalene, it is a presumptive conclusion that this woman is limited in her marginalized psychological bondage.

Oppressive attitudes, conscious and unconscious, limit women in reaching their full potential in many endeavors. In fact, their selfhood may be so drastically compromised that they are paralyzed, immobilized to the extent that they do not believe.

Women can or will realize a manifestation of their God-given potential. Dr. Weems identifies the oppressive forces, "demons," from which Mary Magdalene had to be released before she could become a leader in behalf of the kingdom of God. Dr. Weems (1988, 90) observes: "indeed, the 'demons' that claimed Mary are the same demons that prey on many of us: depression, fear, low self-esteem, doubt, procrastination, bitterness and self-pity." How are such bondage-producing notions formed in one's spirit? They often assume the form of subtle suggestions in the African American community.

The authors of this chapter spent their formative years in a segregated America. One of the authors of this chapter remembers a subtle suggestive message received in her African American populated high school that it took decades to decode. It is a message that creates a menacing feeling of limitation: You are not good enough! The message indicates that no matter how gifted or diligent a female is, she will never achieve on the level of males in similar circumstances. This discouragement surfaces in her spirit at every juncture in her journey, creating stress and strain. Years later, wearied in the struggle and wondering why every achievement is so difficult, the source of the author's dismay becomes clear in a therapeutic encounter. During this time, it became clear that her fear, insecurity, and self-effacing behaviors were products of the high school environment, where she received messages from influential male teachers that were neither encouraging nor affirming. The pattern, in opportunity and verbal encouragement, signified that the girls must stay in their place so that the boys can assume their rightful position, the one that society surely is not going to accord them. While it is true that the society is traditionally oppressive to African American males, this is not an excuse for such attitude to be perpetuated in the community of faith. With renewed minds, the people of God do not conform to the world. The struggle with limitation is destroying gifted, intelligent women. Another testimony of one of the authors of this chapter reveals the fear, doubt and procrastination women encounter on the journey to complete consecration. She reports:

> I knew I felt uncomfortable about being a woman called in ministry. So I adopted the position: If I were really called, then I would feel more comfortable. This would open the door to another round of doubt and paralyzing fear of venturing into "the forbidden," with thoughts that God might just abandon me, leaving me to flounder in error, controversy, or deception. Without consciously thinking about it, there was resignation to a compromise: better just to stay put, not to try to move too fast, or at all! Then there would be the repeat, looking around for affirmation and confirmation amid the same cultural norms and practices that engendered or nourished the fears in the first place.

Under such circumstances, women become counterfeit representatives of the image of God within them.

Commenting from a similar environmental perspective, Dr. Weems (1988, 89) makes the following observation about Mary Magdalene:

> Imagine: Here was an otherwise gifted, intelligent, bright charismatic woman living in a society which had no place for gifted, intelligent, bright, charismatic women. Like many women today, Mary's emotional and physical infirmities were probably symptomatic of the stresses and strains that came in the form of relationships and environments that were neither affirming nor encouraging; stresses that were, in fact, repressive and destructive.

Under such conditions, women continue to experience the paralysis of apathy and unfulfilled dreams. Many do not even recognize that they are denying their Maker and Redeemer opportunity to reflect his image through them, through their faith deficit. It is easier to become a nonentity because then one does not have to war with the oppressor. This false sense of peace is more palatable; the journey to divine destiny comes with a price. In her book *Who Am I Really: A Woman's Journey to God-Significance,* Dr. Lynda Hunter (2001, 148) proclaims:

> The call will cost you. It's easy to sashay through life without hearing and obeying the things God tells you to do. There's a cost to discipleship, and it often involves isolation and misunderstanding. But once you become aware of God's purpose for your life, you're never the same again and nothing else ever quite satisfies.

Most assuredly, misunderstanding accompanies a pursuit of God's purpose. In fact, one of the authors finds that there is a connection between misunderstanding, mistreatment, and validation. Misunderstanding breeds mistreatment, and persons will summarily invalidate individuals they do not understand. Ralph Ellison (1952) wrote *Invisible Man,* depicting an African American male's pilgrimage through psychological bondage and intellectual imprisonment, a kind of limitation; but countless African American women, and women of other cultural backgrounds as well, can attest to the fact that there is also the invisible woman. This occurs most often in the form of mistreatment manifested in omission.

Again, the narrative of one of the authors reflects the issue of validation. Women have experienced a lack of validation through omission, and this presents a barrier in obtaining access to leadership opportunities. The author finds that the struggle simply to be "allowed" a "legitimate" place at the leadership table is wearying. Even though she finds herself at the table, it sometimes comes with hostility, animosity, and suspicion from males and females. As Bishop McKenzie (2001, 117) observes, women pigeonhole each other. "We assign a place to one another." Another testimony from the authors illustrates the pithy results of a lack of validation:

> It is nursing wounds, or an invalidating response to them, that results in a weariness and refusal to unreservedly "stay the course," in tough times. It is being caught off guard, not realizing that the battle scars may involve, not only those "afar off" but some close to you as well.

Bishop McKenzie (2001, 2) suggests that "Many women are wearied by the struggle. They become bitter from the experience just doing what their talent demands." As we reflect on our own experiences, we are reminded that the pain that accompanies this dejection produces a grief situation, which results in depressive moods, frustration, and doubt. Under such pressure, a woman begins to question her humanity, wondering if her affect on others reflects that she is not a positive relational object. What follows is a preoccupation with trying to avoid offending others, and the decision to self-efface becomes paramount. The discomfort that accompanies this deceptive practice is counterproductive and positions the woman as a puppet on the stage of the world, who jumps to the demands of others in order to avoid pain. Invisibility, with the hope of redemptive acceptance, seems to be a better choice rather than open confrontation.

Returning to that place at which this section was initiated, it is profitable to elucidate what the proclaimed plan is as stated in Galatians 3:23–29, which may be referenced as the magna carta of humanity. In this passage, the apostle Paul suggests that a shift has occurred since this faith has come. Thus, in the "coming" (*ĕrchŏmai)* of this expectant hope, this belief in that which is not yet evident, the fallen state of humanity, under the law, has shifted. The former possibilities are renewed because those who have been justified by faith are no longer subject to the limitations of the law, through which no one would have ever been "declared righteous" (*dikaioō*). This declaration of righteousness removes the penalty one would obtain through breaking the law. This justified vessel is furthermore "clothed" (*enduō*) with the garment of righteousness. This new nature comes with reformed possibilities and reconciliation. In this instance, the promise to obtain is to assume leadership in the stewardship of the created causes of God, his world and his salvation plan for the world.

> Therefore, if anyone is in Christ, he is a new creation; the old has gone, the new has come! All this is from God, who reconciled us to himself through Christ and gave us the ministry of reconciliation; that God was reconciling the world to himself in Christ, not counting men's sins against them. And he has committed to us the message of reconciliation (2 Corinthians 5:17–19 NIV 1984).

As God did with the Ninevites, the repentant heart, the one of faith, is thusly restored to the original promise; and this is the proclaimed plan.

THE PURPOSEFUL PRIVILEGE

Following their vocational area in Christian ministry and/or pastoral counseling, the authors offer a pattern of the inner journey from perplexing participation to complete consecration. This is a psychospiritual journey which engages one in soul analysis, and it is an inward movement to truth, which is designed to facilitate growth and self-discovery. As Dr. Lynda Hunter (2001, 136) indicates: "if we're armed, loved, victorious, and growing, we're prime candidates for God to use." Perhaps the model which follows will speak to the hearts of women in the struggle to realize acceptance in their God-ordained assignments.

FROM DISCONCERTED REACTION TO DIVINE REVELATION

Traditional views have deposited in the minds and hearts of women very little vision concerning their possibilities in leadership. These views suggest that certain roles are relegated for men only. As such, large numbers of women continue to deny their gifts in this area and do not consider developing as leaders. Gifted women leaders, then, continue to constitute an underutilized resource. More significantly, however, is the fact that women are often ignoring an aspect of the God-ordained vision for them; and without his vision for them, they are essentially perishing as potential fruit bearers. But, with the vision of God, as exemplified in the life of King Uzziah, women will succeed (2 Chronicles 26:5). God assures his people that he knows the plans he has for them—"plans to prosper you and not to harm you, plans to give you hope and a future" (Jeremiah 29:11b NIV). The movement must be made, however, from poor vision to consecrated completion, by faith.

With poor vision, that which lacks godly hope, trust, and faith, women have struggled with finding an "authentic" presence, voice, and representation. Poor vision is also accompanied by a willingness to accept limitation and unfulfilled dreams. Bishop McKenzie (2001, 5) suggests that the challenge to integrity and character has positive developmental outcomes. She asserts, "Integrity is challenged. Character is molded. Leader style is developed. Vision is sharpened in the event." Instead of the accommodating, self-effacing, false humility to receive access, women can move to a point—through all-sufficient grace—that they recognize that there is a way to reframe the concept of limitation. God-reliance is critical in circumstances where there is human difference, though this is not always the human soul's selection. Sobermindedness with respect to the self and others is the biblical stance in such situations. The apostle Paul is given the following stance by the Spirit of God when his spiritual leadership is challenged.

> My conscience is clear, but that does not make me innocent. It is the Lord who judges me. Therefore judge nothing before the appointed time; wait till the Lord comes. He will bring to light what is hidden in darkness and will expose the motives of the heart (1 Corinthians 4:4–5c NIV).

This is wisdom for women in contentious challenges regarding God's functional role for them in his kingdom work. The patient perseverance, relying on God to keep his promise to provide hope and a future that is, walking by faith is character building and godly character brings hope to the heart!

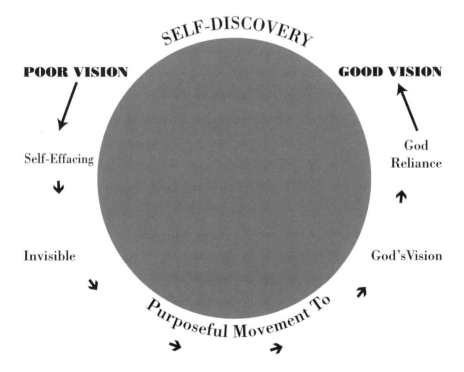

Perseverance can likewise begin a healing process because this stance brings strength that lifts the soul as self-confrontation becomes active behavior. The Word of God illustrates self-confrontation as an approach to re-direct one's thoughts in a more positive direction. Self-confrontation may even deflect the negative ideation. Psalm 43 demonstrates this helpful approach as follows.

> Why are you downcast, O my soul?
> Why so disturbed within me?
> Put your hope in God,
> for I will yet praise him,
> my Savior and my God (Psalm 43:5 NIV 1984).

In this process, self-validation may also evolve as a net benefit, as one relies on God.

> Cast your cares on the LORD and he will sustain you; he will never let the righteous be shaken (Psalm 55:22 NIV).

One does not deny the injury and pain but chooses to employ a strategic approach that is solution-focused. Accordingly, constructive self-dialogue is one approach to initiating healing within the psyche, inner mindset, to consecrated wholeness. God honors, rewards, and empowers those who trust Him with their soul care. This is the mindset whereby women can enter into a healing and conciliatory position, while executing their God-given calls with propriety and by faith.

CONCLUSION

We have surveyed the canon of God's Word with respect to his creative purpose for humankind, examining his positional role for women. We further explained God's original intent for leadership: ruling, reigning, and leading. The overarching activity in the work of God's kingdom is his salvific process; thus, the use of women in spiritual leadership in the unfolding of God's salvation plan and the establishment of his church is amplified in the body of this chapter, with concentration on the leadership skills these women employ. We then presented anecdotal information from our experiences as African American women, which also represent in many ways the universalities in the experiences of women as they engage in leadership assignments. Through these disclosures, we offer a godly outlook for healing injuries, promoting conciliation, and encouraging propriety as women are called to assume roles of spiritual leadership.

The woman with the renewed mind has purpose, propriety, and permission. She functions in an assignment that is God's will for her, and this will manifest itself through affirmation, confirmation, and attribution. Others will affirm her in the role, and this will assure her and help her confirm her assignment from God. Furthermore, the way God anoints her to function in the role will signify that it is especially ordained for her—divine attribution. Such woman is out of order in a role "only when she [sic} uses [sic} her influence against God's will (see Johnson 1996, 225). That is, if a woman is in an assignment that is God's will, his granted permission for her, she is not violating biblical propriety.

The grace gifts granted by the Spirit of God are for use in the salvific work of God's kingdom (Ephesians 4:12). The Word of God does not exclude any of the redeemed, His people of faith, from the gifting process. God's Word declares: "Now to each one the manifestation of the Spirit is given for the common good" (1 Corinthians 12:7 NIV). After this clarification, then the gifts are enumerated. Consequently, if a woman is equipped through spiritual gifting for the assignment she possesses, then she is not disregarding the principle of biblical propriety as she functions in the role. Dr. Lynda Hunter brings clarity to this point in the statement:

> God appoints each of us to duties and purposes for which we were created. He takes our gifting and experiences and desires and rolls them into His central purpose, when we give our lives to Him (2001, 137).

With God's purpose as direction, there is the assurance that all things will work for good (Romans 8:28). There is no need to fear, for the holy Word makes the following promise:

> If you make the Most High your dwelling—
> even the LORD, who is my refuge—
> then no harm will befall you,
> no disaster will come near your tent
> For he will command his angels concerning you to guard you in all your
> ways (Psalm 91:9–11 NIV 1984).

God has not decreed principles that differentiate through human designs of tradition, limitation, and validation. Each individual who believes in Christ has the benefit of unification through faith in Christ. As each person proceeds in God-granted permission and God-given purpose, barriers of tradition, limitation, and validation will be cast aside to the glory of God's immutable design that all humankind are vessels of his image and all the redeemed of him are the called according to his purpose. Are not these free to serve in leadership by faith?

REFERENCES

Adeyemo, T., ed. 2006. *Africa Bible Commentary*. Grand Rapids, MI: Zondervan.

Baker, W. 1994. *The Complete Word Study of the Old Testament*. Iowa Falls, IA: World AMG.

Boyd, Gregory and Paul Eddy. 2009. *Across the Spectrum: Understanding Issues in Evangelical Theology*. Grand Rapids, MI: Baker Academic.

Daane, J. 1991. "Unchangeability of God." *The International Standard Bible Encyclopedia*, ed. G.W. Bromley. Grand Rapids, MI: Eerdmans 4:942–4.

del Mastro, M. L. 2006. *All the Women of the Bible*. Edison, NJ: Castle Books.

Edwards, R. B. 1991. Woman. *The International Standard Bible Encyclopedia*, ed. G. W. Bromley. Grand Rapids, MI: Eerdmans 4:1089–97.

Ellison, Ralph. 1952. *Invisible Man*. New York: Random House.

Gillman, F. 1992. Phoebe. Vol. 5, *The Anchor Bible Dictionary*, ed. D. N. Freedman. New York: Doubleday.

Grenz, Stanley J. and Denise M. Kjesbo. 1995. *Women in the Church: A Biblical Theology of Women in Ministry*. Downers Grove, IL: InterVarsity.

Gundry, Stanley and James Beck, eds. 2005. *Two Views On Women in Ministry*. Grand Rapids: Zondervan.

Hunter, Lynda. 2001. *Who Am I Really: A Woman's Journey to God-Significance*. Nashville, TN: Word.

Johnson, Victoria. 1996. Examining Difficult Passages in the Bible. *Women to Women: Perspectives of Fifteen African-American Christian Women*, ed. Norvella Carter and Matthew Parker. Grand Rapids, MI: Zondervan.

Köstenberger, Andreas J. and Thomas R. Schreiner, eds. 2005. *Women in the Church*. Grand Rapids, MI: Baker Academic.

Lockyer, Herbert. 1995. *All the Women of the Bible*. Grand Rapids, MI: Zondervan.

McKenzie, Vashti M. 2001. *Strength in the Struggle: Leadership Development for Women*. Cleveland, OH: The Pilgrim Press.

Rienstra, M. 1992. "Eve." Vol. 2, *The International Standard Bible Encyclopedia*, ed. G. W. Bromley. Grand Rapids, MI: Eerdmans.

Strong, James. 1996. *The New Strong's Exhaustive Concordance of the Bible*. Nashville, TN: Thomas Nelson Publishers.

Sumner, Sarah. 2003. *Men and Women in the Church*. Downers Grove, IL: InterVarsity.

Thomas, Robert L., ed. 1981. *New American Standard Exhaustive Concordance of the Bible*. Nashville: Holman Bible.

Thompson, Frank Charles, ed. 1991. *The Thompson Chain Reference Bible. New International Version*. Indianapolis, IN: Kirkbride.

Weems, Renita J. 1988. *Just a Sister Away: A Womanist Vision of Women's Relationships in the Bible*. San Diego, CA: Auramedia.

Witherington, III, B. 1992. "Lydia." Vol. 4, *The Anchor Bible Dictionary*, ed. D. N. Freedman. New York: Doubleday.

Chapter 13

PREPARING YOUNG BLACK MALES FOR FUTURE LEADERSHIP

Christopher C. Mathis Jr.

It is important to challenge and offer practical suggestions to older African Americans about how to systematically prepare younger Black males for future leadership. This can be done by:

- Stressing the importance of discipleship;

- Discussing the barriers to Black males success;

- Understanding the need to biblically disciple Black males;

- Exploring sound wisdom necessary for future leadership;

- Discussing the Black church's role in discipling and preparing Black males for leadership; and

- Offering seven steps for preparing young Black males for future leadership

The African proverb—"It takes a village to raise a child"—captures this overall challenge and task. Historically, the African American community has been group-oriented and hence, older Black males particularly need to heed the clarion call to "man up" and take on the challenge of assisting in discipling young Black males in homes, churches, and communities so they can be effective in their future roles.

THE IMPORTANCE OF DISCIPLESHIP

Scriptures tell us that we must properly train our youths, or else they will bring disgrace to the family. Therefore, effective discipleship requires training in a particular manner, custom, or tradition in order to ensure that a certain outcome or order is continued and/or maintained. The New Webster's Dictionary (1991) defines disciple as "one who receives instructions from another; one who adheres to a particular school or philosophy, religious thought, or art." Whereas, Vine (1981) indicates that the Greek word for disciple is mathetes which means "a learner, to learn… one who follows one's teaching." Vine further indicates that "a disciple was not only a pupil, but an adherent; hence they are spoken of as imitators of their teacher."

A synonym for disciple is adherent, and it is defined" as one who adheres; one who follows a leader, party, or profession; a follower, or partisan; believer in a particular faith or church" (www.definitions.net). Thus, a disciple is someone that adheres to a particular leader or a particular faith. Hence, the expected reward of someone being a disciple or adherent to a particular leader or teaching is that someday that person will eventually assume a position of leadership and be successful, given the preparation that has been rendered. This clearly is what we want our young Black males to ultimately achieve in life

For example, Acts 4:20 demonstrates that effective disciples must have hands-on training as well as verbal teaching, in order to master the skills and knowledge imparted. If Jesus had to train his disciples, we must do the same to ensure the success among our young Black males in order to prepare them for the twenty-first century, and the challenges and leadership opportunities to come. Richardson (1991, 1996), for example, has also written extensively in this area.

As I noted in a earlier book chapter (Mathis 1999), Fredrick Douglass, a noted Black male leader in the 1800s stated in an August 4, 1857 speech during the West Indies Emancipation for Freedom, that:

> Those who profess to favor freedom, and yet deprecate agitation, are men
> who want crops without plowing up the ground. They want rain without

the thunder and lightning, or they want the ocean without the awful roar of its waters. This struggle may be both moral and physical; but it must be a struggle, for power concedes nothing without a demand. It never did, and it never will.

The point of this quote, in this context, is that it takes work (hard work) to accomplish any important goal. Effectively impacting young Black males is clearly an important goal and will take a lot of hard work. Hence, as a Black male who has himself been trained and discipled by others for leadership, I call to arms other well-trained Black males and ask them to prepare others for a successful future in both life and leadership (for a discussion of the necessity and reward of risk, see Allen 1996).

UNDERSTANDING THE BARRIERS TO DISCIPLING BLACK MALES FOR LEADERSHIP

Discipling Black males can indeed be a challenge, if not outright intimidating, especially when a person is not grounded in knowing who they are in relationship to God the Creator, humankind, and the broader society. As I have noted (Mathis 1999), here are some of these reasons often mentioned for not getting involved with young Black males:

- "Their priorities are in the wrong place";
- "There's too much risk involved";
- "It's not my problem";
- "I'm too busy";
- "I have raised my children."

Needless to say, I have heard these excuses, along with additional ones such as:

- "They act too thuggish";
- "Their pants are too saggy"; and
- "They appear not to value life."

Although, many of us as Black males have abandoned our responsibility of discipling younger Black males, our history teaches us that if we fail to educate our youth of today, then our future is in jeopardy as well (Armah

1979). Therefore, in order to prepare Black males for future leadership, we must work systematically to turn around the alarming negative statistics that are prevalent in our communities.

For example, the following statistics regarding African American males were shared at the Great Gathering that was held March 1–3, 2010, in the Carolina Coliseum, in Columbia, South Carolina (www.greatgathering.org):

- Eighty-six percent of Black fourth-graders cannot read at grade level;

- On average, African American twelfth-grade students read at approximately the same level as White eighth-graders;

- Although they represent only 17.1 percent of public-school students, in 2006 African American students accounted for 37.4 percent of total suspensions and 37.9 percent of total expulsions nationwide;

- Only forty-one percent of African American males graduate from high school in the United States;

- In 1995, sixteen percent of African American males in their twenties who did not go to college were in jail; a decade later, it has grown to twenty-one percent;

- The arrest rate among African American youth (ages ten to seventeen) was nearly twice the rate of their white peers;

- Nationwide, young Black offenders are more than twice as likely to be transferred to adult court as their White counterparts;

- Nearly sixty percent of young offenders serving time in adult state prisons are African American, although African Americans comprise only fifteen percent of the youth population;

- Nationwide, sixty percent of the 2,380 offenders serving life without parole for crimes they were convicted of committing as children are African American;

Christopher C. Mathis Jr.

- According to the Centers for Disease Control, homicide is the leading cause of death among African American males aged fifteen to thirty-four years;

- According to the Centers for Disease Control and Prevention statistics released in 2008, the homicide rate among Black males ages ten to twenty-four is more than double that of Hispanic and White males in the same age group; and

- North Carolina has spent more money on prisons than on support of the eleven historically Black colleges and universities in the state.

Given the statistics above, as well as the high level of drug use and involvement, gang-related deaths, and Black-on-Black homicides, it is a wonder how we as Black males maintain our sanity in this society.

Curry (1991, 116) points out that "many of our youths never get a chance to be innocent, for they face harsh realities at a tender age." These negative statistics and issues are more than reason enough to sound a loud alarm to the older Black male community of the serious need to disciple our young Black male for greater accountability and effective future leadership roles. This task can be achieved.

Proverbs 19:18 tells us that we should correct our youth while there still is hope and that we should not be concerned whether they enjoy it, for it is the right thing to do in God's sight. Working to change these negative statistics will involve both dedication and risk. Therefore, we must rise up and face this daunting challenge of our present age and be about the business of training and discipling our young Black males for a successful future in both life and leadership.

THE NEED TO BIBLICALLY DISCIPLE
BLACK MALES FOR LEADERSHIP

Jesus says that "For whosoever will save his life shall lose it: but whosoever will lose his life for my sake, the same shall save it" (Luke 9:24 KJV). Losing one's life for a greater cause must be the spirit that drives strong, grounded Black males in every community across the country to take risks and get involved with great seriousness in our community; for without it one can easily predict the results. Most often, as a starter, it only takes a sincere

Christopher C. Mathis Jr.

effort on the part of a strong parent (or guardian), male pastor, mentor, or elder for the younger Black male to listen and adhere to instruction and correction and begin the move in positive direction. There are many examples of this having occurred.

Proverbs 22:6 (KJV) reminds us: "Train a child in the way he should go: and when he is old he will not depart (or turn) from it." Thus, the quality of training a child (Black youth) receives is crucial to their later development, underscoring the importance of proper training. Such a process was referred to as the rites of passages in the traditional African society; for these rites of passage prepared youth for their future leadership roles.

It has become obvious that the practice of rites of passage was crucial to our ancestors. Therefore, as a people of African descent, we must return to our roots (traditional training and practices), as much as possible to assist in the discipleship of our young Black males for maximum effectiveness in the twenty-first century. Moreover, as a people we must continue to design rites of passages programs (as well as expanding other mentoring programs) for our Black males that includes an understanding of our African heritage, history, and spirituality. In addition, as mentioned by Kunjufu (1996), we must consider the African context and/or frame of reference, and belief in the Nguzo-Saba (Seven Principles of Kwanzaa), a Black value system.

SOUND WISDOM AS A NECESSITY IN DISCIPLING BLACK MALES IN PREPARATION FOR LEADERSHIP

Sound wisdom is illustrated throughout the Bible, and particularly in the book of Proverbs. For example, in Proverbs 29:15 (KJV), we are instructed that to avoid shame and reproach, we must be willing to use the "rod" and reproof to give wisdom to sustain throughout life. The point is that, as is often said, "Too often women love their sons, and raise their daughters." Then when their daughter becomes of age to marry, it is difficult to find a Black male suitable to fit the bill, because they have not been properly raised. For if the proper measure is not undertaken, we as a people shall reap what we have sown.

In the foreword to the book *Adam! Where Are You?*, the Reverend Dr. Jeremiah A. Wright Jr. (see Kunjufu 1994, v), states the following:

When God asked the question, "Where are you, Adam? " in the first book of the Bible, there were several factors made the listening audience 5000

Christopher C. Mathis Jr.

years ago a lot different from the reading audience at the end of the 20th century. First, of all, the listening audience who first heard the story understood clearly that God already knew where the man (adamah) was. The problem was that the man did not know where he was.

Unfortunately, the circumstances are the same today as they were when this sacred story was first told. God knows where the black man is. The black man—who is still trying to hide from God—is the one who does not know where he is—even though he *thinks* he knows. Even more tragic, however, is the fact that although the *circumstances* are the same, the *awareness* is not!

That is to say that the listening audience in 3000 B.C. understood that God knew. They were aware that God knew painfully and poignantly where the man was; but the reading audience in the 1990s does not understand. For the most part they were not aware that God knows where the black man is even when the black man (who *thinks* he knows) in reality *does* not know!

These prophetic words by Wright still hold true in the twenty-first century; that is, if the young Black male does not know how to listen to God and understand the Creator, then he is doomed to repeat the past (the mistakes) until he comes to himself and acknowledge God as the Supreme Being of the universe. Then and only then will God allow us to return to our rightful state that he has foreordained before the beginning of heaven and earth.

Furthermore, Wright (Kunjufu 1994, vii) goes on to say:

Chancellor Williams warns us not to forget "our story." In repeating the legend of Sumer, he says the traveler asked the old man, "What happen to the people of Sumer? History teaches us that they were black! Where are they? What happen to them?" "Ah," sighed the old man, "They forgot their story (their history) and so they died."

Given the above, it is my hope that every conscientious older Black male will take up the challenge to disciple younger Black males in their homes, communities, and churches. Knowingly, if we do not answer the clarion call, then what do we expect other to do? The answer is: Nothing.

Consider the following example (Hillard 1995, 72):

[A sheep dog] at birth is separated almost at once from… its family… then placed into a pen where there are nothing but sheep, including the young lambs who are nursing. In its normal drive to satisfy its hunger, it seeks out a ewe and tries to nurse from her, along with other lambs. When it is successful, it continues, and is then raised with sheep as a lamb until it is sufficiently developed to be trained. Notice here that it continues to act like a dog as well … leave the track of a dog and have the speed and strength of a dog. Yet, while it has the intelligence of a dog, it will develop the mind of a sheep! Once that happens, it no longer acts like, or in the interest of itself as a dog, or in the interest of other dogs. Moreover, it will see its own brothers and sister as the "enemy" since this dog does not know them as brothers and sisters.

This story colorfully portrays what transpires when someone is not instructed appropriately by his or her group or family, but rather is educated and reared outside of the family or group in an unfamiliar background. Such unfamiliar training takes the person from a shared history and does not allow the "acumen" of the past nor the future. Rather, it leads to dependency on others for information, the inability to gain knowledge from the experience of one's group (race, religion, etc.), and the feeling of growing up in a foreign environment, which allows one to live in a world of illusions, seeing oneself as something he or she is not.

As African American males in North America, we have to awaken to the significance of affording our young Black males the benefit of learning from our collective experience—for it is one that has beaten the odds, and without it we await our final burial as a people. This point is further echoed by Wright (Kunjufu 1994, vii–viii), when he states that:

We need to *remember* our history, *remember* our story and *retell* our story to our children as Moses warned us, or we too will continue to die?

Judge R. Eugene Pinchman, the retired Appellate Court Judge in the state of Illinois said, "You cannot *be* what you cannot *see!*" One of the reasons so many of our young, African American brothers are "antichurch" and not wanting to be a part of the church—beyond the pressures of the peer group—is that they "cannot see" any strong African American men *in* church, as a part of the church, *loving* the church, *supporting* the church, *tithing* to the church, building up the church and *being* the church — outside of the church building.

Once they being to see that, and once we begin to tell our story, the question that God asks the man (adamad) will begin to have a different answer. We can move from hiding behind fig leaves to rebuild our families and communities as "priests" in our homes!

Given the above, it should become apparent that grounded, God-centered conscious Black males have a charge to keep. In the hymn written by Wesley (1762), he states:

A charge to keep I have,
A God to glorify,
A never-dying soul to save,
And fit it for the sky.
To serve the present age, my calling to fulfill:
O may it all my powers engage to do my Master's will.

This hymn reminds us that we must be faithful to the Creator and glorify him by serving this generation (present age). Then by discipling our young Black male, we can truly say to God that we have fulfilled our calling (charge) and done the Master's (Creator's) will.

Furthermore, this charge is to be a positive role model to the younger Black males as it relates to men in church. This can be done by being a part of the church, by loving the church, by supporting the church, and by being a part of the church outside of the church building. Moreover, we need to tell our story, in order to rebuild our families and communities and be a "priest" in our homes.

THE BLACK CHURCH'S ROLE IN DISCIPLING
BLACK MALES FOR LEADERSHIP

The Black church, as well as the home, has always had an essential function in the instructive development and training (see Curry 1991, S. June 1991, and Richardson, 1996), as well as preparing of our Black males for leadership roles. This is still paramount to ensuring their survival and advancement. Therefore, as a member of the clergy, I employ especially my fellow clergy to become a dedicated transformational leader. By being a leader who loves their congregation, who empowers and trains them to be effective in the culturally and contemporarily relevant real-life ministry, and who have the community's hearts in mind when conducting and developing ministry for young Black males through the church.

Mbiti (1970) shows how religion was an integral part of the whole of African life. We must continue that tradition in America with Christianity in the daily aspects of our life. Not to do so means that we are out of synchronization with our African heritage. Therefore, parents, elders, and others who are entrusted to disciple Black males must make a cognizant pledge to "disciple biblically" within the context of the church. If we are willing to tell the truth, we must admit that one of the main problems that exist in our communities is the woeful lack of admiration toward parents and elders by our youths today.

It was a past practice in South Carolina (my home state) and many other states to teach young Black males to respect their parents and elders. This was a major responsibility of the older Black males in the community or church; when a young male failed to show respect, an elder or peer would routinely correct him. Unfortunately, this type of training and accountability is often viewed as obsolete. Could it be that we have allowed society too much latitude in influencing our decision about doing what "thus saith the Lord"? We must teach young Black males how to reverence their parents and elders, for doing so gives them life. What I like about God's Word is that it repeats itself, thus representing to us the magnitude of a particular concept (see, for example, Deuteronomy 5:16 and Ephesians 6:1–3 respectively). The above passages are substantiating a principle, as well repeating one of God's direct orders, and include young Black males. This is of significance to Black male leaders, for when we fail to carry out God's commandants, there are stern negative outcomes.

SEVEN STEPS IN PREPARATION FOR WORKING WITH YOUNG BLACK MALES FOR FUTURE LEADERSHIP

In my years of working with young Black males and considering the literature on Black males, I offer what I consider to be seven important steps in preparation for working with young Black males for future leadership. They are:

- Develop a personal relationship with the Creator (God) through Jesus Christ.

- Know yourself (be conscious of one's family and ethnic history).

- Develop a strong positive self-image.

- Determine your priorities and set personal goals.

- Make it one of your priorities to mentor a young Black male for future leadership.

- Be persistence in pursuing your goals; and.

- Monitor your health as a way of honoring God.

In embracing these seven steps, it puts us in the right frame of mind to seriously develop and prepare young Black males for future leadership roles in the church, home, and broader society. Further, it gives us clear guidance and instruction regarding how to live our own lives as we prepare for the challenge of being involved in the lives of others.

CONCLUSION

Older Black males who are privileged to work with and around young Black males have a grave responsibility that should not be taken lightly, for we are entrusted with assisting parents. Older African-Americans males, with conscience stirred, must see the importance of discipling younger Black males for effective future leadership. Elder Black males, I urge you again to heed the clarion call to "man up" and take on the challenge of assisting in discipling young Black males in your homes, churches, and communities.

The challenges of "discipling our young Black males are apparent and the pay off for our communities and the kingdom of God is unlimited. Therefore, we must be willingly to provide financial support, sacrifice time, and risk personal gain to help tell and retell our story to young Black males—turning them into God-centered masterpieces who can effectively and willingly take on life challenges so as to ensure a godly presence in the twenty-first century. It is my fervent and continual prayer that older, well-grounded, conscious, and God-centered Black males who are entrusted to train our younger Black males commit themselves to "disciple biblically." God commands it, and the trying times demand it, and future Black male leadership depends on it.

REFERENCES

Allen, H. L. 1996. "Risk and Failures as Preludes to Achievement." *Men to Men: Perspectives of Sixteen African-American Christian Men*, ed. Lee N. June. Grand Rapids, MI: Zondervan.

Armah, Ayi K. 1979. *Two Thousand Seasons*. Chicago: Third World Press.

Curry, B. P. 1991. "The Role of the Church in the Educational Development of Black Children." *The Black Family: Past, Present and Future*, eds. Lee N. June and Matthew Parker. Grand Rapids, MI: Zondervan.

Hillard, A. G. 1995. *The Maroon Within Us: Selected Rssays on African-American Community Socialization*. Baltimore, MD: Black Classic Press.

http://www.definitions.net/definition/adherent

http://www.greatgathering.org/

June, Lee N., and Matthew Parker, eds. 1991. *The Black Family: Past, Present and Future*. Grand Rapids, MI: Zondervan.

June, S. 1991. "The Role of the Home in the Spiritual Development of Black Children." *The Black Family: Past, Present and Future*, eds. Lee N. June and Matthew Parker. Grand Rapids, MI: Zondervan.

Kunjufu, J. 1994. *Adam! Where Are You?* Chicago: Afro-American Publishing Co.

_____. 1996. *Restoring the Village, Values, and Commitment: Solutions for the Black Fa*mily. Chicago: Afro-American Publishing Co.

Christopher C. Mathis Jr.

Mathis, C. C. 1999. "Evangelizing and Discipling Youth and College Students." *Evangelism and Discipleship in African American Churches*, ed. Lee N. June. Grand Rapids, MI: Zondervan.

Mbiti, J. S. 1970. *African Religions and Philosophy*. Garden City, NY: Doubleday.

New Webster's Dictionary and Roget's Thesaurus. 1991. New York: Ottenheimer.

Richardson, Willie. 1991. "Evangelizing Black Males: Critical Issues and How-Tos." *The Black Family: Past, Present and Future*, eds. Lee N. June and Matthew Parker. Grand Rapids, MI: Zondervan.

_____. 1996. *Reclaiming the Urban Family: How to Mobilize the Church as a Family Training Cente*r. Grand Rapids, MI: Zondervan.

Vine, W. E. 1981. *Vine's Expository Dictionary of Old and New Testament Words*, ed. F. F. Bruce. Old Tappan, NJ: Revell.

Wesley, C. 2010. "A Charge to Keep I Have" (1762). *Short Hymns on Select Passages of Holy Scripture*, reprint. Farmington Hills, MI: Gale ECCO.

Wright, J. A. Jr. 1994. Preface in Kunjufu, J. *Adam! Where Are You?* Chicago: Afro-American Publishing.

Chapter 14

SERVANT LEADERSHIP, THE LEADERSHIP STYLE OF JESUS, LEADERSHIP PRINCIPLES OF THE BIBLE, AND THE LEADER AS STEWARD

Lee N. June

In times past, one often heard such descriptions of leadership as charismatic, democratic, autocratic, authoritarian, and laissez faire. For the last several decades, writings and discussions of leadership have led to new descriptions. One such description is the term "servant leadership." Over this period, individuals have also increasingly focused on the leadership style and principles of Jesus Christ and the leadership principles contained in the Bible, as well as on conceptualizing a leader as a steward and as a transformational person. These descriptions, in many cases, overlap and in other instances are independent of each other. The purpose of this chapter is to briefly present and discuss some of these evolving conceptualizations and views of leadership. The reader will note that some of these terms have been used by the contributors to this volume as part of their personal philosophy or as seen or needed in others. This shows that these descriptions are becoming more and more a part of our everyday vocabulary and mode of operation.

SERVANT LEADERSHIP

The term "servant leadership" was coined by Robert Greenleaf in 1970 in an essay entitled "The Servant as Leader". Greenleaf worked for many years in industry and management. Specifically, he worked at A T & T and took an early retirement in 1964. Once he retired from these areas, he devoted his life to teaching and writing about leadership. Greenleaf died in 1990.

According to the Greenleaf Center for Servant Leadership's website (www.greenleaf.org),

> The servant leader is leader first ... It begins with the natural feeling that one wants to serve, to serve first. Then conscious choice brings one to aspire to lead, that person is sharply different from one who is a leader first, because of the need to assuage an unusual power drive or to acquire material possession ... The leader-first and the servant-first are two extreme types. Between them there are shadings and blends that are part of the infinite variety of human nature.

Thus, according to this definition, the person who is a servant leader identifies and is viewed as a servant first. While they are leaders, they see themselves as servants, first and foremost. Viewing oneself as a servant first goes to the motivation for leadership and what are a person's underlying motives and goals for leadership.

In 1996, Don Frick and Larry Spears edited a book entitled *On Becoming a Servant Leader: The Private Writings of Robert K. Greenleaf.* Those who are particularly interested in some of the actual writings and more intimate thoughts of Greenleaf are encouraged to consult this volume.

According to Larry Spears (2010), servant leadership has 10 characteristics. These are:

- Listening
- Empathy
- Healing
- Awareness
- Persuasion
- Conceptualization

- Foresight
- Stewardship
- Commitment to growth of people
- Building community

Spears (1996, 33), in an earlier writing, gave the following definition of servant leadership:

> ... a model that puts serving others as the number one priority. Servant-leadership emphasizes increased service to others; a holistic approach to work; promoting a sense of community; and the sharing of power in decision-making.

Each of these above four characteristics mentioned by Spears (1996) was discussed by Smith (2005) in an effort to give a fuller description of the concept of servant-leader. She also shares additional information on Greenleaf's background and discusses how his theory has been applied in various settings. She indicates that between 33–50 percent of *Fortune* magazine's 100 Best Companies are members of the Greenleaf Center for Servant-Leadership and that the companies that practice servant-leadership include Starbucks Coffee, Southwest Airlines, and several universities. She also appropriately notes that aspects of servant-leadership can be traced back before 1970. Hence, as noted, the term "servant leadership" was coined in 1970, but the concept and principles of servant leadership are longstanding.

While servant leadership is now broadly discussed within society and embraced in a variety of settings, it indeed is what is to be characteristic of the Christian. Just imagine the body of Christ overflowing with individuals who think and behave in this fashion

In the twentieth century, for example, servant leadership was exhibited by Dr. Martin Luther King Jr. As one studies and reviews his life, one sees a person who was thrust into leadership, originally in Alabama (the Montgomery Bus Boycott). People saw in him leadership characteristics and asked him to serve, which he agreed to do. This type of service then became characteristic of the remainder of his life. Dr. King often said that anyone can be great because anyone can serve. Mother Teresa was also one who was committed to servant leadership.

THE LEADERSHIP STYLE(S) OF JESUS AND LEADERSHIP PRINCIPLES FROM THE BIBLE

From a biblical standpoint, Jesus, himself, is the model for servant leadership. There have been a variety of books that have focused on the leadership style and principles of Jesus, and have used various descriptions for his style of leadership. For example, Laurie Beth Jones (1995) entitled her book *Jesus, CEO*. In the preface, Jones (1995, xi) stated that the book

> ... is a practical, step-by-step guide to communicating with and motivating people. It is based on the self mastery, action, and relationship skills that Jesus used to train and motivate his team. It can be applied to any business, service, or endeavor that depends on more than one person to accomplish a goal, and can be implemented by anyone who dares.

Conceptualizing Jesus as a CEO (chief executive officer), she discusses how he exhibited three characteristics—strength of self mastery, strength of action, and strength of relationship. For each of these three areas, a variety of actions are presented, which she believes are reflective of Jesus' style.

In another of her books entitled *Jesus: Life Coach*, Laura Beth Jones (2004), using language typical of this era (the life coach phenomenon), portrays Jesus as a life coach. As a life coach, she discusses the categories of focus, balance, productivity, and fulfillment. For each of these four categories, she lists a series of specific things that one will achieve in each of these areas with Jesus as one's life coach.

Regarding focus, she states that "until we focus, and define what is important to us, we live our lives in a haze of other directed urgencies" (xxi). Regarding balance, she concludes that "without balance, the best gains become burdens, and losses can pull us under. With Jesus as your Coach, you will understand how to strike and maintain a sense of balance in a world that careens and teeters on the edges of our ever shifting desires" (xxi). Regarding productivity, she explains that "productivity is the goal of every leader, manager, and coach. We must learn how to think inside the solution in order to bear fruit and remain alive with constantly expanding new possibilities" (p. xxi). Regarding fulfillment, she notes that "fulfillment is beyond 'success'. Knowing the difference will determine what roads and what actions you choose to take throughout the day" (xxii).

Lorin Woolfe (2002) in her book presents what she believes are *Leadership Secrets from the Bible*. The book is subtitled *From Matthew to Moses—Management Lessons for Contemporary Leaders*. Ten leadership "secrets," and some of the persons believed to have exhibited them, are presented and discussed. The "secrets" presented are:

- Honesty and Integrity
- Purpose
- Kindness and Compassion
- Humility
- Communication
- Performance Management
- Team Development
- Courage
- Justice and Fairness
- Leadership Development

Blanchard and Hodges (2005) published the book entitled *Lead like Jesus: Lessons for Everyone from the Greatest Leadership Role Model of All Times*. In this book, they take the reader through a series of self-assessments regarding leadership and then present what they consider the four domains of leading like Jesus. The four domains are the heart, the head, the hands, and the habits. They believe that when these are aligned that "extraordinary levels of loyalty, trust, and productivity will result" (31). They further state that

> When these areas are out of alignment, frustration, mistrust, and diminished long-term productivity will result. We have found that the biblical books of Matthew, Mark, Luke, John, and Acts are filled with rich examples of how Jesus functioned in each of these domains (31).

With regard to the heart, they believe that leadership is first a spiritual matter of the heart. The heart entails one's motivation for leadership. The head involves one's beliefs and theories regarding leadership. Hands are one's actions. Habits refer to what one does from day to day.

All of the books listed above are great readings for individuals who wish to gain deeper insights into the leadership style(s) of Jesus and/or some of the leadership principles contained in the Bible.

However, let us not forget a classic work in this area, one that precedes all of the above, a book by Bruce (1971), which was originally published in 1871, entitled *The Training of the Twelve*. This book contains valuable lessons on how Jesus trained his disciples over time and the principles he used to refine them and to make them ready for the tasks they will eventually assume. In the Foreword to the second edition of this book, Reverend Olan Hendrix made the following observation:

> The value of this volume is increased today as so many Christian workers are delving into the subject of management. For the first time in church history modern management techniques and principles are being sought out for their application to the local church, the mission, the missionary, and various types of Christian organizations. In the midst of this kind of upsurge of interest in management skills and tools it is increasingly vital that we have firmly fixed in our understanding the *ageless management principles employed by our Lord* in his relationship with his apostles (iii, emphasis mine).

THE LEADER AS STEWARD

R. Scott Rodin (2010), for example, uses the words "The Steward Leader" for the title of his book. The book is divided in three parts— part one, "Becoming a Steward Leader of No Reputation"; part two, "Three Foundations"; and part three, "Four Transformations and Four Trajectories."

In part two, the chapters are:

- "Leading in the Image of the Triune God"
- "The Freedom of the Steward Leader"
- "The Distinctiveness of the Steward Leader"

The chapters under part three are:

- "Stewards of our Relationship with Our Creator God"
- "Stewards of our Relationship with Ourselves"
- "Stewards of our Relationship with our Neighbor"
- "Stewards of Our Relationship with God's Creation"

This book is holistic in its approach to stewardship and discusses the principles and practices of one who would be labeled a steward leader. Rodin is careful to note that this is not a

> ... "how" book on leadership, but a "who" book. It is more about heart than hands, more about transformation than transaction. It does not start with the traits of successful leadership, but with the intent of our Creator and the journey of transformation to which we are called. It is not about what God wants us to do as leaders, but about who God is, and what that means for our self-understanding and our vocation as image bearers of God who are called to lead (7).

In 2009, Zondervan published the *NIV Stewardship Study Bible*. According to the authors, the stewardship Bible "was created to inspire Christians with the broader, holistic vision of biblical stewardship as well as to be a practical guide for pilgrim-stewards who want to become more effective managers of all God has place in their care" (x).

Thus, leading as a steward involves being aware that one is simply a manager (temporarily in charge) of that which belongs to someone else. This concept flows from many passages of Scripture, but one signature passage is Psalms 24:1—"The earth is the Lord's, and the fullness, thereof; the world, and they that dwell therein" (KJV).

CONCLUSION

This chapter is a mere sampling of the vast and evolving literature on servant leadership, the leadership style (s) of Jesus Christ, biblical principles of leadership, and the concept of steward leader. Those familiar with the Bible will readily agree that it is full of leadership principles. For example, it is ripe with examples (good and bad) of leaders; it contains many tips from which leaders can profit; the book of Proverbs can be read from the perspective of abstracting leadership principles, etc. Many persons in non religious settings have used biblical principles in their work without necessarily attributing them to this source.

Observing Jesus' sayings about leadership and those who lead are things we must constantly keep in the fore front. The materials presented in this chapter are consistent with the biblical tradition and are also reflective of what many in the academic world would also embrace. We well remember

Jesus warning the Scribes and the Pharisees about being enamored with titles and the high seats (see Matthew 23:1–12). He also gave a new definition of greatness in his conversation with the mother of Zebedee's children-James and John (see Matthew 20:20–28; Mark 10:35–45). This interaction with them tells us unequivocally that greatness is biblically defined or determined by serving- an observation that Dr. Martin Luther King Jr. made over and over again in the twentieth century, and which was mentioned earlier in this chapter.

REFERENCES

Blanchard, K. and P. Hodges. 2005. *Lead Like Jesus: Lessons for Everyone from the Greatest Leadership Role Model of All Time*. New York: MJF Books.

Bruce, A. B. 1971. *The Training of the Twelve*. Grand Rapids: Kregel Publications.

Frick, D. and Spears, L. C. 1996. *On Becoming a Servant Leader: The Private Writings of Robert K. Greenleaf*. San Francisco: Jossey-Bass Publishers.

Grabill, Stephen J., ed. 2009. *The NIV Stewardship Study Bible*. Grand Rapids: Zondervan.

Greenleaf Center for Servant Leadership (see *www.greenleaf.org*).

Hendrix, O. H. Foreword. In Bruce, A. B. 1971. *The Training of the Twelve*. Grand Rapids: Kregel Publications.

Jones, Laurie B. 1995. *Jesus, CEO: Using Ancient Wisdom for Visionary Leadership*. New York: MIF Books.

_____. 2004. *Jesus: Life Coach*. Nashville: Thomas Nelson.

Rodin, R. S. 2010. *The Steward Leader: Transforming People, Organizations, and Communities*. Downers Grove IL: InterVarsity.

Smith, C. 2005. "Servant Leadership: The Leadership Theory of Robert K, Greenleaf." www.carolsmith.us/downloads/640grrenleaf.pdf

Spears, Larry S. 2010. "Character and Servant Leadership: Ten Characteristics of Effective Caring Leaders." *The Journal of Virtues and Leadership* 1:25–30.

Woolfe, L. 2002. *Leadership Secrets from the Bible*. New York: MJF Books.

NAME INDEX

(Excludes Biblical Persons)